D1557068

# Resilient Communities

In *Resilient Communities*, Jana Krause focuses on civilian agency and mobilization 'from below' and explains violence and non-violence in communal wars. Drawing on extensive field research on ethno-religious conflicts in Ambon/Maluku Province in eastern Indonesia and Jos/Plateau State in central Nigeria, this book shows how civilians responded to local conflict dynamics very differently, evading, supporting, or collectively resisting armed groups. Combining evidence collected from more than 200 interviews with residents, community leaders, and former fighters, local scholarly work (in Indonesian), and local newspaper-based event data analysis, this book explains civilian mobilization, militia formation, and conflict escalation. The book's comparison of vulnerable mixed communities and (un)successful prevention efforts demonstrates how under courageous leadership resilient communities can emerge that adapt to changing conflict zones and collectively prevent killings. By developing the concepts of communal war and social resilience, Krause extends our understanding of local violence, (non-)escalation, and implications for prevention.

JANA KRAUSE is Assistant Professor in the Department of Political Science at the University of Amsterdam.

# Resilient Communities

## Non-Violence and Civilian Agency in Communal War

JANA KRAUSE
*University of Amsterdam*

## CAMBRIDGE
### UNIVERSITY PRESS

University Printing House, Cambridge CB2 8BS, United Kingdom

One Liberty Plaza, 20th Floor, New York, NY 10006, USA

477 Williamstown Road, Port Melbourne, VIC 3207, Australia

314–321, 3rd Floor, Plot 3, Splendor Forum, Jasola District Centre, New Delhi – 110025, India

79 Anson Road, #06–04/06, Singapore 079906

Cambridge University Press is part of the University of Cambridge.

It furthers the University's mission by disseminating knowledge in the pursuit of education, learning, and research at the highest international levels of excellence.

www.cambridge.org
Information on this title: www.cambridge.org/9781108471114
DOI: 10.1017/9781108675079

© Jana Krause 2018

First published 2018

Printed and bound in Great Britain by Clays Ltd, Elcograf S.p.A.

A catalogue record for this publication is available from the British Library.

ISBN 978-1-108-47111-4 Hardback

# Contents

# Figures, Maps, and Tables

# Acknowledgements

This book began with curiosity about how communities located in areas affected by 'religious' conflict remain 'immune' to the conflict dynamics, protect themselves, and preserve spaces of non-violence. While investigating the puzzle of non-violence, interviewing community leaders and residents about their prevention work, and verifying with respondents from gangs and militias why these non-violent communities had not been attacked, I realized that the conflicts in Ambon and Jos did not fit common perceptions of riots. The lethality and ferocity of fighting raised questions as to why and how people could mobilize to such an extent. This book offers an analysis of violence and non-violence in communal war that I hope will make a contribution towards a better understanding of communal militarization and the prevention of such killings. It is based on the accounts, insights, and reflections of my respondents in Ambon and Jos, who shared their precious time, knowledge, and often painful experiences with me with much patience, and at times in the context of continuing conflict. First and foremost, I am most grateful to them. They remain anonymous within this text through the use of pseudonyms. Yet without their reflections, explanations, questions, and memories, this book would obviously not have been possible.

I also owe a debt of gratitude to a great many others who have so generously offered their time, their comments, and their encouragement. I began the process of writing this book at the Graduate Institute of International and Development Studies in Geneva, Switzerland. I am so grateful to my dissertation advisors Keith Krause and Tom Biersteker at the Graduate Institute for their guidance, patience, encouragement, intellectual energy, and support throughout the research process. I am also indebted to Jeff Checkel, whose input proved invaluable and who pushed me towards greater analytical clarity. The research later led to an international research consortium on the gender dimensions of conflict and peacebuilding with research partners in Indonesia and Nigeria. I am very grateful to Arifah Rahmawati and Wening Udasmoro as well as Joy Onyesoh and Mimidoo Achakpa; the many discussions with them sharpened my arguments.

My fieldwork was made possible by a long list of people who offered indispensable advice along the way. I would like to express my gratitude to the Centre for Security and Peace Research at Gadjah Mada University in Yogyakarta, Indonesia, for hosting me during my research in 2009 and 2010. I am grateful to Jeroen Adam, Gerry van Klinken, and Rizal Panggabean for very helpful advice before embarking on fieldwork in Indonesia. Arifah Rahmawati greatly facilitated my research in Ambon, patiently discussing with me her research and mediation experiences and introducing me to friends and former colleagues in Ambon. I warmly thank Jemmy, Herry, Merry, and Onya in Ambon for showing me this beautiful place and aiding my research at various stages. I am also grateful to academic colleagues at Ambon's Pattimura University for sharing their expertise with me, and to the staff at Ambon's Interfaith Centre, Lembaga Antar Imam Maluku, who discussed their peacebuilding work with me at length. I thank my Indonesian language teachers at Wismah Bahasa in Yogyakarta for their enthusiasm and patience, advice, and encouragement. I gratefully remember Ibu Heru for her warmth and generosity; her homestay in Yogyakarta offered a place to which to retreat, reflect on interviews, and reconnect with very helpful friends. I also thank Aan for his excellent transcription and translation assistance.

I am grateful to the staff at the Small Arms Survey, most notably Robert Muggah, Anna Alvazzi del Frate, Luigi De Martino, Eric Berman, and Carole Touraine, for their wonderful support of my research in Nigeria. I am also grateful to Adam Higazi, Yakubu Joseph, and Philip Ostien, who provided invaluable advice in preparation of research in Jos and detailed critical feedback on my findings. I thank the office of the Friedrich Ebert Foundation in Abuja for having facilitated my work. In Jos, I am especially grateful for the insights and support provided by Sister Helena McEvilly of the Franciscans. I thank my research assistant, who remains anonymous, for his excellent work. I am also deeply grateful to all the colleagues from NGO peacebuilding initiatives in Jos – and in Ambon – who discussed their work and the lessons they have learned with me in numerous meetings. I greatly admire their unwavering energy, hope, and resolve.

I am grateful to the Department of Political Science and International Relations at the Graduate Institute, which provided a supportive environment and funded part of my research. I thank the colleagues, friends, and academics there who were so generous in sharing helpful comments and lending a patient ear to my fieldwork experiences: Assia Alexieva, Rachelle Cloutier, Cecilia Cannon, Elena Gadjanova, Janis Grzybowski, Heidi Hardt, Stephanie Hofmann, Jasna Lazarevic, Thania Paffenholz, Chris Stevenson, and Achim Wennmann.

The Program on Order, Conflict, and Violence at Yale University provided a very welcoming and immensely stimulating environment to further develop the arguments and analysis of this book. Stathis Kalyvas offered invaluable support and advice when this project was in its early stages, and Libby Wood, as always, was extremely helpful with her guidance, questions, feedback, and encouragement. I also thank Regina Bateson, Francesca Grandi, Adi Greif, Seraina Grünewald, Corinna Jentzsch, Megan Lynch, Colin Nippert, Livia Schubiger, Alex Shukov, and Jessika Trisko Darden for very helpful conversations on this project.

The War Studies Department at King's College London, and in particular the Conflict, Security and Development Research Group, was a very welcoming and supportive place in which to finalize this manuscript. I am deeply grateful to Mats Berdal, Christine Cheng, Rebekka Friedman, Kieran Mitton, and Oisín Tansey, as well as Claudia Aradau and Vivienne Jabri for their encouragement and critical feedback on arguments developed in this book.

Finally, in Amsterdam, where I completed this manuscript, I am indebted to Kars de Bruijne, Simone Datzberger, Ursula Daxecker, Marlies Glasius, Marieke de Goede, Imke Harbers, Beste Isleyen, Romain Malejacq, Michelle Parlevliet, Ingrid Samset, Philip Schleifer, Abbey Steele, Niels Terpstra, and Darshan Vigneswaran, for making my research stronger.

I was very fortunate to receive a large number of excellent comments on this book at various stages from Nadine Ansorg, Susanna Campbell, David Chandler, Erica Chenoweth, Eric Hieraji, Roger Mac Ginty, Zachariah Mampilly, Juan Masullo, Emily Meierding, Henri Myrttinen, Oliver Kaplan, Scott Straus, and two anonymous reviewers, as well as numerous participants in seminars and workshops at the University of Amsterdam, the University of Denver, Gadjah Mada University, the German Institute of Global and Area Studies, the International Committee of the Red Cross in Geneva, the Käte-Hamburger Kolleg at the University of Duisburg-Essen, the London School of Economics, SOAS University of London, the United Nations Development Program in Abuja, and Yale University.

I gratefully acknowledge generous financial support for this work from the Graduate Institute's Political Science and International Relations Department, the German Academic Exchange Service, the Small Arms Survey, the German Foundation Villigst, and the Swiss National Science Foundation.

I thank my editor John Haslam and the team at Cambridge University Press for their excellent guidance and support, and Jenna Marangoni and Jeremy Grove for their assistance with this manuscript as well as Jillian Luff for producing the maps.

Earlier versions of some of the material from Chapters 6 and 7 were previously published in 'Non-Violence and Civilian Agency in Communal War: Evidence from Jos, Nigeria', *African Affairs* 116(463) (April 2017); and 'A Deadly Cycle: Ethno-Religious Conflict in Jos, Plateau State, Nigeria', Report, Geneva Declaration Secretariat (2011b). I thank the Small Arms Survey in Geneva and the publisher of *African Affairs* for their permission to use this material.

In chapters four and five, part of my analysis draws on interviews conducted by Arifah Rahmawati in the context of a joint research project, as stated in the footnotes, and I am very grateful for the excellent collaboration.

This book would not have been possible without those who have provided their friendship, encouragement, and support over the years. I am grateful to my parents, and to Nataly Scheer, Chris Rétif, Fairlie Chappuis, Anke Draude, Diana Priese, and the late Marianne Abt.

# Abbreviations

| | |
|---|---|
| BBM | Buton, Bugis, and Makasser (Muslim migrants on Ambon Island, Indonesia) |
| BECO | Berom Educational and Cultural Organization (Nigeria) |
| CAN | Christian Association of Nigeria |
| COCIN | Church of Christ in Nigeria |
| COKER | Cowok Keren ('Handsome Boys', a gang in Ambon, Indonesia) |
| FKAWJ | Forum Komunikasi Ahlus Sunnah Wal Jama'ah (Communication Forum of the Followers of the Sunnah and the Community of the Prophet, Indonesia) |
| ICMI | Ikatan Cendekiawan Muslim se-*Indonesia* (Association of Indonesian Muslim Intellectuals) |
| JDA | Jasawa Development Association (Nigeria) |
| KOPASSUS | Komando Pasukan Khusus (Special Forces Command, Indonesia) |
| LGA | Local Government Area (Nigeria) |
| PDI-P | Indonesian Democratic Party – Struggle |
| PDP | People's Democratic Party (Nigeria) |
| RMS | Republik Maluku Selatan (Republic of South Maluku, Indonesia) |
| TNI | Tentara Nasional Indonesia (Indonesian Army) |

# Introduction

I first arrived in Jos in November 2010, at the end of one of the worst years in the central Nigerian city, to conduct interviews on the dynamics of communal violence and prevention strategies. Having passed several military checkpoints on the drive from Abuja to Jos, I entered what looked like a war zone, a city with a heavy military presence at all major junctions and near previous areas of fighting. Along main streets and within neighbourhoods, long lines of burned and half-destroyed houses were a testament to the ferocity of the clashes. More than 1,000 people had been killed in Jos and nearby villages in ethno-religious violence around the Christian–Muslim clea-vage during that year – a fatality rate commonly associated with the civil war threshold.[1] Most people I met were eager to discuss the conflict situation, trying to make sense of atrocities in the name of religion. They reflected on their everyday struggles in navigating a vibrant city with many 'no-go areas' defined by religion. Once my respondents and I had discussed the conflict, one final interview ques-tion often caught them by surprise: 'Do you know of a religiously mixed and vulnerable neighbourhood in Jos where no killings have taken place?' Respondents started to think out loud, and most named the community of Dadin Kowa, in the south of Jos, a large religiously, ethnically, and socio-economically mixed neighbourhood. However, they had more questions than answers about this place of 'local peace'. After initial interviews in Dadin Kowa, I was referred to one highly respected community leader, and arrived at his home to meet a middle-aged man who led a local church. Timothy, whose name I have changed to protect his identity, was very confident and articulate. He explained how he decided to actively keep his neighbourhood safe. In January 2010, a Christian militia group from surrounding villages and neighbourhoods approached Dadin Kowa to kill Muslims.

---

[1] For a detailed discussion of victim estimates, see Chapter 5.

Timothy came out to meet the armed men and persuaded them not to attack. The same men had been involved in heavy fighting with Muslim groups in a nearby market area the previous day, but when Timothy forbade them from entering Dadin Kowa, they returned to their villages without killing. As I listened – at first in disbelief – to Timothy's account, I came to understand that not permitting an armed group entry into the neighbourhood for killings was only the most dramatic part of laborious, decade-long efforts to prevent fighting in Dadin Kowa. Behind the religious leader who confronted a militia and averted an attack stood a carefully maintained social network that allowed Timothy to speak in the name of Christian men in Dadin Kowa and refuse collaboration with external armed groups.

Previously, in 2009 and 2010, I had conducted research on communal war and non-violence in Ambon, Indonesia. Ambon is the capital of the maritime Maluku Province and the historic Spice Islands. When I arrived seven years after the 2002 Maluku peace agreement, which ended a local 'religious war' between the Muslim and Christian populations, the remnants of burned and bullet-ridden houses were still visible in the city centre, standing among newly built and renovated homes and shops. My first respondents were interested in meeting the foreign student but reluctant to discuss the conflict because my questions reopened a matter that many considered closed and dealt with. Several studies of the Maluku conflict had been published by that time. Often respondents' answers repeated what studies had identified as 'causes' of the Maluku conflict, such as long-standing religious tensions and local political and economic competition. These 'causes' seemed to lead to more questions than answers. I soon detected what I would call a 'standard narrative' of the conflict, often centred on the 'provocateur theme'. This theme was common in many conflict regions of Indonesia and alleged that political and military elites close to the former dictator General Suharto in the capital, Jakarta, 'provoked' the troubles for their own political gain, masterminded them, and 'directed the local conflict actors like a *dalang*', the famous Indonesian puppet master.[2] The perceptions and actions of ordinary people during the three years of communal war in Maluku were remarkably lacking in these accounts. The provocateur theme holds some insights, in that local and national elites – politicians, religious leaders, and military officers –

---

[2]  See Human Rights Watch 1999; Purdey 2004.

fuelled the conflict either intentionally and in pursuit of political gain, or through incompetence. However, this should not lead us to conclude that elites 'played' local people against each other without the latter being actors themselves whose actions impacted the course of war. My efforts to direct conversations beyond this standard narrative to learn more about how ordinary people experienced the conflict situation and responded to a changing war environment first appeared to go nowhere. This changed when I asked my interview partners about the community of Wayame, the only religiously, ethnically, and socio-economically mixed neighbourhood in Ambon not devastated during the local war. Suddenly, the provocateur theme no longer held answers. Respondents tried to explain – often to themselves as much as to me – why community leaders and ordinary people in other mixed and vulnerable areas did not respond to the conflict like the residents of Wayame, and why some instead supported militia groups and facilitated attacks and killings. In these conversations, my respondents and I were able to focus on ordinary people's perceptions, action and inactions, and the consequences; we discussed *civilian agency* to understand violence and non-violence in communal war.

## Puzzles

The study of non-violence or negative cases of armed conflict has offered limited systematic analysis to date. Numerous anthropological, journalistic, and scholarly accounts have demonstrated that while cases of non-violent communities are rare, they do exist within a remarkable range of conflicts.[3] For example, during the genocide in Rwanda, in a cluster of communes around Giti, where the mayor was a member of the ruling party but did not carry out orders, organize militias, or start killings, no massacres took place because the mayor calmed people down and resisted violence.[4] During the civil war in Burundi, one commune escaped killings during the initial war years because civilian leaders persuaded Hutus not to pursue violence against Tutsis.[5] Accounts such as these exist for a large number of cases, but many

---

[3] Garcia 1997; Nordstrom 1997; Hancock and Mitchell 2007, 2012; Anderson and Wallace 2013; Kaplan 2013, 2017; Barter 2014; Idler, Garrido, and Mouly 2015; Arjona 2016a; Dudouet 2015; Hallward, Masullo, and Mouly 2017; Masullo 2017.
[4] Janzen 2000; Straus 2006, pp. 85–87.     [5] Lynch 2014.

lack systematic and comparative analysis. These accounts tend to be descriptive and often refer to so-called islands of peace. Some evoke an image of a closed and self-sustaining community that somewhat miraculously escaped the war dynamics of the region.[6] The researcher investigating non-violence is faced with the methodological challenge of making sense of a phenomenon that is relatively rare in conflict zones and does not lend itself easily to comparative analysis and generalization. Moreover, accounts of the few known cases tend to be ambiguous, conflicting, and anecdotal. This is not surprising, given the delicate nature of such information in the context of war. Just as narratives of violence are complex and multifaceted, explanations for non-violence require systematic comparative analysis and triangulation.

In recent years, a substantial body of literature has demonstrated that the level and intensity of violence varies within civil wars.[7] Research suggests that most conflict-prone regions include pockets of non-violence. Stathis Kalyvas' theory of selective violence in civil war, which seeks to explain local-level variation in levels of violence, prominently integrated civilian agency but primarily focused on 'negative' agency in the form of denunciations to armed groups and indirect contributions to violence against other civilians. Kalyvas argued that civilians and armed groups jointly produce violence because civilians provide target-relevant information and denounce others,[8] thereby 'killing by the tongue'.

By contrast, peace research has documented so-called zones of peace and emphasized 'positive' civilian agency for violence prevention, i.e. civilian resistance to war dynamics and attempts to preserve safe spaces within war zones.[9] Recent research into non-violent communities in the Columbian civil war by Ana Arjona[10] and Oliver Kaplan[11] offered more systematic analyses and valuable insights into civilian self-protection strategies and interaction with armed groups. Both Arjona and Kaplan concluded that institutional capacity of local communities is key because it would allow them to settle their own disputes and enable collective action and resistance against armed groups. Both

---

[6] One case study on the Maluku conflict also refers to the only mixed community not devastated by clashes as an 'island of civility'; see Braithwaite 2010.

[7] Wood 2003b; Kalyvas 2006; Varshney 2007; see also Nordstrom 2007.

[8] Kalyvas 2006.      [9] Hancock and Mitchell 2007; Hancock 2017.

[10] Arjona 2016a.      [11] Kaplan 2017.

studies further stressed incentives among armed groups to respect civilian preferences, such as broad reliance on civilian collaboration and long-term perspectives to govern a particular territory, as necessary preconditions that allow civilians bargaining power. These recent studies of non-violence in the context of the Colombian civil war substantially illuminate civilian–armed group interaction. However, how such communities and their institutional capacity emerge, and how people preserve non-violence in the context of a changing conflict zone – often over years – which means maintaining institutions for decision-making and social cohesion to repeatedly negotiate with armed groups, remains underexplored. The context of communal war in Ambon and Jos, which this book addresses, also raises further questions. None of my case study communities could rely on a pre-established institutional framework and capacity to resist armed groups. Instead, civilians developed social orders within their communities that would prevent killings in the wake of the outbreak of the conflict, and then continuously adapted prevention strategies within a rapidly changing conflict zone.

During my field research in Ambon and in Jos, I found that one ethnically, religiously, and socio-economically mixed community in each city had remained non-violent. In both cities, each non-violent community was located in the second most violent local district. The non-violent communities of Wayame in Ambon and Dadin Kowa in Jos were both almost contiguous to a similarly mixed community that had equally undertaken violence prevention efforts but was eventually devastated by clashes and thereafter remained religiously segregated.

Unfortunately, the effective prevention work of people in Wayame and Dadin Kowa remained exceptional. As is discussed in further detail in what follows, neighbouring similarly mixed communities that equally tried to prevent killings suffered clashes when external armed groups attacked, with support from some residents of the targeted area against their neighbours. In Jos, only some upper-middle-class mixed areas remained intact while in Ambon, no other mixed community escaped killings and displacement.

Both conflicts escalated quickly from brawls and local fights to killings perpetrated by well-armed mobile gangs and militias, often in coordinated attacks, resulting in large victim numbers and massive displacement. In 2001, the first clashes in Jos killed more than 1,000 people in five days, while the local war in Ambon and tiny Maluku Province cost an estimated 1,460 people their lives in 1999, out of a population of about 1.1 million. At the height of the conflict in Maluku, at least 350,000 people were displaced.[12]

How to explain such conflict escalation? Beyond the puzzle of non-violence, this book analyses civilian mobilization and conflict escalation in *communal war*. Communal war, as I define it, refers to non-state armed conflict between social groups that results in casualty numbers that reach the civil war threshold. As is demonstrated in this volume, much of the violence in communal wars escalates from neighbourhood-based pogroms against the minority population, in which neighbours may kill neighbours, to frontal battles between armed groups, and joint attacks of mobile gangs and militias in coordination with some civilians from targeted areas.

This book investigates local-level violence and non-violence in communal 'religious' wars. It develops theoretical frameworks for the study of civilian mobilization and (1) regional conflict escalation to the level of a communal war, and (2) community-based non-escalation and the outcome of non-violence in the context of communal war.

## Arguments

Why were people in Wayame and Dadin Kowa able to prevent killings while surrounded by atrocities taking place, when many among their own youths wanted to participate in fighting and external armed groups threatened to attack? In order to theorize non-escalation and prevention, I first clarify assumptions and definitions.

'Non-violence' is a term with strong positive connotations, rooted in the conflict resolution literature, where it refers to 'social change and increased justice through peaceful means'.[13] Non-violent resistance encompasses 'an abstention from using physical force to achieve an aim, but also a full engagement in resisting oppression, domination and any other forms of injustice'.[14] The growing body of literature on non-violence warrants further definition of the term. Civil resistance research has defined 'non-violent resistance' as 'the application of

---

[12] See www.internal-displacement.org/south-and-south-east-asia/indonesia/new
-archive/conflict-and-displacement-in-and-from-maluku-and-north-maluku
-1999–2004. Last accessed 13 November 2017.
[13] Lederach 2005, p. 15.    [14] Dudouet 2008, p. 3.

unarmed civilian power using nonviolent methods such as protests, strikes, boycotts, and demonstrations, without using or threatening physical harm against the opponent'.[15] By contrast, I study *non-violence* as an *outcome* – the absence of conflict-related violence in areas located within conflict zones – and as a *process*, i.e. non-escalation. Non-violence does not need to imply pacifist attitudes, a lack of threats to physical violence, or a complete absence of any form of inter-personal violence. On the contrary, as is demonstrated later in this book, non-violence in Wayame in Ambon and Dadin Kowa in Jos was an outcome preserved partly through repression and physical punishments of those who wanted to instigate killings.

Theoretically, non-violence as an outcome can result from geographic factors and/or the strategies of armed groups. Empirically, non-violence is not usually a coincidental by-product of armed conflict but the direct result of civilian self-protection and prevention efforts. Since civilians are mostly viewed as victims of armed conflict, their intrepid mobilization, successful engagement with armed groups, and prevention of killings is counterintuitive and requires explanation.

In a nutshell, I argue that at the onset of conflicts, Wayame and Dadin Kowa were *vulnerable* communities because part of their own youth wanted to mobilize and fight, and external armed groups threatened to attack. Based on continuous prevention efforts, these areas *became resilient communities* that successfully adapted and mitigated their vulnerability, albeit under severe duress, as is demonstrated in what follows. Although prevention efforts were embedded within a specific conflict context, factors such as geography, demography, or a timely intervention by security forces did not predict non-violence. Instead, preventing killings was an adaptive social process contingent on individual leadership and collective agency. Community leaders and residents countered polarization and developed inclusive cross-cleavage identities; established internal social control, persuading residents to support prevention efforts and formulating rules and procedures for conflict management; and engaged external armed groups for negotiations and the gathering and dissemination of information. In so doing, they established social orders different from violence-prone neighbourhoods that came under the influence and control of armed groups.

---

[15] Chenoweth and Cunningham 2013, p. 271.

I draw on resilience research of communities exposed to climate change and develop a *resilience lens* that focuses on adaptation. Socio-ecological research has pioneered the idea to describe how communities adapt to environmental change and placed emphasis on the significance of generic dynamics of social knowledge and learning, self-organization, anticipation, and imagination that would support community adaptation to adversity. Resilience has also made significant inroads into policy research on armed violence and development. Within the World Bank and other donors, a discourse has emerged on 'making societies more resilient to violence' in order to foster social and economic development.[16] Non-violent communities in Ambon and Jos adapted to a rapidly changing conflict environment characterized by the mobilization of vigilantes, criminals, and gangs organized around political actors; deeply polarized ethnic and religious relations; and the formation of militias and a growing militarization of local order. Civilian prevention efforts emerged first through individual leaders who negotiated neutrality within and beyond their communities. Their courageous and high-risk initiatives sparked community-based social movements when ordinary people joined their efforts. Community leaders were guided by *social knowledge* concerning the organization of violence and *lived experience* in other conflict zones prior to the conflicts in Ambon and Jos. Throughout their prevention work, they demonstrated *social learning* with regard to conflict dynamics, imagination of threats and challenges, and continuous *scenario-building* of potential attacks to *anticipate* and mitigate consequences, thus sustaining prevention.

To date, the distinction between causes of conflict onset and causes of violence against civilians, as developed in the civil war literature, has not been fully integrated into communal conflict research. Most studies of communal violence focus on riots as sporadic phenomena of urban violence linked to urban elite politics, and urban bias often prevails in the field.[17] However, communal violence in and around Ambon and Jos took place over several years, driven by interlinking dynamics of urban and rural violence. In Indonesia and Nigeria, almost half of all casualty numbers resulted from rural communal clashes. Riot research

---

[16]  Marc 2009.
[17]  See also Kalyvas 2006, pp. 38–48, for a discussion of urban bias in civil war research.

neither analyses urban–rural violence dynamics nor does this body of literature offer convincing explanations for non-violent communities within these conflict zones. Understanding escalation and causes for violence endogenous to conditions at conflict onset[18] is a crucial first step for theorizing non-escalation and factors of restraint.[19] Conceptualizing the conflicts in Maluku Province in Indonesia[20] and Plateau State in Nigeria as communal wars allows me to theorize civilian agency as causal for violent and non-violent outcomes in neighbouring communities. This analysis builds on the recent micro-turn in the study of civil war and genocide, which emphasized the complexity and non-linearity of escalation and non-escalation,[21] and the enduring social legacies of war and violence that impact post-conflict political order.[22]

## Research Design

At the turn of the century, Indonesia and Nigeria appeared to exemplify an apparent global trend in 'ethnic' and 'religious' conflicts, with both countries seemingly disintegrating. In 1998, within the course of three weeks, the authoritarian military regimes in Jakarta and Abuja fell, and both countries embarked on a democratization process. In the wake of the transitions, communal conflicts with a strong transnational religious dimension along the Christian–Muslim cleavage ravaged both states and sent shock waves through the regions.

Indonesia and Nigeria have been selected for their similar background factors. Both post-colonial countries are populous, leading regional powers characterized by a high level of ethnic heterogeneity and religious and cultural diversity. My research focuses on two regional conflicts that escalated in the context of regime change and democratization processes, weakened security forces, transnational religious movements, and religious conflict discourses.

The conflict in Ambon, capital of Maluku Province in eastern Indonesia, was one of the worst conflicts during the transition. Between 1999 and 2002, almost 3,000 people were killed in Ambon

---

[18] Kalyvas 2009.  [19] E.g., Straus 2012.
[20] Barron, Azca, and Susdinarjanti 2012 also previously referred to the Maluku conflict as a 'communal war'.
[21] Fujii 2009; Kalyvas 2009; Straus 2012.  [22] Wood 2008, 2015.

and rural Maluku out of a population of about 1.1 million.[23] In the city of Jos, the capital of Plateau State in central Nigeria, clashes subsequent to a controversial local political appointment transformed into a deadly cycle of killings along the religious divide. In Jos and rural Plateau State, at least 7,000 people died between 2001 and 2016.[24] The violence in Ambon escalated when well-organized militias and paramilitary troops launched sophisticated attacks on urban and rural communities. In Jos, a heavy military presence contained escalation before gangs and vigilantes transformed into militias in control of the city. However, in rural areas, well-armed militias continued attacks and atrocities.

While Indonesia's democratic consolidation is widely seen as stable, Nigeria has repeatedly been referred to as 'teetering on the brink of collapse'.[25] Since the transitions, political struggles over the place of religion in public life and the formation of religious extremist movements have been an important domestic feature in both countries. The critical junctures of the transitions, the weakening of political institutions and security forces, economic decline, and the general climate of uncertainty resulted in an enabling environment for the escalation of violence both in Ambon and in Jos.[26] Both communal conflicts had significant national repercussions; extremist religious groups, such as Laskar Jihad in Indonesia and Boko Haram in Nigeria, directly referred to 'the killing of Muslims' in Ambon and in Jos, respectively, to justify terrorist acts in other parts of the countries.

Table I.1 summarizes my cross-case and within-case paired comparative approach. I studied non-violent communities in a paired comparison to an almost contiguous community that was similarly mixed, where community leaders tried to prevent killings, but devastating clashes eventually took place. Paired comparison is a widely used method distinct from single-case studies and multi-case analysis.[27] Also referred to as 'controlled case comparison'[28] or 'matching

---

[23] Estimates based on data from the Indonesia National Violence Monitoring Program; see Chapter 4 for a detailed discussion.

[24] Estimates based on my dataset of violent incidents for Plateau State; see Chapter 6 for a detailed discussion.

[25] Campbell 2013.

[26] How the Indonesian regime change created an enabling environment for the Maluku conflict, and other cases of communal violence in Indonesia, has been discussed at length in Bertrand 2004, Sidel 2006, and van Klinken 2007.

[27] Tarrow 2010.     [28] Bennett and George 2005.

Table I.1 *Cross-case and within-case paired comparison*

| Cross-Case Comparison | | Within-Case Comparison | |
| --- | --- | --- | --- |
| | | VIOLENT COMMUNITY | NON-VIOLENT COMMUNITY |
| COUNTRY | PROVINCE/STATE | | |
| Indonesia | Ambon – Maluku | Poka–Rumahtiga | *Wayame* |
| Nigeria | Jos – Plateau | Anglo Jos | *Dadin Kowa* |

cases',[29] this method supports assessing whether findings derived from an in-depth case study can travel.

Prior to the conflicts, Ambon and Jos had a strong reputation for peaceful coexistence of their almost equal numbers of Muslim and Christian populations. There were no histories of significant clashes despite long-standing tensions between ethnic and religious groups. Consequently, my case selection allows me to exclude potential effects of legacies of previous clashes on the escalation and non-escalation processes that this book analyses.

The material for this book was collected during nine fieldwork stays in Indonesia and Nigeria between the years 2009 and 2015, during which I conducted more than 200 interviews. I visited Ambon four times and conducted a total of 83 interviews with 52 individuals, including community and religious leaders, residents and journalists, non-governmental organization (NGO) representatives and academic colleagues at the local universities, militia leaders and members, and, of course, residents from my case study areas. My repeated visits allowed me to interview key respondents twice or more to probe memories and verify details. In Jos, I conducted a total of 125 interviews with 98 community members and leaders, religious and ethnic group leaders, journalists, NGO workers, politicians, and gang members. My interview respondents came from the worst-affected neighbourhoods in the centre of Jos and my case study communities. My presence in Jos at the end of one of the worst years in a continuing conflict also allowed me to collect valuable ethnographic observations, particularly in the non-violent neighbourhood of Dadin Kowa. These interviews form the evidentiary backbone of this book.

---

[29]  Gerring 2007.

In addition, I analysed event data for both conflict regions. For Indonesia, I utilize data collected by the Indonesia National Violence Monitoring System (NVMS).[30] For Nigeria, I have collected and verified reporting from the Armed Conflict Location and Event Data Project (ACLED), Human Rights Watch, Nigeria Watch, and information from local community representatives.[31] My descriptive statistics capture geographical and temporal conflict trends. They demonstrate the spread of militia attacks and their reach, thus providing valuable information on the urban and rural dynamics of violence in communal war.

## Why Read This Book

Are individuals who prevent killings driven by moral commitment and inclusive values, or by instrumental motives of self-protection and personal benefit? Can we only expect non-violence if individuals driven by a sense of moral obligations and outstanding courage are present? To what extent can ordinary people and potential bystanders prevent killings, for example because they want to protect themselves and their families? These questions and potential explanations imply different policy approaches to strengthening local prevention efforts in conflict zones. Nascent civil war research on civilian agency suggests that individuals who engage in violence prevention are driven by motives of self-interest and self-protection.[32] However, self-protection and fear are also key motivations for joining militias or participate in genocide.[33] Furthermore, genocide research on rescue behaviour during the Holocaust concluded that individuals who performed extraordinary and courageous rescue deeds 'were ordinary people' from 'all walks of life'.[34] Consequently, as Oliner and Oliner first formulated in 1988 in their preface for *The Altruistic Personality*, 'if we can understand some of the attributes that distinguished rescuers from others, perhaps we can deliberately cultivate them.'[35] This book is motivated by the concern that the emergence of non-violence and civilian agency and their implications for the protection of civilians overall remain poorly understood.

---

[30] This dataset was compiled by the Indonesian Ministry of Welfare in cooperation with the World Bank: www.snpk-indonesia.com/
[31] See Chapter 5 for more details.      [32] Chenoweth and Cunningham 2013.
[33] Straus 2006; Guichaoua 2007.      [34] Oliner and Oliner 1992.
[35] Oliner and Oliner 1992.

For the reader interested in non-violence and local peacebuilding, this book contributes to a more nuanced theoretical reflection and empirical analysis of the phenomenon. Non-violence has emerged as an important research theme in the field of political violence, but its dynamics, limitations, and legacies deserve further research. Moreover, how violence prevention practices impact the civilian population over months and years calls for further critical attention. This book offers a systematic comparative analysis of effective and failed civilian violence prevention efforts in the context of communal war.

Second, most research on collective violence has been state-centric, with a primary focus on civil wars and interstate violence. Yet the consequences of non-state conflict also result in civilian victimization, large-scale displacement, economic devastation, grievous injury, and death.[36] Communal violence affects many democratizing states, particularly in Sub-Saharan Africa and South/Southeast Asia. It can escalate so dramatically as to reach casualty numbers beyond the yearly civil war threshold only within days of fighting. Despite this intensity of violence, the social processes of escalation, civilian responses, and their legacies for state-building, democratization, and peaceful coexistence have received limited research attention. For the reader interested in communal conflict and political violence research more broadly, this book offers a new conceptualization of large-scale communal violence as warfare 'from below', emerging not only from elite manipulation and in the context of elections, but importantly from the mobilization of ordinary people in response to first acts of killings. The book further moves beyond the urban bias of the riot literature and integrates the rural dimension of communal violence into its analysis.

For the reader interested in the dynamics of 'religious' conflict, particularly in the context of regime change and democratization, I hope to provide a fresh analysis of the emergence of 'religious conflict' narratives and their causal effect on armed group formation and conflict escalation. The risk of mass violence perceived and framed as 'religious conflict', and the potential of religious leaders to effectively prevent violence, remain of primary policy concern, as for example the conflict in the Central African Republic reminds us.

Lastly, for the reader interested in resilience research, this book advances the empirical study of social resilience in conflict and

---

[36] Sundberg, Eck, and Kreutz 2012.

implications for peacebuilding. Since the World Bank adopted the term in the context of state fragility and conflict prevention, there has been an explosion of resilience-based policy programmes in international security and development. The term 'resilience' has come to attract considerable popularity, provoking substantial criticism on its vagueness and potential neo-liberal policy implications.[37] There is now a substantial field of critical security and resilience research but careful application of the concept's core ideas to empirical cases is lacking. This book addresses this gap. It offers an in-depth analysis of how vulnerable communities become resilient. In many war zones, security forces or international peacekeepers often deploy late and in insufficient numbers,[38] forcing civilians into self-protection for survival. The book provides a discussion of the normative implications of social resilience, civilian protection, and survival in war zones.

## Organization of This Book

The following chapter defines communal war and offers a typology of the patterns of violence in communal conflicts. I distinguish patterns of violence along five dimensions: the geography of violence (urban/rural); the type of conflict (one-sided/dyadic) and of violent incident (pogroms, battles, [joint] attacks, massacres); the categories of armed actors; the national context and the role of the state; and the repertoires of violence employed by armed civilians and reported per incident. This typology supports a more nuanced analysis of civilian mobilization and the organization of violence in communal war, which should inform prevention efforts.

Chapter 2 offers a brief summary of resilience research and introduces the 'resilience lens', which directs the analytical focus towards community adaptation and the role of generic social dynamics of social knowledge, learning, scenario-building, and threat anticipation in the context of an adverse environment. I review civil war and genocide research on civilian prevention and self-protection and distinguish two main arguments: the institutional capacity of local communities, which enables resistance to conflict dynamics; and leadership and rescue agency of individuals who act courageously and altruistically to

---

[37] E.g., Norris et al. 2008, p. 125; Chandler 2014.
[38] Corbett 2011; Harragin 2011; Williams 2013; Gorur 2013.

prevent killings despite high risks to their lives. I combine both arguments in my theoretical framework of civilian mobilization and non-escalation. Using the resilience lens, the framework shows how individual and collective agency enables community adaptation to mitigate vulnerability and sustain prevention. Chapter 3 offers a discussion of my fieldwork in the context of continuing communal conflicts in Indonesia and Nigeria. It focuses on the research design and process, the context of my interviews and ethnographic observations, and the challenges and limitations of this field research.

Chapter 4 turns to the empirical analysis of communal war in Ambon and Maluku Province, eastern Indonesia. After a brief summary of the conflict, I explain the emergence of communal violence from below and militia formation. The next chapter examines violent and non-violent outcomes in the similarly mixed and contiguous neighbourhoods of Poka–Rumahtiga and Wayame in Ambon. It details how leaders in Wayame established a new social order while in Poka–Rumahtiga, ad hoc prevention efforts failed when, under the influence of refugee populations, some residents started to arm themselves and mobilize for attacks as much as for self-defence. I show how in Wayame, one community leader's rescue agency enabled collective mobilization that sustained prevention.

Chapters 6 and 7 turn to the analysis of the Jos conflict in Plateau State, central Nigeria. Chapter 6 examines civilian mobilization and conflict escalation in Jos and briefly contrasts these findings to the case study of Ambon. Chapter 7 comparatively analyses violent and non-violent outcomes in the almost contiguous mixed neighbourhoods of Anglo Jos and Dadin Kowa, demonstrating how people in Dadin Kowa mobilized to prevent clashes. Dadin Kowa's successful prevention work later informed NGO peacebuilding efforts in Jos.

Lastly, my concluding chapter reviews the arguments presented and discusses their implications for researchers and policy makers, and the prospects of resilience building.

# 1 | *Communal War*

In September 2001, communal clashes in Jos, a city of about 1.5 million people in central Nigeria, killed at least 1,000 people during five days of violence commonly referred to as 'riots'. Subsequent to the Kenyan national elections in December 2007, communal clashes in the capital, Nairobi, and many other parts of the country cost more than 1,000 people their lives over several weeks. The 2005 Paris 'riots' did not lead to a single casualty during eighteen days of unrest, while the 2011 London riots killed one person. In the 2013 Stockholm riots, several police officers were injured but no one was killed. This global snapshot demonstrates that 'riots' can refer to very different phenomena. Riot researchers have long noted that the term often sharply underestimates the real level of violence.[1] A death toll of at least 1,000 people per year marks the civil war threshold if one party to the conflict is the state. In Jos, this fatality threshold was reached in only five days when civilians mobilized and fought, armed with knives and machetes, while state security forces failed to intervene effectively to bring the killings to a halt. This intensity of violence resembles local dynamics of genocide. For many residents from the cities of Ambon in eastern Indonesia and Jos in central Nigeria, the sudden escalation of long-existing communal tensions remained incomprehensible. We know much about the causes of communal conflicts and the conditions under which they are likely to break out, but *how* conflicts escalate to the level of a civil war within only days has received too little scholarly attention.

Time and again, large-scale communal violence appears to erupt out of nowhere in cities previously praised for 'communal harmony', and clashes quickly result in hundreds or even thousands dead. For example, in 1992, one of the worst episodes of Hindu–Muslim violence in India took place in the state of Gujarat. The riot-prone city of

[1] Wilkinson 2009, p. 331.

16

Ahmedabad witnessed yet another episode of killings, while in Surat, a city nearby without a history of communal violence, similar atrocities took place for the first time, to the shock of its residents.[2] The outbreak and dramatic escalation of violence in Jos and Ambon deeply disturbed people in Indonesia and Nigeria because these cities were not known as 'riot-prone'. Instead, Ambon manise ('sweet Ambon') and Jos, the 'home of peace and tourism', as the two cities had long been referred to, had been praised for peaceful communal relations. Unlike in Surat, however, fighting in Ambon and Jos did not end after a few days of killings. Instead, the clashes sparked years of violence, carried out in part by well-organized mobile militias, particularly in the rural areas of Maluku Province and Plateau State.

This chapter explains communal war. Focusing on how communal violence emerges 'from below', I examine civilian mobilization and conflict escalation. By 'communal war', I mean non-state conflict between two or more social groups that results in casualty numbers that reach the civil war threshold. After days of mass killings, it may seem as if 'civilian destroyers' simply return to their everyday lives and neighbourly existence.[3] Yet, even though communal violence often ends after days of atrocities, at least if security forces intervene effectively, the killings leave behind legacies that can profoundly impact social structures and increase vulnerability to further clashes. When fighting breaks out, atrocities and extreme brutality in killings often take place during the very first hours and days, leaving those affected outraged and traumatized. Social interactions across the conflict cleavage can break down and trade and economic development may suffer, resulting in deepening poverty and instability. Neighbourhood communities may mobilize and raise funds for acquiring weapons to protect themselves in the context of weak or unprofessional security forces. Community leaders may openly align with vigilantes, and even with thugs and gangs, linking themselves to men who carry a well-established reputation for violence for fear of another episode of killings. These developments encourage communal militia formation and endogenously cause further escalation beyond the initial clashes that may or may not have been instigated by political elites. If state and security forces do not decisively bring communal conflicts under control, which is particularly challenging in contexts of regime change or

---

[2] Chandra 1993, p. 1883.    [3] Tambiah 1990, p. 744. See also Tilly 2003, p. 11.

civil war, and if community leaders and authorities do not halt escalation, conflicts can transform into communal wars.

This chapter lays out an analytical framework for the study of communal war. Leaving the imprecise riot terminology behind, I first present a typology for analysing the patterns of violence in communal conflicts along four dimensions: geography, the type of violence, the categories of armed actors, and the national context and role of the state. In addition, I distinguish repertoires of (non-)lethal violence by incident.[4] These dimensions facilitate a more nuanced analysis of the production (and prevention) of violence in communal conflicts and its organization, civilian mobilization, and conflict (de-)escalation. The second part of this chapter demonstrates why civilian agency is causal for the production of violence in communal conflicts. Instrumentalist approaches in riot research have long acknowledged that individuals may follow elites into violence to pursue their own personal agendas, while civil war research has emphasized personal – often malicious – motives to explain why civilians would denounce others and kill. However, the causal role of (collective) civilian agency and mobilization has remained under-theorized. The last part of this chapter offers a theoretical framework of civilian mobilization and conflict escalation to communal war. The framework builds on three social processes of escalation: the political mobilization of 'everyday violence networks', the polarization of social identities, and the formation of communal militias and the militarization of local communities.

## What Is Communal War?

Scale is the main distinguishing characteristic of a communal war. A communal conflict is a non-state conflict between social groups. If such a conflict reaches casualty numbers of or beyond the civil war threshold, I define it as communal war. The majority of communal conflicts take place in Africa, with Nigeria topping the list.[5] Although casualty numbers of communal conflicts usually rise into the hundreds, some conflicts stand out with more than 1,000 victims per year. This deadliness of communal violence particularly applies to countries also

---

[4] Here, I take inspiration from the typology on patterns of violence in civil war developed by Gutiérrez-Sanín and Wood 2017.
[5] See data on non-state conflict collected by the Uppsala Conflict Data Program, and Allanson, Melander and Themnér 2017.

affected by civil war, such as the Democratic Republic of the Congo (DRC) and South Sudan. The communal wars in Ambon and rural Maluku Province in Indonesia and in Jos and rural Plateau State in Nigeria took place in the context of states facing regional insurgencies and the threat of disintegration. In Indonesia after the end of authoritarian rule, the civil war in Aceh escalated while separatist conflict in Papua remained unresolved and communal violence also affected other provinces of the archipelago. The Nigerian state was challenged in the Niger Delta to the south and later by the Boko Haram insurgency in the northeast.

Communal conflicts are fought over (local) government control and/ or over local territory. Rural land for agricultural production, resource extraction, and cattle herding is often contested, and traditional and state laws over landownership may conflict. In cities, urban land is fought over for residence, business, and trade opportunities, and for the control of local government areas for winning elections and accessing state budgets. Ethnic and religious violence is often a form of political cleansing that takes place to establish territorial control over a specific area, although individual motives for participation in such violence may differ and instead reflect private motives, as in civil war.

'Riot' is a term used for various forms of communal conflict and suffers from a number of limitations. It can refer to protests turned violent, pogroms against a minority group, clashes between almost equally strong social groups, ethnic cleansing, and atrocities. 'Riot' initially referred to events of collective action that threatened public order and state control.[6] Subsuming episodes of non-state armed conflict with widely varying casualty numbers under the same terminology lumps together very different forms of collective action that deserve nuanced and careful analysis. An uncritical use of the word 'riot' can further imply adopting the language used by authorities and hinder analysis of the organization of violence and the responsibility of the perpetrators.[7]

Riot research generally lacks precision regarding the patterns and organizational dynamics of violence. Riots in India predominantly mean one-sided violence of Hindu activists against Muslims, with support from police forces, also referred to as 'pogroms'.[8]

---

[6] Wilkinson 2009.    [7] Tilly 1986, p. 168.
[8] Brass 1997, 2003; Berenschot 2011b; Ghassem-Fachandi 2012.

By contrast, communal conflicts in Indonesia and Nigeria have involved two similarly strong communal groups. The patterns of violence in primarily one-sided conflicts, and the dynamics of civilian mobilization and conflict escalation, may differ from conflicts fought between similarly strong groups. A more precise terminology that addresses these varying forms of communal conflict is imperative for careful analysis. Furthermore, research reports and scholarly analyses have provided numerous victim accounts with gruesome details of the atrocities perpetrated, but analysis of perpetrators' motives and perspectives is less prominent in the field.[9] We also know relatively little about why and how people support such fighting. For example, women often cook for large groups of armed men before the latter launch an attack against another community, or women may assemble and repair weapons before fighting continues. Lastly, the riot literature is characterized by urban bias and lacks a thorough discussion of rural dynamics of violence. In Indonesia and Nigeria, urban communal violence sparked massive rural clashes while this rural violence in turn reinforced urban conflict. To date, communal violence in rural areas has received far less attention than urban riots.

The terms 'riots' and 'communal violence' are further often applied interchangeably with descriptive terms of armed conflict, such as 'ethnic' and 'religious' conflicts or 'sons-of-the-soil' conflicts over land-ownership and rural livelihoods.[10] Research into non-state conflicts in Africa often applies the term 'electoral violence',[11] generally understood as 'forms of political violence in which the dynamics of electoral competition shape the motives of perpetrators, the identification of targets, and the forms and timing of physical violence'.[12] Social conflicts are typically labelled on the basis of what is perceived as the overarching cleavage dimension: ideological, ethnic, or religious.[13] Terms such as 'ethnic' or 'religious' conflict, 'electoral violence', and 'sons-of-the-soil conflict' label conflicts according to an overarching cleavage that often not only describes a particular form of collective violence but also assigns a motive to it.[14]

However, communal conflicts are complex phenomena with multiple conflict patterns. The early violence in Ambon and in Jos could be

---

[9] But see Scacco 2010; Claassen 2014.   [10] Fearon and Laitin 2011.
[11] E.g. Höglund 2009; Straus and Taylor 2009; Boone 2011; Bekoe 2012.
[12] Klaus and Mitchell 2015.   [13] Tambiah 1996; Kalyvas 2006.
[14] Kalyvas 2009; Wilkinson 2012.

referred to as 'ethnic' conflict between two ethnically defined groups, and as 'religious' conflict once the Christian–Muslim cleavage became salient and interpretations of 'religious' violence influenced many residents. Furthermore, both conflicts could also be categorized as cases of electoral violence, given that a political appointment related to an electoral cleavage as well as local government elections first sparked the fighting in Jos, while electoral mobilization for the first democratic local elections after decades of authoritarian rule triggered the violence in Ambon. Finally, the term 'sons-of-the-soil' conflict equally holds explanatory value, given that both conflicts showed strong polarization between those who regarded themselves as 'indigenes' of Jos and Plateau State, and Ambon and Maluku Province, and those who were regarded as immigrants and settlers. In Ambon and in Jos, and in surrounding rural areas, however, all of these conflict cleavages overlapped and reinforced each other. Crucially, none explains why conflict escalated to the level of a communal war, or how some vulnerable mixed communities could have prevented violence.

I understand communal violence as armed conflict between social groups that define themselves along identity lines, such as ethnicity, religion, language, or culture. A previous definition of communal war comes from the Correlates of War Project (COW), which defined 'intercommunal wars' as one form of intra-state wars, alongside civil wars and regional internal wars, as long as inter-communal wars reached the threshold of 1,000 fatalities among combatants (not civilians) within twelve months from the onset of violent conflict.[15] By contrast, I use the term 'communal war' to refer to communal conflicts that reach casualty numbers around the civil war threshold without distinguishing between 'combatants' and 'civilians'.

Communal violence has further been understood as one form of non-state conflict, as coded in the Uppsala Conflict Data Program (UCDP), i.e. 'conflict between two organized groups, neither of which is the government of a state, which results in at least 25 annual battle-related deaths'.[16] Apart from fighting between rebel groups in the context of a civil war, the UCDP non-state conflict category includes election-related violence fought by armed groups mobilized around political actors and/or parties, and fighting between communal armed groups or communal militias.

[15] Sarkees 2014.  [16] Sundberg, Eck, and Kreutz 2012, p. 352.

22 *Communal War*

In communal wars, as I define them, armed civilians fight either as members of gangs, vigilante groups, or militias, or as 'ordinary people' who temporarily join a more established armed group for killings. I distinguish between armed and unarmed civilians rather than combatants and civilians because civilian behaviour can change from the adoption of unarmed to armed and 'back to unarmed strategies during the course of conflict, depending on patterns of civilian mobilization and the timeliness and effectiveness of prevention initiatives.

## Patterns of Violence in Communal Conflicts

Communal wars are large-scale, non-state conflicts that consist of numerous interlinked episodes of collective violence, often referred to as 'sequences of riots'. Stanley Tambiah described riots as 'organized, anticipated, programmed, and recurring features and phases of seemingly spontaneous, chaotic, and orgiastic actions'.[17] Donald Horowitz defined a riot as 'an intense, sudden, though not necessarily wholly unplanned, lethal attack by civilian members of one ethnic group on civilian members of another ethnic group, the victims chosen because of their group membership', that can be 'as brief as a day or two or as long as several weeks'.[18] Paul Brass described riots as 'a grisly form of dramatic production in which there are three phases: preparation/rehearsal, activation/enactment, and explanation/interpretation'.[19] Although these descriptions capture important similarities across conflicts, they remain vague on how violence is organized and how episodes of violence are interlinked. Analysing the patterns of violence leads to questions such as how communal violence is organized, prepared, and sustained, and reintegrates civilian agency as a causal factor.

In the following, I provide a typology of the patterns of violence in communal conflicts along four dimensions: geography, type, categories of armed actors, and the role of the state. In addition, I distinguish repertoires of (non-)lethal violence.[20] I then illustrate how such analysis supports understanding the variation of violence in communal conflicts.

---

[17] Tambiah 1996, p. 230.   [18] Horowitz 2001, pp. 1–2.   [19] Brass 2003, p. 15.
[20] Drawing on the typology of patterns of violence developed by Gutiérrez-Sanín and Wood 2017.

Table 1.1 *Patterns of violence in communal conflicts*

| Dimension | Spectrum | |
|---|---|---|
| Type | (One-sided) Pogrom | (Dyadic) Communal Clashes |
| | *Attacks; Massacres* | *Battles, (Joint) Attacks; Massacres* |
| Geography | Urban – Peri-Urban – Rural | |
| Armed Actors | Neighbours – Vigilantes – Thugs – Gangs – Communal Militias – Security Forces | |
| National Context | E.g. Regime Change – Civil War – Democratization – Elections | |
| Repertoires of (Non)-Lethal Violence | Homicide; Sexual Violence; Forced Displacement; Torture; Kidnapping; (Sexual) Slavery, etc. | |

Reports of communal conflicts, for example concerning Maluku in eastern Indonesia, often note that violence 'erupted', 'spread', and 'escalated' across a particular conflict region, but provide limited information about *how* violence spread and escalated without the presence of organized rebel groups seeking to conquer territory. The mobilization dynamics and the organization behind the spread of violence remain unclear. Studies do not answer *why* communal violence escalated and affected more and more urban neighbourhoods and rural vicinities. The Maluku conflict started in Ambon, the provincial capital of a maritime and remote province with numerous small islands, at a time with little to no mobile phone use and few Internet connections. How violence 'spread' remains unclear until we focus on civilian mobilization and the organization of violence. How did people hear about atrocities in Ambon? How did they *respond* to the news? Why did a narrative of 'religious war' emerge rather than the interpretation that thugs fought each other in Ambon? Did violence spread because people mobilized against their own neighbours of a different ethnic or religious background, or did armed groups from Ambon attack in rural areas and thus spread the violence? When Christian or Muslim militia groups emerged, did they rely on information from residents for targeted attacks or did they massacre entire villages? Behind expressions such as 'the conflict escalated' and 'violence spread' stand processes of civilian mobilization that can result in distinct patterns of violence, which require tailored intervention strategies.

Riot researchers have emphasized the difficulties of scholarly analysis in an environment where for every violent incident often at least two distinct narratives exist. Paul Brass noted, 'by the time the social scientist arrives on the scene, the riot exists only in memory and interpretation and its principal actors ... are either not to be found or are born liars.'[21] However, unlike in civil wars, in communal conflicts, those who fight are usually men (rarely women) who remain husbands, brothers, and sons deeply embedded within their communities. While they may fight in areas outside their immediate neighbourhood, and may not always personally know those whom they kill, perpetrators are not faceless phantoms or rebel fighters recruited from different parts of a country. A detailed analysis of the patterns of violence supports nuanced scholarly analysis and verification of how violence was organized and where the perpetrators came from for understanding agency and responsibility. Moreover, questioning why some areas within a conflict zone did *not* suffer from communal violence can offer important insights into the location, reach, and limitations of thugs, gangs, or communal militias.

To study the patterns of violence in communal conflicts, research needs to distinguish whether such violence took place in the form of pogroms or two-sided battles; whether violence was perpetrated primarily by armed civilian supporters of political groups or organized communal militias; whether clashes took place in urban and/or in rural areas, and how these clashes may interlink; and whether and how the state was complicit in the organization of violence. All these dimensions can vary significantly within particular cases. In the following, I discuss each dimension in more detail.

## Geography of Violence: Urban and Rural Conflicts

Riots are predominantly understood as 'an urban phenomenon ... lacking significant retaliation',[22] but such descriptions mostly capture the nature of pogroms in urban areas. Donald Horowitz gave rural communal violence a passing but illuminating note: if communal violence does take place in rural areas, 'it tends to be relatively well organized, lasts longer, and is more difficult to end'.[23] For India-

---

[21] Brass 1997, p. 10.    [22] Kalyvas 2006, p. 23.    [23] Horowitz 2001, p. 382.

focused researchers, the city has traditionally been the unit of analysis.[24] According to Varshney and Wilkinson's dataset based on *national* newspaper reporting, more than 96 per cent of deaths from communal violence in India take place in cities.[25] However, there are examples of rural communal violence even in India. The much-studied violence in the state of Gujarat in 2002 did not only affect the cities of Ahmedabad and Surat but also spread to rural areas.[26] Clashes took place over the course of three months and hit 154 out of 182 electoral districts in Gujarat. Furthermore, the balance between urban and rural violence is striking; Ward Berenschot's analysis relies on documents that found that 151 towns and 991 rural remote villages were affected.[27]

I analysed event data collected from *local* Indonesian newspapers and demonstrate that almost half of the recorded casualty numbers for the Maluku conflict stem from killings in rural areas, where violence was more deadly. Similarly, in Plateau State in Nigeria, several massacres and some of the deadliest clashes took place in rural areas or smaller towns, at times wiping out entire village populations. My event dataset on violent incidents for Plateau State covering the years 2001–2016 shows that more than half of the number of violent incidents took place in rural areas and small towns. In Maluku and in Plateau State, respondents agreed that urban and rural violence dynamics were inextricably linked even though the cause of grievances and local conflicts may differ.[28] These linkages eventually resulted in a deadly cycle of killings.

Analysing the geography of communal violence does not concern only the distinction between patterns of urban and rural conflict but also the variation of violence within a conflict-affected area. Riot research has long noted that communal violence 'almost never' engulfs entire cities, but this 'obvious and elementary character of collective violence' has remained under-theorized.[29] For example, Paul Brass noted that in the riot-prone city of Aligarh in the state of Uttar Pradesh in India, 'most of the Muslim population lives

---

[24] Varshney 2002; Brass 2003; Wilkinson 2004, 2013; Berenschot 2011a, 2011b.
[25] Varshney 2002, p. 6.      [26] Human Rights Watch 2002.
[27] Oommen 2005, cited in Berenschot 2011b, p. 20.
[28] See also Adam Higazi's (2016) research on rural communal violence in Plateau State.
[29] Brass 2003, p. 149.

south–southwest of the railway line in enormously congested *mohallas*.'[30] Political administrators had compiled classifications of the city's neighbourhoods in which most of the riotous activities took place into five categories: '[communally] sensitive; riot-hit, but not crime-prone; crime-prone, but not riot-hit; riot-hit and crime prone; sensitive and crime-prone, but not riot-hit'.[31] For residents, community activists, and political administrators in riot-prone cities, and for those who lived in Jos and Ambon, the uneven spread of violence was common knowledge that informed their business and trade activities as much as their daily social lives. The neighbourhood-level variation of violence informed civilian coping strategies and NGO prevention and peacebuilding work.

Rural violence spread very unevenly through Plateau State over the conflict years. After the 2001 violence in Jos, the rural areas most affected by fighting were in lower Plateau State, while some areas closer to Jos maintained a well-functioning local dispute resolution framework to settle conflicts between predominantly Christian farmers and Muslim herders.[32] However, years of fighting impacted the civilian population and eroded interethnic conflict resolution in some previously peaceful rural areas. After the 2010 urban violence in Jos, the rural areas most severely affected were no longer the lower parts of Plateau State but villages on the Jos Plateau close to the city, and rural conflict dynamics were also affected by regional farmer–herder conflicts beyond Plateau State.[33] In sum, a thorough analysis of the geography of communal violence enables a more nuanced understanding of civilian mobilization and the legacies of previous clashes, with important implications for timely intervention and prevention efforts, as I demonstrate in Chapters 4 and 6 on communal war in Ambon and in Jos.

## Type of Killings: Pogroms, Battles, (Joint) Attacks, and Massacres

Communal conflict refers to armed violence between social groups, often understood as 'ethnic groups in conflict'.[34] However, this notion does not specify whether violence and victimization are predominantly

---

[30] Brass 2003, p. 153.     [31] Brass 2003, p. 162.     [32] Blench 2003b.
[33] See Higazi 2016 for a detailed analysis.     [34] Horowitz 1985.

one-sided and directed against a minority, or whether violence takes place between similarly strong groups. This distinction is vital for analysing the dynamics of civilian mobilization and killings. Scholars of Hindu–Muslim violence have emphasized that 'riot' and 'communal violence' can be politically charged labels that obscure understanding the organization of violence and perpetrator responsibilities. In India, as Paul Brass noted, the press and state authorities refer to 'riots' rather than 'pogroms' even though 'mostly Muslims are killed, mostly by the police'.[35] Even more to the point, Parvis Ghassem-Fachandi referred to the 2002 violence in Gujarat as 'the Gujarat pogrom'.[36]

The UCDP dataset defines one-sided violence as 'the use of armed force by the government of a state or by a formally organised group against civilians which results in at least 25 deaths in a year'.[37] In communal conflicts, non-state armed groups perpetrate one-sided violence against a minority, often with complicity from the state. In order to distinguish such patterns from the context of civil war, for one-sided violence in communal conflicts, I use the term 'pogrom'. The distinction of pogroms and two-sided violence is fundamental for a detailed analysis of violence in communal conflicts that can counter politically motivated interpretation of killings and explain conflict escalation, civilian mobilization, and prevention.

My analysis of violence in communal war focuses on conflict between similarly strong groups that I refer to as 'dyadic' or 'communal clashes'. Within dyadic communal conflicts, *pogroms* against unarmed civilians of the other group can take place alongside battles between armed groups from both sides, and joint attacks coordinated by external armed groups with some residents from a targeted area. For example in Jos, at the onset of the first major clashes, residents in predominantly Muslim and mainly Christian neighbourhoods killed or expelled the ethno-religious minority. Subsequently, when no further Muslims or Christians were left to kill within the immediate vicinity, armed civilians mobilized and supported Christian or Muslim groups in other areas of the city, resulting in *joint attacks* against unarmed civilians as well as *battles* between armed civilians.

Communal conflicts can further include massacres as a distinct form of attack. 'Massacres' refers to the simultaneous killing of individuals,

---

[35] Brass 2003, p. 10.   [36] Ghassem-Fachandi 2012.
[37] UCDP, www.pcr.uu.se/research/ucdp/definitions/#One-sided_violence.

as when people seek protection in religious buildings that are subsequently burned down, or when armed groups raid villages and kill all of the inhabitants they can find, as reported from rural areas in Plateau State. In contrast to joint attacks, massacres tend to be perpetrated by armed groups strong enough to carry out the killings without unarmed civilian support. In communal conflicts, massacres may be particularly prevalent in rural areas, where security forces have more difficulties stopping militias and containing fighting.

In sum, within one region affected by communal conflict, the type of killings can vary significantly. Patterns change with levels of civilian mobilization, displacement, and the location and capacity of security forces.

## Categories of Armed Actors

'Riot' tends to be associated with spontaneity of violence, which is misleading because such violence is always embedded into larger communal tensions and relies on some form of organization. Communal violence has been defined as 'a violent clash between two groups of civilians, often characterized as mobs'.[38] 'Mobs' has often been taken to suggest spontaneity of fighting, even though scholars largely agree that riots, even if they are small and less deadly, follow some preparation.[39] The term 'civilians' does not inform us whether violence is primarily carried out by thugs who may have been bussed into the locality for killings, whether neighbours and local youth groups take up arms to fight and kill within their immediate vicinity, or whether communal militias face each other in battles.

The perpetrators of communal violence are variously referred to as 'thugs', 'armed civilians', and simply 'neighbours'. Yet these very different categories of perpetrators imply distinct patterns of mobilization. The UCDP non-state conflict database distinguishes between two types of informal (non-rebel) armed groups. The first type is defined as 'groups composed of supporters and affiliates to political parties and candidates', and the second type as 'groups that share a common identification along ethnic, clan, religious, national or tribal lines'.[40] As we see in what follows, when studying civilian mobilization in

[38] Varshney 2007.    [39] Brass 2003; Wilkinson 2004; Berenschot 2011b.
[40] http://ucdp.uu.se/downloads/nsos/ucdp-nonstate-25-2016.pdf.

communal conflicts, these two types of armed groups can significantly overlap and interlink once conflict escalates. Armed supporters and affiliates to political parties and candidates, i.e. thugs and gangs, may initially instigate communal clashes. If conflict escalates, such groups may transform and mobilize more civilians along ethnic or religious lines for further violence, resulting in the second type of informal armed groups, or communal militias. Whether perpetrators are primarily groups of thugs related to political actors, neighbours who take up arms against neighbours, or well-organized and mobile communal militias implies distinct levels of conflict escalation that call for different intervention strategies. In addition, state security forces often appear as perpetrators whose actions add to the lethality of communal violence. In Ambon and Maluku Province, police and military forces were deeply drawn into the conflict and repeatedly supported attacks, while in Jos, security forces significantly increased the death toll through arbitrary killings.

In the context of civil war, militias have been defined as armed groups, civil militias, or paramilitaries that fight against insurgents, operating alongside state security forces or independently.[41] In the context of communal conflict, however, I understand communal militias as armed groups that fight against opposing militias and unarmed civilians. Communal militias rely on support from unarmed civilians and may have varying links to the state.

Even though a communal conflict may be characterized as two-sided, communal militias on both sides may mobilize civilians differently. For example, in the Maluku conflict, Christian militia groups were primarily based in the city of Ambon and used the extensive and centralized network of the Protestant Church in Maluku for civilian mobilization. Christian militias from the city also fought in rural areas and organized targeted attacks on villages. By contrast, Muslim militias were less centralized in their command structures, and some were based in rural areas. In order to understand the production of violence, both the variation in civilian mobilization and the organizational structures of armed groups need careful analysis.

---

[41] Jentzsch, Kalyvas, and Schubiger 2015.

## National Context

Riot researchers emphasize the role of the state in determining whether riots break out and what deaths tolls are produced. Paul Brass located the origins of Hindu–Muslim violence in the political order of the Indian state, where 'the whole political order in post-Independence north India and many, if not most, of its leading as well as local actors ... have become implicated in the persistence of Hindu–Muslim riots' because of 'concrete benefits for particular political organizations as well as larger political uses'.[42] Steven Wilkinson's theory of electoral incentive structures and communal violence emphasized that the role of the state determines the occurrence and deadliness; depending on institutional incentive structures, elites would have strong or weak motivations to instruct security forces to intervene decisively and stop killings.[43] According to Brass, intense political competition along ethnic lines explains communal conflict, while 'an administration that does not have instructions or its own will to act decisively to prevent or control rioting' explains whether mass killings take place.[44]

The communal wars in Indonesia and Nigeria took place in the context of *regime change* from a military to a civilian regime, within a weakened state and with the security forces in disarray. While Indonesia consolidated a democratic and stable regime, the Nigerian state remained perpetually weak. An immediate and professional intervention of security forces would most likely have brought initial fighting to a halt, but such an intervention did not take place. Instead, security forces were drawn into the conflict on both sides in Ambon and in Jos. While the Indian state has repeatedly been accused of complicity in communal violence, scholars of Indonesian politics have argued that communal violence in Maluku and elsewhere resulted from the state's weakness during regime change and the unravelling of patronage networks.[45] Back in 1999, the very first report on communal violence in Ambon concluded that conspiracy theories, which saw members of the old political regime in Jakarta as orchestrators of communal violence in remote Maluku Province, had little credibility because the state and its security forces hardly seemed capable of such

[42] Brass 2003, p. 6.    [43] Wilkinson 2004.    [44] Brass 2003, p. 149.
[45] Van Klinken 2001, 2007; Bertrand 2004; Sidel 2006; Tajima 2013; Barron, Jaffrey, and Varshney 2016.

conduct during the transition.[46] In other states, such as the DRC, the Central African Republic (CAR), or South Sudan, large-scale communal violence took place in the shadow of civil war or the threat thereof, with the state primarily fighting rebel groups.

The role of the state is central for understanding the escalation and lethality of communal violence. Periods of regime change, democratization and institutional transformation, contested elections, or the context of civil war are often associated with communal violence. States may fail to protect their populations from killings for various reasons that call for different intervention and support strategies.

## Repertoires of Violence

Complementing the analysis of patterns of violence in communal conflict, and adding further nuance to our understanding, repertoires of violence can be distinguished.[47] Francisco Gutiérrez-Sanín and Elisabeth Wood define patterns of violence by armed groups in civil war along dimensions of repertoires as well as targeting, frequency, and technique; together, they display a group's 'violent signature'. In communal conflicts, however, armed groups are less clearly defined; only some are fought by communal militias with strong organizational structures. Repertoires relate to specific actors; in the case of communal conflicts, armed civilians most broadly defined. I focus here on changing repertoires reported for a chain of violent incidents. Armed civilians and communal militias may have more fluid command structures than rebel groups. The observed *repertoires* of violence in communal conflicts may not always include lethal forms of violence and may vary with levels of conflict escalation and armed group organization. Armed civilians may primarily organize an attack to expel and displace members of an ethnic group rather than for mass killings. For example, residents from religiously mixed villages in Maluku reported that neighbours warned them of imminent attacks and delayed the start of violence to allow victims to flee and save their lives before their belongings were looted and their houses were burned down.[48]

Non-lethal acts of communal violence, or the threat of attacks, are an important conflict dimension. The strategic displacement of civilians can secure an electoral win for a political group in a contested election

---

[46] Human Rights Watch 1999.    [47] See Gutiérrez-Sanín and Wood 2017.
[48] Interviews with residents in Ambon, 2009–2014.

or resolve conflicts over land rights through violent means. Furthermore, rape and other forms of sexual violence may significantly vary across and within communal conflicts. For example, for the city of Jos, few reports of sexual violence during clashes exist while for rural areas of Plateau State, significant levels of rape and sexual slavery have been reported.[49] Accounts of communal violence in India repeatedly include reports of rapes of women,[50] while for Maluku Province in Indonesia, rape, torture, and mutilation of men have been reported.[51]

Incidents of communal violence may also display significant variation in the *targeting* of victims, depending on the organization of violence and civilian mobilization. For instance, in some areas, all members of an ethnic group may be killed in an attack regardless of their relationships with neighbours and position within the community. However, respondents frequently stated that community members would mark the houses of those to be attacked by perpetrators from outside the neighbourhood community, which gave neighbours significant leverage over the life or death of potential victims. Thus, communal violence can be indiscriminate when all members of an ethnic group are targeted, for example in massacres, and selective when some members of the targeted group are spared because of social position, social networks, or individual favours.

The *technique* of violence that armed civilians use against their victims relates directly to the forms and levels of civilian mobilization and the role of the state. In both Ambon and Jos, victims during the first clashes were killed with knives and machetes, but civilian communities soon acquired firearms, significantly raising the death tolls. The *frequency* of violent incidents may vary during communal conflicts. Riot researchers have long noted that lulls of months and years can separate one period of violence from another. These lulls do not mean that episodes of communal violence are unconnected. A focus on the impact of violence on civilian mobilization, the changing level of organization of armed groups, and unarmed civilian support for attacks show that periods of violence separated by lulls are interlinked. Thus, reflecting on the frequency of violent incidents may allow for important insights into the dynamics of mobilization and prevention.

[49] Human Rights Watch 2004.   [50] Narula 2002.
[51] Interviews with residents in Ambon, 2009–2014.

## Summary

In order to understand why some communal conflicts escalate to the level of a communal war, and how to halt and reverse escalation, an analysis of (changing) patterns of violence is a crucial first step. I distinguish communal wars from communal conflicts more broadly according to scale. Communal war is often characterized by interlinking dynamics of urban and rural violence. Rural violence may be particularly deadly because it tends to be perpetrated by well-organized communal militias rather than by the thugs and gangs associated with politicians in urban areas. Escalation to the level of communal war can further imply changing civilian mobilization, as when armed civilians associated with political actors transform into militias that pursue violence and ethnic cleansing independently of the control of the state or specific political actors.

## Individual and Collective Agency in Communal War

Research has demonstrated that riots are more likely to break out if electoral incentives on the levels of the local constituency and of the government that controls the security forces align,[52] and that political elites use political–criminal networks to instigate violence.[53] Research has also long recognized that 'ordinary people' may pursue their own agendas under the cover of a conflict narrative and the chaos of a riot, and may not necessarily be following elites into violence.[54] Beyond elite instigation that may explain the onset of communal violence and individual, often malicious, motives for participation, less attention has been paid to collective civilian agency and its causal impact on conflict escalation or de-escalation. Approaches to communal conflict predominantly explain its onset. If they integrate civilian agency, they often do so only to a limited extent.

Studies of communal violence draw on primordialist, instrumentalist, constructivist, or institutionalist approaches, at times combining several perspectives.[55] By now, there is near consensus that no mono-causal theory will account for the complexity of communal violence,

[52] Wilkinson 2004.    [53] Brass 1997, 2003.
[54] Fearon and Laitin 2000; Brass 2003.
[55] Fearon and Laitin 2000; Varshney 2007.

and few scholars seriously argue that ethnic identity is primordial or that it is devoid of any intrinsic value and is used only as a strategic tool.[56] Constructivist approaches emphasize that collective identities are constructed and fluid and can therefore be adapted to defuse social polarization; instrumentalist approaches recognize the primary responsibility of the state and political elites to prevent killings and de-escalate communal relations; and institutionalist approaches identify structural incentives for the instigation of communal violence, such as electoral systems and legal pluralism regarding land rights. Instrumentalist approaches with a focus on elite behaviour have successfully discredited primordialist assumptions of 'ethnic' or 'religious' hatred that explain neither communal violence nor ethnically framed violence against civilians in civil war or genocide.[57] Instrumentalist approaches are prominent in the field and build on rationalist understandings of ethnic politics as building a 'winning coalition of minimal size on the basis of ethnic identities to maximize political control and socioeconomic gain, particularly with regard to electoral democracies'.[58] From a rationalist perspective, electoral mobilization of ethnic groups serves to secure scarce benefits, such as access to government employment, funds and contracts, political representation, and higher education.[59] Political entrepreneurs would have incentives to provoke communal violence for political purposes, and institutions may incentivize or deter such politics.[60]

Instrumentalist approaches, such as the work of Paul Brass and Ward Berenschot, have combined the instrumentalist perspective with a focus on state structures and local political networks. Brass' analysis of the 'institutionalized riot system' identifies the regularities of collective action in reports from different riot cases. He describes the system as 'a perpetually operative network of roles whose functions are to maintain communal hostilities'; 'mobilize crowds to threaten or intimidate persons from the other community'; 'recruit criminals'; and 'let loose widespread violent action'.[61] However, the assumption is problematic that political elites can stir up as well as control communal tensions, let violence loose, or supress and prevent it independently of civilian responses to conflict. Furthermore, whether riot networks in

---

[56] Varshney 2007, p. 292.   [57] Straus 2006; Fujii 2009.   [58] Posner 2005.
[59] Bates 1983, p. 171; Fearon 1999.   [60] Wilkinson 2004, p. 6.
[61] Brass 2003, p. 258.

riot-prone cities are really a cause or rather a consequence of previous rioting remains an empirical question.[62]

Ward Berenschot's study of communal violence in the Indian state of Gujarat in 2002 moved beyond some of these limitations, analysing the roots of riot networks and their performance beyond riot periods. He argued that riot networks also manage everyday local politics within the neighbourhood during peaceful times. They would comprise local politicians as intermediaries for residents with state institutions, as well as police officers, bureaucrats, and local criminals, who all feed off a network that manipulates state institutions and their revenues. Local neighbourhood leaders and elders would not confront such networks when violence was instigated because they depended on these intermediaries. We would therefore 'misinterpret the nature of riot networks if we viewed them solely as "institutionalized riot systems" because these networks were not created for the specific purpose of fomenting violence; they formed themselves in response to the difficulties that citizens face when dealing with state institutions'.[63] Berenschot detailed how community leaders roamed neighbourhoods in preparation for violence, giving hate speeches in private homes and recruiting thugs for the instigation of killings. His analysis offers important insights into neighbourhood politics and social processes during 'peace times' and noted a key role for civilian agency.

Some of Brass' empirical evidence can also be read with a more pronounced emphasis on civilian agency in the production and prevention of communal violence. For example, he discussed journalistic accounts that allude to the relevance of civilian agency for the absence of renewed fighting. When major riots hit Mumbai in 1992, Aligarh remained surprisingly calm. Local journalists reportedly noted that 'people in general were simply fed up with communal riots here' and that 'peace committees had been activated in Aligarh well in time'.[64] My respondents in Ambon and Jos similarly stated that in violence-prone areas, people became tired of everyday life in the face of violence and devastation, and this sentiment eroded unarmed civilian support for armed groups. Brass attributed incidents of tensions without violent outbreaks solely to a lack of political incentives for violence or the awareness and will of the administration to prevent killings. Yet, in

---

[62] Wilkinson 2009, p. 339.    [63] Berenschot 2011b, p. 11.
[64] Brass 2003, p. 139.

Ambon and Jos, many local peacebuilding efforts targeted ordinary people in order to end support for armed civilians. According to local peace activists, it was crucial to reach young men and women to break the cycle of mobilization for renewed fighting.[65] In sum, the predominant instrumentalist perspective implicitly acknowledges the causal role of civilian agency, assuming that civilians may often follow elites into violence for reasons unrelated to elite politics and conflict narratives, but lacks in-depth analysis of the impact and legacies of civilian agency.

Civil war research has studied individual civilian agency more prominently, emphasizing that violence against civilians is often 'jointly produced' by the interaction of armed groups and civilians.[66] I argue that in communal wars, the collaboration between armed and unarmed civilians, the former sometimes killing in neighbourhoods or rural areas they do not live in and the latter often being residents with in-depth knowledge of their neighbours, similarly accounts for a large share of victim numbers, as I show in the empirical chapters.

The intimate character of the local dynamics of violence in communal conflicts, civil war, and genocide has long been regarded as deeply disturbing. 'Everyone lives in fear of his neighbour,' one BBC journalist titled a report on events in Jos after the January 2010 clashes.[67] 'Neighbours' was the title of Jan Gross' study of Jews killed in a Polish village under Nazi German occupation,[68] and Lee Ann Fujii titled her study of individual participation in the Rwandan genocide 'Killing Neighbours'.[69] In order to explain civilian collaboration with armed groups in the production or prevention of civil war violence without a full causal recourse to primordialist discourses of ethnic and religious hatred, individual and private motives come to the fore. Stathis Kalyvas argues that civil wars are so violent partly because they provide opportunities for indirect violence to the local population. Referring to the 'dark side of social capital', he claims that civilians will denounce neighbours to armed groups for what often appear to be private and malicious motives.[70] Denunciation is based on the intimacy of neighbours, family members, colleagues and friends because familiarity with the denounced person is necessary for information about them. Civilian-on-civilian denunciation can have political and

---

[65] Krause 2018.    [66] Kalyvas 2006.    [67] Walker 2011.    [68] Gross 2001.
[69] Fujii 2009.    [70] Kalyvas 2006.

ideological or malicious personal motives. The absence of denunciation may explain the absence of violence from a particular community in civil war, as I discuss in Chapter 2.[71]

In communal conflicts, clashes similarly provide 'opportunities for persons and groups ... to take violent action that would otherwise be prevented by the village leaders or, in some cases, by the police as well'.[72] Individual malicious motives and grievances over political opportunities or land rights may explain why civilians, at least initially, follow elites into violence. Local grievances and land conflicts certainly fuelled the violence in and around Ambon and Jos. However, many people in conflict zones do not take violent actions against others even when opportunities to do so arise. In many religiously mixed neighbourhoods of Ambon and Jos, residents I interviewed stated that they did not fear their immediate neighbours taking up arms to kill them; instead, they feared that their neighbours might allow or even support armed groups from other neighbourhoods to enter their area and kill them. Thus, they feared indirect violence and denunciation in the form of providing information that would allow for and facilitate killings. Some respondents explained that people would have been too ashamed to kill their own neighbours directly.[73] Thus, while communal violence is often referred to as 'neighbours killing neighbours', in my case studies, respondents emphasized that people would kill in areas where they did not personally know their victims, supported by some local residents, rather than directly kill their own neighbours. A thorough analysis of patterns of violence brings such dynamics to the fore.

The riot literature assumes that violent acts within riots are spearheaded and often perpetrated by a small number of 'specialists of violence',[74] not by ordinary people. However, as my research demonstrates, in some neighbourhoods ordinary people made fighting possible, even if they did not kill. In the mixed urban neighbourhoods of Ambon and Jos, where residency was not strictly segregated, gangs and militia groups relied on local informants for the correct targeting of 'enemy populations'. Even where residency was largely segregated and settlement information was of lesser value, armed groups would rely on

[71] Kalyvas 2006, p. 179.   [72] Brass 1997, p. 20.
[73] Interviews in Ambon, 2009–2014.   [74] Brass 1997.

local informants to organize attacks. They collected information regarding the potential resistance of the opposite group, local strategies of security forces within and around that neighbourhood, and information on which houses to loot.[75] The more information armed groups have available, the lesser the risks for the perpetrators involved. Collaboration from residents is further crucial in the aftermath of an attack; unarmed civilian support often ensures a safe return for fighters to their own neighbourhood. This return can be as dangerous as an attack in another community because the opposing armed groups can be equally mobile, and state security forces may deploy and arrest or kill whomever they find on the streets. Thus, mobile fighters may need unarmed civilians to hide them – sometimes for days, if necessary – until a safe return to their communities is possible.

Motivation to support or take part in violence may further change during the course of conflict, beyond initial individual malicious motives and local grievances. Interviewing perpetrators from Rwanda's genocide, Straus noted that fear and the need for self-protection were important motives for joining the killings.[76] Scacco concluded that in Jos, young men who took part in the 2001 clashes often sought to protect their neighbourhood against armed groups from other areas.[77] In addition to motives of protection, my respondents often referred to emotions of pride, loyalty and belonging to one's religious group, which hardened during the course of conflict, as well as revenge for previous atrocities. Consequently, analysis of civilian agency needs to take the full range of changing motives into account.

A social constructivist perspective emphasizes motives relating to group identity and collective action. While the social construction of ethnic identities is to some extent 'obviously right',[78] a focus on mobilization supports analysis of the causal relevance of collective identities and narratives. Social constructivism reminds us that ethnic boundaries are often activated and strengthened by the political mobilization of identities and the use of collective violence. Ethnic or religious groups may not be the densely knit communities with a high in-group information flow they tend to be portrayed as in ethnic discourses, particularly in larger mixed urban settings. Many people who would be members of

---

[75] Information collected from interviews with residents and militia leaders in Ambon and Jos, 2009–2015.
[76] Straus 2006.   [77] Scacco 2010.   [78] Brubaker 2004, p. 3.

a particular ethnic or religious group may not hold this social identity as particularly salient and may maintain social networks that include few members of 'their' ethnic or religious groups until the outbreak of violence forces them to break up inter-group ties.

In sum, approaches that either neglect civilian agency or limit its relevance to individual motives and grievances are too narrow to account for conflict escalation to the level of communal war and its patterns of violence. Mass communal violence does not take place without civilian mobilization. Furthermore, the common assumption of 'neighbours killing neighbours' in communal conflicts is too narrow to account for the causal role of unarmed civilian support in the organization of violence. In the last part of this chapter, I present a theoretical framework for the analysis of civilian mobilization and conflict escalation to communal war.

## Civilian Mobilization and Conflict Escalation

Periods of relative calm have often been observed between riots. Yet studies tend to neglect the analysis of people's responses to previous killings during such lulls. For example, for Stanley Tambiah, riots are 'mercifully short-lived', not only because the police and army, after initial chaos and paralysis, can assert their dominance but also because the riots would have a short life cycle in any case.[79] There is an assumption that what happens during lulls is not causally relevant for conflict escalation or de-escalation. From an instrumentalist point of view, communal violence does not take place as long as political elites do not instigate violence or instruct police forces to suppress killings.[80] However, this focus on a negative peace as the absence of lethal violence ignores how local communities often remain deeply polarized and support or tolerate conflict narratives and the circulation of weapons. Thugs, gangs, and vigilantes, i.e. individuals and groups who may have initiated communal clashes, and the conflict narratives that 'other' and dehumanize members of another ethnic or religious group, do not simply cease to exist outside episodes of killings. For example, in Jos, residents described the period between the clashes in 2001 and 2008 as a 'graveyard peace', knowing that the absence of violence in no way meant that the conflict was resolved. Instead, strong tensions, religious

[79] Tambiah 1990, p. 744.    [80] Brass 2003; Wilkinson 2004, 2013.

conflict narratives, and community armament for self-protection prevailed. Equating the absence of communal violence in such settings with 'peace' forecloses understanding the legacies of violence, civilian responses, and mobilization for or against further fighting. This limited focus on lethal violence further ignores that in the face of violent outbreaks, some civilians may respond with local prevention efforts with the potential to cause de-escalation and restraint.[81] Birgit Bräuchler discussed the many small peacebuilding efforts that residents in Ambon initiated, often only days after the first clashes broke out, which eventually supported a grassroots peace process.[82] Analysing how people respond to the aftermath of communal violence, and why violence prevention efforts do not take place or have limited impact on conflict escalation, supports understanding of the escalation process and its prevention.

Recent genocide research has adopted a broader analytical perspective that encompasses genocide as a complex social process beyond a narrow analysis of elite behaviour and killings. Examining how the process of genocide unfolds allows for a more nuanced analysis of its prevention.[83] As a process, the Rwandan genocide 'ceases to be a clearly demarcated temporal period of mass slaughter and becomes instead a messy agglomeration of actions taken and not taken, decisions made and unmade, perceptions reinforced and transformed', whereby shifting contexts and actors with multiple and contradictory motives mean that 'this process need not be linear, for the violence can speed up, slow down, claim new targets, and abandon the old.'[84] Thus, factors and processes of restraint, de-escalation, or non-escalation come into view. I adopt this perspective on communal war as a complex process and focus on the social dynamics before, during, and after acts of killings to understand civilian mobilization and conflict escalation. How civilians respond to tensions and killings may determine the patterns of violence, conflict duration, lethality, and legacies, such as displacement and a changing economy. Beyond the root causes of conflict and elite incentives, it is civilian mobilization, i.e. armed and unarmed support for collective violence, which explains communal war.

[81] See Straus 2012.  [82] Bräuchler 2015.  [83] Rosenberg 2012, p. 17.
[84] Fujii 2009, p. 11.

In the following, I provide a theoretical framework of civilian mobilization and conflict escalation that draws on concepts and mechanisms developed within the social movements and contentious politics literature. Conflict escalation means 'an increase in the frequency and scale of attacks or a widening of the repertoire or the targeting of violence'.[85] Conflict escalation results from social processes that transform and reconfigure social networks, aligning unarmed civilians with those who take up arms. Elisabeth Wood's analysis identified six wartime processes for the context of civil war: political mobilization; military socialization; polarization of social identities; militarization of local authorities; the transformation of gender roles; and the fragmentation of the local economy. All of them reconfigure social networks to a varying extent, often with profound legacies after the conflict.[86] Social mechanisms are the events that link effects to causes and compound into larger social processes, which 'assemble mechanisms into combinations and sequences that produce larger-scale effects than any particular mechanism causes by itself'.[87] This approach takes into account that mechanisms that cause processes of escalation and de-escalation can take place in parallel, which needs to inform the analysis of non-violence and restraint as well as targeted intervention strategies.

In the context of communal war, I identify three key processes of civilian mobilization and conflict escalation: the political mobilization of what I term 'everyday violence networks'; the polarization of social identities and traumatization; and the formation of communal militias and the militarization of local communities, which also deepens polarized and unequal gender relations. To what extent these processes impact the civilian population and conflict dynamics, and how deeply they transform a conflict region, depends on the response of security forces and the role of the state as well as the strength and perseverance of local prevention and peacebuilding initiatives that have the potential to halt and reverse escalation.

## Political Mobilization of Everyday Violence Networks

Although communal clashes are often described as anomic and 'sudden' outbursts of killings, perpetrators do not appear out of nowhere and atrocities do not take place without a conflict narrative.

---

[85] Wood 2015, p. 475.   [86] Wood 2008.   [87] Tilly and Tarrow 2007, p. 214.

Table 1.2 *The social processes of escalation*

| Social Process | Mechanisms |
| --- | --- |
| Political Mobilization of 'Everyday Violence Networks' | *Alignment* of thugs, gangs, and vigilantes with political actors *Recruitment* of ordinary youth through ethnic and religious networks |
| Polarization of Social Identities | *Othering* *Traumatization* *Moral Outrage* |
| Militia Formation and Militarization of Local Communities | *(further) Recruitment of ordinary men (women, children) Unarmed civilian support to armed groups Suppression of dissidents* |

Communal violence is rooted in what I term 'everyday violence net-works'. These networks consist primarily of groups of thugs and gangs, which often extend to vigilante youth. Their availability explains how 'sudden' but massive violence is possible even in apparently peaceful and harmonic places without a legacy of communal killings. In ethnically and religiously polarized environments, everyday violence networks link to political actors and parties. The collaboration between ethnic and religious leaders with political actors during elec-tion times is a widespread phenomenon in both Nigeria and Indonesia, and many other countries of the global south, and represents a central challenge to meaningful democratization.[88] It is common for ethnic and religious leaders to give voting advice and endorse politicians. This collaboration between political actors and ethnic and religious leaders links ordinary youth groups organized around ethnic and religious lines to violence networks. Such linkages result in a large number of predominantly men, and sometimes women, being mobilized for vio-lence, including a few 'specialists in violence' and many who may follow them into fighting. Beyond the politicization of vigilantes, thugs, and gangs and their instrumental *alignment* with political actors, the collaboration between political actors and ethnic/religious leaders

[88] Staniland 2014.

provide legitimacy for the consolidation of violence networks around politicians and political agendas and the recruitment of youth along ethnic and religious lines.

In Indonesia and Nigeria, the recruitment of vigilantes and thugs around political actors and state institutions has long been common practice. In Indonesia, during and after the transition from the authoritarian regime under Suharto in 1998, most political parties had some form of active paramilitary wing and associated groups.[89] Thugs and gangsters expanded their networks along ethnic and religious lines as patronage structures unravelled and took control over public places for exploitation, such as bus terminals and food markets.[90] The Ambon conflict broke out at the city's central bus terminal and market where well-known *preman* groups (thugs) competed for territorial control. With the return to civilian rule in 1999, Nigeria similarly witnessed 'a proliferation of vigilantism'.[91] Vigilante groups have organized around various identities, from lineage to ethnicity and religion. Ethnic militias serve as vigilantes in their own neighbourhoods and as thugs for politicians.[92] Most urban neighbourhoods have groups of adolescents who are accepted within the community and perform certain social and public services, such as collecting rubbish and protecting against thieves.[93] Neighbourhoods with poor policing rely on 'local security providers',[94] such as vigilante groups, for protection. Beyond fighting crime and providing community protection, vigilantes have become 'synonymous with the fractured and violence-ridden image of Africa's most populous nation'.[95] Young men who have not yet established a 'career' based on their hired muscle power often join for the benefits of social status in the neighbourhood and small incomes provided.

Everyday violence networks form the basis of armed group mobilization and militia formation in communal warfare. This politicization of violence networks transforms networks of vigilantes, street gangs, and thugs into groups aligned with political actors and agendas. *Recruitment* of ordinary youth through neighbourhood ethnic and religious networks broadens violence networks beyond the core of 'violence specialists'. In sum, the political mobilization of an everyday violence network builds on the mechanisms of *alignment* of such

[89] Ryter 1998; Lindsey 2001; Wilson 2006.     [90] Wilson 2006, p. 270.
[91] Pratten 2008, p. 1.     [92] Agbu 2004, p. 35; Bratton 2008.     [93] Ya'u 2000.
[94] Scacco 2010.     [95] Ya'u 2000.

networks around political actors and the further *recruitment of ordinary youth* from ethnic and religious networks. The process results in social network reconfigurations that link violence specialists and ordinary youth who may not have used violent means before to political actors and ethnic/religious leaders, thus providing the organizational capacity for mass violence.

## Polarization of Social Identities

Polarization is a key concept in the study of group conflict.[96] I conceptualize polarization as a social process of civilian mobilization and conflict escalation, which deepens with the traumatization of victims. This process renders civilians more likely to support armed groups in fighting. Polarization of social identities and conflict narratives influenced by trauma and moral outrage mobilize civilians along with an emotional response to previous clashes. Meaning-making and interpretation after initial clashes can change conflict narratives and subsequent violence dynamics. The Ambon riots broke out as ethnic clashes against non-Ambonese migrants. Only when a 'religious war' narrative emerged did the conflict escalate to the level of a communal war and pull many ordinary civilians in. An international environment characterized by a polarization along the Christian–Muslim cleavage further deepened this local conflict narrative and contributed to escalation. In Ambon and Jos, ethnic, and particularly religious, relations between Muslims and Christians were polarized long before the outbreak of violence. Both regions had a history of ethnic and religious polarization linked to competing political claims even though no previous major clashes had taken place. The polarization of social identities intensified with the onset of violence. High levels of polarization resulted in increased civilian support for armed groups and segregation of the population.

Theoretically, mild polarization of social identities can emerge from political mobilization around ethnic and religious identities and increases with narratives of threat and exclusion. A basic social psychological mechanism that causes polarization is '*othering*', which has been well documented in ethnic conflict and genocide research to explain how ordinary people can turn into perpetrators,[97] and also in

[96]  Nordlinger 1972; Kalyvas 2009; Wilkinson 2012.
[97]  Waller 2007; Chirot and McCauley 2010; Monroe 2008, 2012.

feminist security studies on gender, race, and peacebuilding.[98] Othering draws on social identity theory and in-group bias. Social identity theory assumes that individuals strive to maintain a positive and distinct group identity based on in-group and out-group categories. Tajfel defined social identity as 'the individual's knowledge that he belongs to certain social groups together with some emotional and value significance to him of his group membership'.[99] In-group bias is a fundamental and omnipresent feature that structures inter-group relations.[100] 'In-group bias' refers to the systematic tendency to evaluate one's own membership group or its members more favourably than a non-membership group or its members, and can encompass discrimination, prejudice, and stereotyping.[101] In-group bias 'can be compatible with a range of attitudes toward corresponding out-groups, including mild positivity, indifference, disdain, or hatred'.[102] Consequently, inter-group relations are not inherently prone to violence, and social categorization and group identifications do not in themselves cause violent behaviour towards members of the out-group. Some scholars argue that in-group identification is a necessary condition for the successful organization of perpetrators for mass killings and genocide.[103] Increased in-group bias can contribute to violence because it results in distorted perceptions and hinders a neutral analysis of a conflict situation.[104] Polarized communities are more likely to support armed groups for community protection and for revenge killings.

Strong polarization emerges endogenously, as a result of atrocities and victimization. It can severely weaken inter-group networks and strengthen the bonds of intra-group collaboration. It is an important component of escalation because it may distort civilians' perspectives and perceived choices about protection and the (im)possibility of prevention. *Traumatization* explains dramatically increased in-group bias, othering and dehumanization. Trauma can contribute to a more profound and exclusive sense of community. In trauma research, it has been argued that the experience of sudden, unusual, and extreme suffering can become the defining factor of social identities and render

---

[98] Hudson 2014. [99] Tajfel 1972, p. 292. [100] Tajfel and Turner 1979, p. 56.
[101] Hewstone, Rubin, and Willis 2002, p. 576. [102] Brewer 1999, p. 430.
[103] Chirot and McCauley 2010.
[104] Fearon and Laitin 2000, p. 854; Christie et al. 2008, p. 546.

groups of victims feeling 'set apart and made special', thus strengthening group boundaries.[105] Kai Erikson's research on collective trauma found that community members' perceptions of situations were distorted through the traumatic experience: 'They come to feel they have lost a natural immunity to misfortune and that something awful is almost bound to happen.'[106] Traumatized people thus become unusually vigilant and anxious. In both Ambon and Jos, even during times without fighting, rumours circulated. Many community peace activists stated that they aimed to facilitate a professional approach to rumours that would support people with verification and overcome the dynamics of anxiety and outrage that could easily spark further violence. Traumatization contributes to conflict escalation because people are more likely to believe rumours and support armed groups for self-protection. Furthermore, severe harm caused by people can have a qualitatively different traumatic dimension than harm caused by natural disasters. Killings and destruction perceived as brought about by other human beings 'not only hurt in special ways but bring in their wake feelings of injury and vulnerability from which it is difficult to recover'.[107] The 'inhumanity' that people experience comes to be seen as a natural feature of human life.

*Moral outrage* over atrocities can further deepen the traumatization and further align civilians with armed groups based on loyalty.[108] Perpetrators in Rwanda often noted anger and outrage as their motives for participating in killings.[109] Polarization leads to segregation and ethnic cleansing, which further changes social networks and results in more homogenous communities and strengthens in-group bias. Polarization and traumatization align unarmed civilians more profoundly with armed groups for their own community protection but also for revenge seeking. Extensive support from ordinary people makes the formation of communal militias and the militarization of local order possible.

In sum, the mechanism of *othering* supports the polarization of social identities and conflict narratives, while *traumatization* and *moral outrage* deepen polarization and sustain dehumanizing outgroup narratives. Although the traumatization of the victimized civilian population is an obvious feature of armed conflict, its social

---

[105] Erikson 1995.    [106] Erikson 1995, p. 195.    [107] Erikson 1995, p. 237.
[108] Wood 2008.    [109] Straus 2006.

psychological effect deserves careful analytical attention because it endogenously causes further escalation, deepening and accelerating support for armed civilians and enabling the consolidation of communal militias.

## Militia Formation and Militarization of Local Communities

The emergence of local militias as compact and often well-trained combat units is a key explanatory factor for the escalation of clashes into communal war. In Ambon and Jos, gangs and militias established social control within neighbourhoods, and widely recruited ordinary men and – in Ambon – young children. They established influence and control within ethnic and religious communities through collaboration with some community leaders and repression of those who opposed the militarization of local order and recruitment.

Armed groups in and around Ambon and Jos have been variously referred to as 'vigilantes', 'gangs', and 'militias'.[110] We can distinguish vigilantes as those groups oriented towards the protection of a circumscribed locality and militias as those oriented towards offence, who launch attacks 'either within or beyond the immediate locality of the village or town'.[111] However, even though armed groups in Jos were primarily referred to as 'gangs' or 'vigilantes' rather than 'militias', neighbourhood-based armed groups went out on coordinated attacks into other parts of the city.

The political mobilization of civilian networks in support of gangs and militias reshapes social networks.[112] In the contexts of Ambon and Jos, initial political mobilization took place along ethnic and predominantly religious cleavages prior to local elections after a regime change. Civilians aligned themselves with gangs and militias and mobilized for self-protection or the protection of religious kin. This civilian realignment and unarmed support often resulted in attacks on other neighbourhoods and villages, wrapped into narratives of self-defence. Militia members purchased weapons with

[110] Best and von Kemedi 2005.    [111] Higazi 2008, p. 119.
[112] Wood 2008, p. 545.

money collected from community members who contributed for their own protection.

Militia formation and the militarization of local communities are based on mechanisms of broader recruitment of ordinary men, and sometimes women and children, widespread civilian support, repression of individuals and leaders opposed to further fighting, and peer group pressure among men to join militias. Participation in fighting also provides unemployed young men with a significant rise in social status as protectors of their communities. Militia members in both places explained that local communities would prepare food before men went into battles, and that as militia members they could 'ask' for money from local politicians. Joining armed groups offered significant economic benefits. Further important emotional motivations included a sense of obligation to protect one's religious community, the need to prove one's 'manhood', and shame over not participating. Some former fighters I interviewed explained that men could not stay in their houses knowing that other men were going into battle.

The formation and transformation of gangs and militias is linked to the militarization of community order. Local communities became particularly militarized in Ambon, where gang leaders rose to positions of leadership and influence alongside religious and community leaders. Their active recruitment of children into militia groups exemplifies the militarization of local order. Militarization was based on *recruitment* of ordinary men, women, and children, on *unarmed civilian support* of armed groups for community defence, and on the *suppression* of civilian leaders who tried to oppose militarization. Many community leaders supported gangs and militias either out of a desire for protection and/or potentially opportunistic motives. The militarization of local authority often has a strong generational dimension; young men are put into a position to challenge their parents' generation, elders, and traditional leaders. Ordinary people – men and women – are drawn directly into fighting, or indirectly into supporting fighting through organizing food, manufacturing ammunition, or attending to wounded fighters.

In sum, the transformation of gangs and the formation of militias, as well as the militarization of community order, resulted in an alignment of ordinary people with armed groups that made communal war possible.

## Conclusion

This chapter developed the concept of communal war to explain why and how conflicts in and around Ambon and Jos could escalate from initial violence between thugs and gangs into fighting that killed on the level of a small civil war. If communal violence causes casualties in the thousands rather than in double-digit figures, it relates to distinct organizational dynamics of violence networks. In order to distinguish communal wars from other forms of communal conflict and analyse the organization of violence and its prevention, I presented a typology of patterns of violence in communal conflicts along four dimensions: geography; type of violence; level of organization among armed civilians; and the role of the state and the national context. In addition, I integrated an analysis of the repertoires of violence that armed civilians employ. Even though episodes of collective violence may only last for several days, the consequences of group polarization and traumatization, the formation of militias, and the displacement of large populations result in legacies that often increase vulnerability and endogenously cause further violence. Analysing the changing patterns of violence is an important first step towards understanding civilian agency, conflict escalation, and prevention. The chapter then demonstrated that civilian agency is a key causal factor for violence in communal wars and argued for its comprehensive analysis along a range of motives in the context of changing conflict dynamics. Communal conflicts partly kill on the level of civil wars because armed groups collaborate with unarmed civilians, whose support is vital for the organization of large-scale attacks. Building on the typology of patterns of violence in communal conflicts and the causal role of civilian agency, the chapter lastly offered a theoretical framework of civilian mobilization and conflict escalation to analyse how large-scale communal violence emerges from below. The next chapter presents a complementary typology of civilian mobilization and non-escalation for the analysis of resilient communities.

# 2 | Resilient Communities

In many conflict zones, civilians try to escape or resist war dynamics. They seek to evade the reach of armed groups by fleeing temporarily or choosing long-term displacement. They adopt coping practices such as maintaining temporary shelters, night commuting, or establishing bush camps away from villages, as has been reported from Uganda,[1] Sudan and South Sudan,[2] and Myanmar,[3] to name just a few cases. On their own and without organized support, however, civilians stand little chance of surviving and escaping a conflict zone.[4] Collective civilian protection strategies increase the likelihood of survival, but they raise the classic collective action problem.[5] People's protection and prevention efforts are often contingent on strong leadership, maintaining social cohesion, and context-related factors. Even when civilians try to collectively resist war dynamics they may fail.[6]

In the previous chapter, I have argued that conflicts escalate to the level of a communal war once violent incidents endogenously cause widespread civilian mobilization and support to armed groups that results in further violence, for example by providing armed groups with target-relevant information, by cooking for armed men when they assemble for attacks, and by hiding perpetrators from security forces in the aftermath of an attack. Unarmed civilian support is crucial for the formation of communal militias and reflects a militarization of local order. Conflict escalation builds on the social processes of political mobilization of everyday violence networks of thugs, gangs, and vigilantes; the polarization of social identities, including traumatization; and militia formation and the militarization of local communities.

In this chapter, I explain the outcome of non-violence in ethnically, religiously, and socio-economically mixed and *vulnerable* communities

---

[1] Baines and Paddon 2012.    [2] Corbett 2011.    [3] Hull 2009; South 2010.
[4] Tec 1993; Kaplan 2017.    [5] Arjona 2016a; Kaplan 2017; Masullo 2017.
[6] Lynch 2014; Kaplan 2017; Khamidov, Megoran, and Heathershaw 2017; Krause 2017.

as the result of a process of non-escalation and adaptation. Drawing on evolutionary resilience research, I construct a *resilience lens* to analyze adaptation to an adverse environment. The resilience literature has linked community adaptation to the generic social dynamics of social knowledge and learning, lived experience, anticipation of threats and challenges, and scenario-building. I apply this resilience lens to non-violent communities and theorize individual agency in the form of visionary leadership and collective agency or mobilization against violence.

I understand individual behaviour in armed conflict along a range of potential options from rescuing victims to evading, participating in, or actively organizing killings.[7] My focus is on individual agency and leadership as high-risk and altruistic rescue agency, drawing on previous research on rescue behaviour during genocide. I combine this focus on individual rescue agency with an analysis of collective agency for violence prevention, which I understand as motivated primarily by the desire for self-protection. Non-escalation results from three social processes of civilian mobilization and violence prevention: the depolarization of social identities; the establishment of social control within communities, including persuasive advocacy of non-violence, the formulation of rules and procedures for conflict management, and the repression of those who want to fight; and engagement with external armed groups for negotiation and refusal to collaborate in attacks.

In the following, I first discuss why the riot literature does not explain non-violence in *vulnerable* mixed communities and rule out alternative explanations for non-violence. Next, I examine arguments for civilian agency and non-violence presented in the civil war and genocide literature. While genocide research has primarily focused on individual agency in the form of rescue behaviour and stressed the causal role of norms and moral values, civil war research has examined collective agency and emphasized institutional capacity as key to resisting war dynamics. How institutional capacity emerges, however, and how institutions and social cohesion are sustained during months and years within a changing war zone has received limited attention to date. Third, I provide a brief review of the resilience literature and develop what I term the 'resilience lens', which emphasizes adaptation

---

[7] Drawing on Kristen Monroe's work 2001a, 2012. See also Fujii's 2009 conceptualization.

as a complex and non-linear process within the context of adversity. Rooted in evolutionary resilience and climate change research, community adaptation has been shown to rely on generic dynamics of social knowledge and learning, meaning-making, and social organization that draws on visionary thinking and supports constructive coping strategies and conflict resolution.

In the second half of the chapter, I situate individual agency and leadership aimed at violence prevention within a broader understanding of perspective and socialization, emphasizing the significance of altruistic behaviour. I argue that non-violence emerges through strong leadership rooted in social knowledge of conflict dynamics and lived experience in conflict zones. A more altruistic perspective results in courageous and risk-tolerating leadership that persuades others to join in violence prevention. Even though strong leadership is necessary for the emergence of prevention efforts, communities cannot sustain prevention over months and years without collective agency and widespread mobilization for non-violence, which results in at least weak forms of institutionalized conflict management.

## Why the Riot Literature Does Not Explain Non-Violence

To date, there is limited research into the localized absence of clashes in conflict zones and bottom-up peace initiatives. Riot research on India implies four potential explanations for the absence of violence in communities located in conflict zones. First, according to Brass, the absence of an 'institutionalised riot system' within a mixed neighbourhood may explain the absence of killings. Thus, neighbourhoods that do not host strong gangs or groups of thugs that politicians can mobilize may be significantly less vulnerable to communal violence. Second, according to Varshney, neighbourhoods with high levels of cross-cleavage civic engagement and peace committees – and in particular middle-class neighbourhoods – should be much less vulnerable to clashes. Third, according to Berenschot, violence should be absent from communities that prevent politicians from instigating clashes and armed groups from entering the neighbourhood. Finally, according to Steven Wilkinson's work as discussed in Chapter 1, the timely intervention of security forces could also explain the absence of violence.[8] None of

---

[8] Wilkinson 2004.

these theories accounts for how the ethnically, religiously, and socio-economically mixed communities of Wayame in Ambon and Dadin Kowa in Jos, which were both vulnerable to clashes from within and from external armed groups, remained non-violent during the course of several years.

Ashutosh Varshney's work focused on civic engagement in Indian cities to explain why some cities are not riot-prone. In analogy to Brass' 'institutionalised riot system' discussed in the first chapter, Varshney argued that an 'institutionalised peace system' based on cross-cleavage civic engagement can mitigate communal tensions and prevent riots.[9] Civic networks would promote communication and the temporary formation of peace committees that can police neighbourhoods, neutralize rumours, and collaborate with local state authorities.[10] Everyday forms of inter-ethnic civic engagement would make violence prevention possible. However, associational forms of civic engagement – such as business organizations and unions – would be sturdier in resisting riot instigation. In sum, 'interethnic networks are agents of peace.'[11]

Varshney's work offers a valuable bottom-up perspective, but a number of theoretical and methodological issues arise. First and foremost, just as it is difficult to ascertain whether Brass' 'institutionalised riot system' is a cause or an effect of communal violence, we cannot verify whether higher percentages of inter-ethnic engagement are cause or effect of the absence of riots in the cities Varshney studied. It is noteworthy that in one of his samples from a peaceful town, 84 per cent of Hindus and Muslims stated they visit each other regularly, while in the violence-prone counterpart, 60 per cent said they did so.[12] Furthermore, by using the city as its unit of analysis, the study cannot demonstrate that civic engagement explains non-violence within neighbourhoods of riot-prone cities. He assumed that neighbourhood-level peace committees during times of tensions would simply be 'an extension of the pre-existing local networks of engagement'.[13] This argument is illustrated with the case of Surat, where, in 1992, a riot hit the slums while middle-class neighbourhoods remained peaceful. According to Varshney, in the slums, 'where workers worked exceptionally long hours . . . there are few institutionalized

---

[9] Varshney 2002.   [10] Varshney 2002.   [11] Varshney 2002, p. 363.
[12] Varshney 2002.   [13] Varshney 2001, p. 388.

settings for building civic ties', while in middle-class areas, 'peace committees were quickly formed'.[14] However, the formation of peace committees is no explanation of non-violence because it remains unclear whether such neighbourhoods were threatened in the first place. In Jos, middle-class areas did not host strong vigilante or gang networks and were under reasonable police protection. Residents did not consider such areas as *vulnerable*. Furthermore, not only poor people riot. In Surat, 'a new low was registered in the Hindu middle class association with communal violence as well-off men and women joined in the looting of Muslim shops' and 'stories began to circulate of middle class men and women ... defying the curfew and returning home with the choicest booty'.[15] Some have dismissed the relevance of people's peace efforts altogether, arguing, 'even where elements of civic engagement do exist in civil society in India, they cannot withstand the power of political movements and forces that seek to create inter-communal violence.'[16] Others have noted that the argument is specifically about Hindu–Muslim relations because the 'peaceful' cities in Varshney's sample have seen 'brutally violent incidents along lines of caste (low-status versus high-status Hindus) and sect (Shia versus Sunni Muslims)'.[17]

Brass' work on communal violence also includes incidents of prevention. For example, he refers to an article about how a Hindu woman intervened when a mob tried to kill a Muslim group; the woman was able to prevent killings and shelter the group in her house until the police could take them to safety. For Brass, this was an exceptional case for which he had 'no similar reports in the history of post-independence rioting in Aligarh'.[18] Residents in Ambon and Jos, however, frequently reported how neighbours intervened, hid them, and saved them from attackers.[19] Furthermore, Brass noted that in one vulnerable neighbourhood in the city of Aligarh, communal violence was prevented despite heavy tensions. He explained the local absence of violence solely as the absence of instigation: 'the district administration in Aligarh at the time was very much aware of the potential for an outbreak of violence at this site, was on top of the situation, and was determined to ensure that no significant violence did in fact break

[14] Varshney 2002.   [15] Chandra 1993, p. 1884.   [16] Brass 2006, pp. 68–69.
[17] King 2004.   [18] Brass 2003, p. 142.
[19] Human Rights Watch 1999; Tertsakian and Smart 2001.

out.'[20] However, the perspective of residents from the neighbourhood is not documented. The potential alternative explanation – people's violence prevention efforts – remained underexplored.

Ward Berenschot's study investigated the variation of violence within the city of Ahmedabad and identified one neighbourhood, Raamrahimnagar, which did not suffer clashes between its Hindu and Muslim populations.[21] In this area, a local neighbourhood committee of twenty-three members controlled many of the activities in the locality, acted as an intermediary to state institutions, politicians, and parties, and physically attacked anyone who came into the community to instigate fighting. During the Gujarat killings, neighbourhood youth patrolled the entrances into the area while elder leaders addressed tensions and convinced people not to fear each other or start killings.[22] Although Berenschot's discussion of the actual dynamics of violence and non-violence is limited,[23] it demonstrates that neither the existence of an institutionalized riot system nor of an institutionalized peace system explains communal violence and its absence. Berenschot concluded that the absence of violence was in part due to the integration of local leaders into patronage networks not organized around religious divisions, making Raamrahimnagar 'an island of communal harmony'.[24] By contrast, I find that the non-violent communities of Wayame in Ambon and Dadin Kowa in Jos were by no means places of communal harmony. As discussed in Chapters 5 and 7, violence prevention remained contingent on people's constant conflict management and prevention efforts.

In sum, none of these approaches explains my empirics. First, while Wayame and Dadin Kowa did not host strong gangs or groups of thugs, they did have significant numbers of unemployed youth at risk of being mobilized. In both non-violent communities, in the context of high levels of regional civilian mobilization for violence, some of the youth wanted to take up arms against their neighbours. Thus, both communities were vulnerable to killings. Second, both were socio-economically mixed areas with middle-class and poor houses, but lacking private security guards. Due to the dynamics of communal war and strong mobile militias, in Ambon, no mixed middle-class neighbourhood – and indeed no mixed area except Wayame – escaped

---

[20] Brass 2003, p. 146.    [21] Berenschot 2011a, p. 223; 2011b.
[22] Berenschot 2011b.    [23] Mehta 2013.    [24] Berenschot 2011a, p. 228.

the clashes. In Jos, some middle-class settlements remained peaceful, but people in Jos never regarded these areas as vulnerable to violence in the first place. These were upper-middle-class settlements in the south of the city with relatively large compounds and well-laid-out streets, private security guards, and good police protection. Given that the Nigerian military brought the clashes in Jos under control better than the Indonesian military did in Ambon, urban armed groups did not consolidate into communal militias strong enough to attack and over-whelm any urban neighbourhood, as they did in Ambon. Third, both communities could not rely on the timely intervention of security forces for their protection. The establishment of some form of community organization and the prevention of instigations of violence does explain the absence of violence in Wayame and in Dadin Kowa. Yet, under-standing how these vulnerable communities established and main-tained such institutions and prevented clashes during several years of fighting needs careful theorization of collective agency in the context of vulnerability in a changing conflict zone. In order to do this, I first draw on research into non-violent communities in civil war and genocide and examine individual and collective agency for non-violence. I then develop a theoretical framework of mobilization for non-violence, using a resilience lens to conceptualize adaptation within the context of a changing conflict environment.

## How People Prevent Killings

Genocide and civil war research has emphasized the roles of values and normative commitments on the one hand, and the relevance of institu-tional local capacity on the other hand, for explaining non-violence in conflict. I combine both arguments in my theoretical framework, but first examine both in more detail. Examples of communities that pre-vented killings abound from a range of civil wars. 'Zones of Peace' research spearheaded investigation into civilian agency and non-violence, emphasizing how peace communities in the Philippines helped people overcome a sense of helplessness and hopelessness in the midst of war.[25] However, these peace zones were also ignored at times and overrun by armed groups during the course of the conflict.[26]

---

[25] Hancock and Mitchell 2007, 2012; Hancock 2017.
[26] Garcia 1997; Hancock and Iyer 2007.

Case study research has documented how, in Sierra Leone, one village community located in a conflict-affected area reportedly forged a sense of unity, carefully avoided collaboration with the Revolutionary United Front (RUF), and managed conflicts between elders and youth so that rebels would not be able to exploit tensions, as they did in many other villages.[27] Reports from Syria show that during the early years of the civil war, which began in 2011, community leaders repeatedly negotiated local ceasefires with armed groups to lessen the impact of fighting on the civilian population.[28] As discussed in the first chapter, civil war research has predominantly focused on 'negative' agency such as denunciations that enable killings.[29] According to Stathis Kalyvas, civilians would make denouncements often for private or malicious motives or to settle local scores.[30] However, reports of civilians who protect others in conflict and who preserve localized non-violence while tolerating risks to their own lives call for a theorizing of protective and preventive agency in war.

Why would individuals not denounce others and collaborate with armed groups? Fear of retaliation is one credible motive, but one account cited in Kalyvas, which refers to a non-violent community during the Guatemalan civil war, pointed to the significance of ideas, values, and relations among civilians: 'Despite the army occupation, almost no one died in Chimbal, in contrast to all the towns around them' because people in Chimbal were '"good people", good "Christian believers" who had not denounced one another to the army as people had elsewhere'.[31]

## Norms, Values, and Rescue Agency

Why not denounce neighbours to armed groups when it is relatively safe to do so during armed conflict, especially when communities are ripe with social conflicts and no places of harmony? Scholarship on non-violence and civil resistance has emphasized motives of self-interest and self-protection rather than moral obligations when civilians prevent killings.[32] Some have argued that non-violent communities 'opted out of war' based on the perceived benefits of

---

[27] Dixon and Mokuwa 2004.
[28] Turkmani, Ali, Kaldor and Bojicic-Dzelilovic 2015.   [29] Kalyvas 2006.
[30] Kalyvas 2006, p. 209.   [31] Watanabe 1992, p. 182.
[32] Anderson and Wallace 2012; Gray 2012; Chenoweth and Cunningham 2013; Lynch 2014.

neutrality;[33] 'practiced peace' as a 'self-protective measure';[34] or believed that 'preventing violence against others was the most effective way to prevent violence against themselves'.[35] Acknowledging the desire for self-protection leads to further questions, such as how people come to believe in non-violence as a preferred self-protection strategy, and why some pursue prevention and protection even when not themselves threatened. Why risk one's own life, as some community leaders in Ambon and Jos did when confronting gangs and militias to prevent killings, as 'rescuers' did when protecting Jews during the Holocaust, or as some Muslims did when protecting Tutsis from genocide in Rwanda?[36]

Rationalist approaches hardly explain actions for which the opportunity costs are evidently high.[37] The few existing studies of rescue behaviour in genocide have emphasized the causal role of values and beliefs for civilian resistance to killings. For example, reports of the Muslim minority in Rwanda during the genocide stated that many Muslims hid Tutsis in their houses and mosques, built barriers around their quarters to protect refugees from approaching militias, and pleaded with the Interahamwe paramilitaries for the lives of those they protected.[38] Muslim religious leaders reportedly facilitated resistance to killings through several sensitization campaigns, using sermons and radio broadcasts that urged people to resist ethnic polarization and stressed the value of every human life. A number of mayors, local administrators, and church officials also resisted the approaching militias, at least initially.[39] Resistance among the Muslim community was reported to have been collective; Muslims took advantage of their religious networks and rotated refugees among families and the local mosque for protection.[40]

Additional support for the causal relevance of ideas, values, and moral obligations emerges from the literature on the Holocaust. Nechama Tec's account of the Bielski brothers in Belorussia, who established a forest community of fugitive Jews, a story turned into a Hollywood movie starring Daniel Craig,[41] cited Tuvia Bielski, the key

---

[33] Anderson and Wallace 2012.    [34] Gray 2012.    [35] Lynch 2014.
[36] See Oliner and Oliner 1992; Monroe 2012. On Rwanda, see Wax 2002; Doughty and Ntambara 2003.
[37] Monroe 2001b; Wood 2003a.    [38] Doughty and Ntambara 2003; p. 7.
[39] Straus 2006; Longman 2010.    [40] Doughty and Ntambara 2003.
[41] *Defiance* (2008).

leader, as having stated, 'I wanted to save, not to kill.'[42] In 1941, German forces invaded the Soviet Union and occupied western Belorussia. In areas near forests some Jews fled into the woods where they had to secure food and shelter and were vulnerable to attacks by German forces and local peasants.[43] During the first months of German occupation, the Bielski brothers – themselves Jewish escapees – established a forest community and assured everyone's survival. They sent scouts to the nearby ghettos to encourage Jews to flee from certain death even though more civilians joining their community increased the burden of protection. At the end of the war, Bielski had succeeded not only in surviving the genocide but also in rescuing more than 1,200 Jews.[44]

According to Tec, herself a survivor of the Holocaust, actions such as those demonstrated by Tuvia Bielski rely on a particular sense of self, a key explanatory factor for such extraordinary behaviour. Rescuers were more reliant on their own self-approval and moral values than on the approval of others.[45] She also emphasized individual perception of a situation to explain why some people were overcome by fear while others proactively protected and prevented: 'People who are exposed to extreme dangers may be paralyzed into inaction,' but whether this occurs is in part 'contingent on the extent to which they define a situation as hopeless'.[46]

In the largest survey of rescuers, non-rescuers, and rescued survivors during the Holocaust, Samuel and Pearl Oliner estimated that between 50,000 and 500,000 non-Jews risked their lives, and frequently those of their families, to help Jews.[47] They argued that rescuers were more aware of Jews in their neighbourhood and their plight than those who did not rescue them:

Although rescuers and nonrescuers knew similar facts, at some point rescuers began to *perceive* them in a personal way. ... Awareness became attention, and attention became focused concentration on what was happening to particular people in specific contexts. Although rescuers and nonrescuers perceived the risks to themselves and their families as similarly high, their actions differed markedly.[48]

---

[42] Tec 1993, p. 64.    [43] Tec 1993.    [44] Tec 1993.    [45] Tec 1986.
[46] Tec 1993.    [47] Oliner and Oliner 1988, p. 1.
[48] Oliner and Oliner 1988, p. 123.

Many rescuers came from families with strong moral values of a prosocial orientation and a sense of inclusiveness and empathy with the suffering of people outside their own in-group. Rescuers were also characterized as having a sense of responsibility to live up to their own moral principles. Bystanders, by contrast, 'were overcome by fear, hopelessness, and uncertainty', despite their hostility to the Nazis.[49] After the war, rescuers' relations to others continued to differ from those who did not rescue Jews. Rescuers tended to be more involved in community activity and more focused on other people's suffering.[50] Oliner and Oliner concluded that the altruistic personality 'is a relatively enduring predisposition to act selflessly on behalf of others, which develops early in life'.[51]

These arguments have been further developed in Kristen Monroe's research into rescuers, bystanders, and perpetrators during the Holocaust. In contrast to the Oliners, Monroe concluded that an individual's worldview, values, and self-image are 'far more important than background characteristics, early childhood socialization, or even traumatic events in explaining the variation in wartime treatment of others'.[52] Self-image and self-concept were the central psychological variables that dramatically differed between rescuers and bystanders: 'rescuers had a strong sense of themselves as people who were connected to others through bonds of common humanity.'[53] For rescuers, 'any cost–benefit analysis became secondary to the hierarchy of values already deeply integrated into a sense of self, which demanded spontaneous rescue activities.'[54] She concluded that the rescuers' sense of self, moral obligation, and a belief in agency gave them the confidence to act and tolerate high risks to their own lives.[55]

## Institutional Capacity and Collective Agency

In contrast to genocide research and theories of individual rescue behaviour, recent civil war scholarship has investigated collective civilian agency and stressed the key significance of community institutions and capacity of conflict management over individual normative commitments to explain non-violence during war. Two studies with a focus

---

[49] Oliner and Oliner 1988, p. 146.    [50] Oliner and Oliner 1988, p. 223.
[51] Oliner and Oliner 1988, p. 3.    [52] Monroe 2012, p. 8.
[53] Monroe 2008, p. 711.    [54] Monroe 2012, p. 201.    [55] Monroe 2012.

on Colombia and civilian self-protection have emphasized the causal role of community social coherence and institutional capacity over norms and values against killings. Ana Arjona concluded that only if rebel groups display internal discipline and a long-term time horizon with the will to establish social order, can civilians collectively organize and resist rebel rule.[56] Civilian communities with strong institutions for conflict management and dispute resolution would be more likely to collectively resist the influence of rebel groups because civilian preferences for resistance would be determined by the quality of pre-existing institutions in the community when an armed group arrives.[57] She further assumed that a community's capacity for collective resistance would hardly change in the presence of an armed actor unless communities received support from NGOs. This emphasis on armed groups' time horizons and civilian institutions for conflict management and resistance against rebel governance may be particularly important in the contexts of long civil wars, as in Colombia or the Philippines. Arjona's argument in part relies on in-depth qualitative evidence from a natural experiment based on three neighbouring villages within the same politico-administrative unit, with a shared history of peasant mobilization and collective resistance against armed groups during *La Violencia*. Thereafter, leaders of the former peasant movement congregated in one village, which later collectively resisted the Revolutionary Armed Forces of Colombia (FARC). According to Arjona, in Zama, 'the incidental concentration of leaders' had an effect on institutional quality, making resistance more likely. One could also read this case study in part as the influence of exceptional leaders who knew how to assume command and persuade people to follow them into non-violent resistance, which may have enabled them to organize and institutionalize new forms of resistance during the FARC's presence.

Oliver Kaplan similarly argued that social cohesion among civilian communities in Colombia and elsewhere afforded them greater chances of keeping armed groups out. Kaplan emphasized that well-functioning organizations would be able to withstand the loss of any single individual, and would therefore be more likely to enable resistance to armed groups.[58] While individual leaders might be particularly capable of leading non-violence efforts, they would usually be 'produced by

---

[56] Arjona 2016a.    [57] Arjona 2016a, p. 75.    [58] Kaplan 2017, p. 40.

especially cooperative and visionary communities'.[59] According to Kaplan, civilians would combine several resistance strategies according to context and external environment, such as supporting a culture of peace; implementing local conflict resolution mechanisms to limit the risk of denunciation; establishing local investigatory mechanisms to gather information; publicly protesting against armed groups and seeking international assistance; establishing early warning mechanisms; and deciding to arm themselves for self-protection.[60] Although these strategies are richly illustrated, we do not learn whether they are path-dependent and how they may be causally linked.

The previous brief examples from Syria and Sierra Leone demonstrate that engaging potential fighters early during the onset of conflict to establish influence and control over them can be crucial for preventing killings. Furthermore, they suggest that at the onset of conflict, communities that eventually preserve non-violence and develop social resilience may not already have strong institutions in place. Instead, civilians may establish them based on their anticipation of threats and their social knowledge of conflict dynamics. When institutions are built and reinforced over the course of war, communities may emerge with stronger institutional frameworks that allow them to repeatedly resist armed groups.

## The Resilience Lens: Vulnerability and Adaptation

My case studies of Wayame in Ambon and Dadin Kowa in Jos show that both did not have strong pre-existing institutional frameworks that set them apart from other areas. On the contrary, residents and community leaders recounted how they established new institutions, rules, and procedures to deal with emerging threats. Key leaders in these non-violent communities were individuals who had previously lived through an armed conflict and had experience of dealing with civilians mobilizing for violence. I argue that this social knowledge and lived experience enabled them to see violence prevention as the most promising self-protection strategy and to establish effective community organization to prevent killings. Their prevention efforts resulted in collective mobilization for the prevention of killings. Broad-based resistance and adaptation to changing conflict dynamics sustained

---

[59] Kaplan 2017, p. 41.      [60] Kaplan 2017, pp. 42–61.

prevention. Adaptation is the key theoretical concept of resilience research, which has made inroads in many disciplines but so far has hardly been systematically studied in conflict and peacebuilding. In the following, I briefly summarize key debates of the resilience field and then focus on the concepts of adaptation and evolutionary resilience.

## What Is Social Resilience?

Climate change research has popularized the notion of resilient communities based on adaptation to threats and adversity. Studies into the evolutionary resilience of ecosystems argue that adaptation is a process partly driven by social dynamics of human interaction, such as social knowledge, social learning, anticipation, self-organization, and imagination. These generic dynamics render the concepts of adaptation and social resilience applicable to war and violence research. For example, the World Bank and other large donors have long adopted the term 'resilience' as part of their core terminology on fragility, peacebuilding, and development. Even before the adoption of the term in policy making, resilience made major inroads into a vast diversity of disciplines, including economics and finances, urban planning, psychology and trauma healing, risk management, development policy, and national security. As such, resilience has become 'a pervasive idiom of global governance'[61] and resilience research in international security and peacebuilding has exploded.[62] I provide only a brief overview here and then focus on evolutionary resilience and its key concept of adaptation.

The critical security studies literature sees resilience as 'an increasingly prominent organizing principle in political life'.[63] As a neo-liberal governance strategy, it would allow states to abdicate responsibility in times of crisis, resulting in calls for social resilience as a response to the consequences.[64] Such policies would sell the need for resilience to local communities in the developing world as part of the neo-liberal project of governance.[65] By contrast, civilian protection research has approached resilience as a necessary and potentially useful concept.

---

[61] Walker and Cooper 2011, p. 144.
[62] For a brief overview, see Joseph 2013; Aradau 2014; Chandler 2014; Duffield 2012; Bourbeau 2015; Cavelty, Kaufmann, and Kristensen 2015.
[63] Cavelty, Kaufmann, and Kristensen 2015.
[64] Hall and Lamont 2013; Bourbeau 2015.   [65] Duffield 2012.

64                                                    *Resilient Communities*

Resilience could offer 'a useful way of thinking about how to reduce violence against civilians in contemporary war zones'.[66] The notion of resilience emphasizes bottom-up community self-protection strategies to complement top-down efforts by external actors to protect civilians. However, in conflict and peacebuilding research, the concept of resilience has remained under-theorized and lacks empirical application.

The idea of resilience emerged within various disciplines within recent decades, including ecology, physics and engineering, psychology, and child development. These disciplinary legacies have resulted in distinct approaches to resilience. In common usage, resilience either refers to (1) 'the capability of a strained body to recover its size and shape after deformation caused especially by compressive stress', or (2) 'an ability to recover from or adjust easily to misfortune or change'.[67] The first understanding is often used with a negative connotation, for example the resilience of autocratic regimes. The second notion holds the positive connotation of coping despite challenges. It is this latter understanding that I engage with.

Resilience in the psychological literature on child development describes individuals who thrive in adult life despite poor background conditions. Over several decades, psychologists and education scientists have investigated how and why some children and youth respond with non-violent practices and positive adaptation to significant difficulties arising from their immediate social environments. Their family backgrounds were characterized by poverty and social exclusion, low education standards, crime, and substance abuse. The most comprehensive definition within this literature defines resilience as a 'dynamic process encompassing positive adaptation within the context of significant adversity', further specifying two critical conditions: '(1) exposure to significant threat or severe adversity; and (2) the achievement of positive adaptation despite major assaults on the developmental process'.[68] Thus, resilience should be understood as a *process* that is qualitatively different from risk and vulnerability.[69] Public health and disaster management research developed this idea of individual resilience into the concept of social and community resilience.[70]

[66] Williams 2013, p. 291.    [67] Merriam-Webster online dictionary.
[68] Luthar and Cicchetti 2000.
[69] Almedom, Brensinger, and Adam 2010, p. 130.
[70] Krug, Dahlberg, Mercy, Zwi, and Lozano 2002; Norris et al. 2008, p. 127.

Some of the most innovative and productive research on social resilience has emerged from ecology and a focus on 'humans in nature'. Socio-ecological resilience integrates human agency.[71] A prominent understanding of social resilience refers to 'the ability of communities to withstand external shocks to their social infrastructure', such as environmental as well as social, political, or economic upheaval.[72] According to the Stockholm Resilience Centre, one of the leading think tanks on resilience research, social resilience is the 'the ability of human communities to withstand and recover from stresses, such as environmental change or social, economic or political upheaval'.[73]

Early empirical research in psychological resilience and in climate change was based on a perceived dualism of risk and resilience, assuming that they represented opposite ends of a single spectrum.[74] Empirical research based on this dualism draws on the concept of social capital. Network-focused studies proposed that social networks composed of 'bridging' links to a diverse web of resources strengthen a community's ability to adapt to change. In turn, networks composed only of local 'bonding' links that impose constraining social norms and foster group homophily could reduce resilience.[75] Bridging social capital would allow actors to access outside information and overcome social norms with support from outside their local network, while bonding capital would provide the group the resilience needed to absorb the benefits of bridging capital. These approaches echo Robert Putnam's argument that communities with a good stock of social capital are more likely to benefit from lower crime rates, better health, higher educational achievements, and better economic growth.[76] Thus, communities with a high level of social capital would also be more resilient to violent conflict. Critics have remarked that the mere sum of bridging and bonding ties is unlikely to predict how well a community will be able to adapt to adversity. Social capital as a concept appears to be 'imbued with highly positive connotations conveying an image of helpful, friendly interactions between individuals based on personal knowledge and face-to-face contact'.[77] However, in the context of armed conflict, 'the dark side of social capital'[78] may enable violence against civilians because it facilitates denunciations. The question

---

[71] Davoudi et al. 2012.    [72] Adger 2000, p. 361.
[73] Stockholm Resilience Centre 2017.
[74] Rutter 1987, p. 316; Killian 2004, p. 43.    [75] Newman and Dale 2005.
[76] Putnam 1995.    [77] Leonard 2004, p. 929.    [78] Kalyvas 2006.

remains whether high levels of social capital are a cause or an effect of conflict prevention, democratization, or development.

## Social Resilience as Adaptation

We would trivialize the idea of social resilience as a dynamic and open-ended process if we only equated the concept with the sum of buffering factors or coping strategies.[79] Social resilience research rooted in complexity theory called for 'dynamic' theoretical approaches.[80] C. S. Holling called resilience research 'the science of surprises'.[81] The idea is that resilience is an emergent property of a complex system and cannot be predicted from examining the system's parts, thus requiring approaches that move beyond linear thinking.[82]

I construct a *resilience lens* to analyze adaptation as a complex and non-linear process and apply this lens to study the outcome of non-violence in conflict. The resilience lens identifies the emergence of new forms of coping strategies and collective agency as well as community adaptation to changing conflict dynamics. The key element of socio-ecological resilience is *adaptation*. In biological usage, adaptation refers to 'the process whereby an organism fits itself to its environment', whereby 'experience guides changes in the organism's structure so that as time passes the organism makes better use of its environment for its own ends.'[83]

Adaptation in socio-ecological research has been linked to the social dynamics of human interaction, 'a process of deliberate change in anticipation of or in reaction to external stimuli and stress'.[84] Advances in climate change research have sought to integrate human agency and perspective as crucial components of adaptation because 'turning a crisis into an opportunity requires a great deal of preparedness, which in turn depends on the *capacity to imagine alternative futures*'.[85] Evolutionary resilience incorporates a creative capacity with regard to renewal, reorganization, and development within communities and societies.[86] External shocks or disturbances bear the

---

[79] Pfefferbaum, Reissman, Pfefferbaum, Klomp, and Gurwitch 2005; Zimmermann and Brenner 2010, p. 283; Rutter 2012.
[80] Berkes, Colding, and Folke 2003, p. 5.   [81] Holling 1986.
[82] Berkes, Colding, and Folke 2003, p. 7.   [83] Holland 1995, p. 9.
[84] Nelson, Adger, and Brown 2007, p. 395.   [85] Davoudi et al. 2012, p. 303.
[86] Folke, Colding, and Berkes 2003.

'potential to create opportunity for doing new things, for innovation and development'.[87] The social dynamics of resilience include 'social learning and social memory, mental models and knowledge-system integration, visioning and scenario-building', as well as 'leadership', 'adaptive capacity' and 'systems of adaptive governance'.[88] Social learning refers to 'the capacity and processes through which new values, ideas, and practices are disseminated, popularized, and become dominant in society or [...] a local community', and social organiza-tion as 'the propensity for social collectives to form without direction from the state or other higher-level actors'.[89] These generic social dynamics of adaptation render the concept of evolutionary resilience meaningful for the study of conflict and violence. Consequently, the resilience lens emphasizes the importance of social knowledge, mean-ing-making, and social learning for communities adapting to adversity. In the following, I use the resilience lens to understand civilian mobi-lization and non-violence.

## Civilian Mobilization, Non-Escalation, and Community Adaptation

Chapter 1 established that communal war is a complex social process resulting from civilian mobilization and escalation. The chapter pre-sented a theoretical framework based on three interlinking processes: the political mobilization of everyday violence networks; the polariza-tion of social identities; and militia formation and the militarization of local order. Research has paid limited attention to the social processes of non-escalation and restraint in war.[90] Non-violent communities in Ambon and Jos were vulnerable communities threatened both from within, when youth wanted to mobilize for killings, and from external armed groups. My theoretical framework emphasizes the emergence of civilian prevention efforts in contexts where civilians have few pre-existing institutions to rely on once threatened.

I draw on Kristen Monroe's 'perspective paradigm', a meta-theoretical perspective that moves beyond a dualistic understanding of rational choice versus altruism and treats utility-maximizing beha-viour as one option on a behavioural continuum.[91] Fujii's ethnographic

---

[87] Folke 2006, p. 253.    [88] Folke 2006, p. 253.    [89] Pelling 2010, p. 59.
[90] But see Straus 2012, 2015; McLoughlin 2014.    [91] Monroe 2001b, p. 151.

research has shown that civilian behaviour does not fit neatly into binaries of killing or participation in killings versus evading or rescuing. Instead, individual behaviour may vary according to situational context, ranging from evading to protecting and rescuing victims to participating in killings.[92] In order to theorize wartime civilian agency for violence and prevention, I adopt a theoretical perspective that includes self-interested and altruistic behaviour as subsets of behavioural choices informed by the individual's perspective.

I argue that civilians' understanding of war dynamics, i.e. social knowledge and social learning, affects their ability to make decisions that protect lives. Even when communities have strong institutional capacity and legitimate institutions in place, which was not the case in Wayame and Dadin Kowa, the leadership needs to persuade community members not to collaborate when an armed group arrives. If civilian leaders make misjudgements, lives may be lost and the legitimacy of decision-making procedures and institutions may erode. My theory of non-escalation as a social process explains how vulnerable communities adapt to a changing conflict environment and prevent killings. This theory combines individual high-risk agency, in the form of leadership, with the social processes of civilian mobilization that sustain non-escalation and prevention. Using the resilience lens, I emphasize the social dynamics of knowledge, learning, and anticipation of threats that allowed communities to adapt to a changing conflict zone and temporarily mitigate vulnerability. The outcome of non-violence is contingent on civilian agency, and resulted from the depolarization of social identities, the consolidation of civilian control, and negotiations with external armed groups. Civilian violence prevention efforts emerged with individual leaders who negotiated local peace and neutrality within and beyond their communities to prevent killings. Their initiatives motivated ordinary people to join and sustain the prevention efforts.

## Individual Agency: Leadership and Rescue Agency

Community leadership, i.e. the ability to persuade residents and the confidence to confront armed groups and negotiate with them, is crucial for the outcome of localized non-violence. This prompts me to

[92] Fujii 2009.

further analyse high-risk agency for prevention. Why does fear lead some people to perceive violence prevention to be in their best interest, while others choose to evade or actively take part in killings? Self-protection may motivate both violence and violence prevention. Some scholars argue that individuals who engage in violence prevention are driven by motives of self-interest and self-protection,[93] but protection seeking can also motivate the joining of militias or participation in killings.[94]

Nascent research on wartime experiences has emphasized altruism and the potential legacies of prosocial behaviour after exposure to war.[95] For example, individuals whose households experienced more intense violence during Sierra Leone's civil war were more likely to attend community meetings, to join local political and community groups, and to vote.[96] In Liberia, individuals and communities with high levels of exposure to violence during the civil war were shown to be less biased against out-group refugees and more responsive to the distress of Ivorian refugees who entered the country during the 2010 post-election crisis.[97] The example of Liberians supporting Ivorian refugees suggests that experience of wartime violence can increase empathy, altruism, and identification with other people's suffering.

These findings again underline the question of why, in similar circumstances, some individuals perceive violence prevention to be in their self-interest and avert killings while others facilitate and/or participate in them. In order to explain both collective violence and violence prevention, I argue that analysis needs to focus on how people *perceive* a conflict situation to understand their responses. How do civilians make sense of their environment and their behavioural options, and how do previous *experience* and *knowledge* guide them in meaning-making? Because individuals can potentially adopt the roles of perpetrators, bystanders, and rescuers during the course of a war, a theory that explains wartime individual agency needs to start with 'a conceptualization of the self that allows not only for the times when the actor will respond as a self-interested individual but also for those times when the actor conceives of himself or herself as part of a collective

---

[93] Chenoweth and Cunningham 2013.
[94] Straus 2006; Guichaoua 2007; Longman 2010.
[95] Bellows and Miguel 2009; Blattman 2009; Bateson 2012.
[96] Bellows and Miguel 2009.     [97] Hartman and Morse 2018.

or even as an altruist'.[98] Kristen Monroe's micro-level theory of rescuers, bystanders, and perpetrators starts with the perception of self in
relation to others: 'Our perception of ourselves in relation to others sets
and delineates the range of options we find available, not just morally
but empirically.'[99] Behavioural consequences are thus related to identity and self-perceptions. Within this theoretical framework, actors
have multiple identities, and their prominence can vary according to
cultural and situational contexts.[100] External factors can draw
a particular part of this complex identity into political salience.
Understanding how people perceive, comprehend, and interpret the
sociopolitical world – and a particular conflict environment – is thus
a crucial analytical task. Perception and situational context may
explain why individuals sometimes act out of self-interest and at
other times pursue group interest or altruism. This is a particularly
fruitful entry for theorizing non-violence and civilian agency because it
accounts for motivations of both self-interest and self-preservation as
well as motivations arising from beliefs, values, and moral obligation.

What is recue agency? I adopt Monroe's perspective paradigm,
according to which identity constrains choice and the range of possible
actions individuals perceive as available to themselves. Rescue agency
relies on a relatively stable moral framework and a strong and consis-
tent belief in agency and the ability to effect change. Monroe's theory of
agency and moral choice starts from the assumption that we each have
'a moral framework through which identity sifts and filters perceptions
to set and delineate the possible choices we find available and thus can
act upon'.[101] This ethical framework serves as cognitive scaffolding,
filled in by life experiences. Key aspects are self-image, worldviews, and
moral values.[102] Rescuers displayed a strong sense of human connection and cognitive categorization beyond in-/out-group distinctions,
a worldview in which all human beings were placed within
a fundamental category of worth and deserved equal protection.
The deep anchoring of key moral values into the rescuers' sense of
self 'effectively created boundaries in the self-image and then limited
and foreclosed debate about transgressing these values'.[103] It follows
that 'ethical acts emanate not so much from conscious choice but rather

---

[98] Monroe 2001b, p. 160.    [99] Monroe 2001b, p. 157.
[100] Monroe 2001b, p. 159.    [101] Monroe 2012, p. 504.    [102] Monroe 2012.
[103] Monroe 2008, p. 716.

from deep-seated instincts, predispositions, and habitual patterns of behaviour that are related to our central identity.'[104]

Consequently, the rescuer's perception of self enables a sense of efficacy in controlling one's destiny. According to Monroe, belief in the ability to effect change is intrinsically linked to an individual's perspective on, knowledge and social learning about, and response to crisis situations. Thus, the social dynamics that climate change researchers associate with effective adaptation in resilience research – social knowledge, social learning, imagination, and anticipation – link to an altruistic perspective, prosocial orientation, and the confidence to act, prevent, and protect.

By contrast, Monroe characterized bystanders as having a *perceived* lack of choice or agency. She found the worldviews of perpetrators and bystanders to be marked by a sense of fatalism, helplessness, and a lack of agency, a passive self-image that translated into a perception that the suffering of others was a phenomenon outside of their control and that they lacked the ability to respond to the plight of victims. This sense of powerlessness would result in ignorance and inaction. Lee Ann Fujii's research on rescuers, bystanders, and perpetrators during the Rwandan genocide found a similar sense of low efficacy among bystanders.[105] However, for bystanders and for those who join in killings, identities may not circumscribe the options they see available for themselves as clearly as for rescuers.[106] Bystanders and joiners may change their behaviour and sometimes kill, but under different circumstances rescue friends or strangers. While rescuers' behaviour may be very stable, non-rescuers' actions may be much more indeterminate, 'making them potentially benign and threatening at the same time'.[107]

Although most people likely prefer to interact with other people non-violently, even during the onset of conflict,[108] they also fear for their lives and are often overcome by a sense of helplessness. Consequently, to set the process of non-escalation and violence prevention into motion, the display of rescue behaviour, at least at the outset of prevention efforts, is essential for building trust and convincing people of the sincerity of the commitment to prevention. Leadership that grows out of rescue behaviour may be more courageous, more persuasive, and more visionary than leadership based more narrowly on very

---

[104] Monroe 2009, p. 435.    [105] Fujii 2009.    [106] Fujii 2012.
[107] Fujii 2012, p. 417.    [108] Straus 2012, p. 346.

understandable motives of self-protection and fear. I argue that key community leaders in Wayame and Dadin Kowa displayed such rescue agency. Their courageous intervention and willingness to tolerate high levels of risk to their lives made them persuasive leaders. For the majority of community members, however, the desire to protect themselves and their immediate family members may be more than sufficient motivation to support a leader's violence prevention efforts if these are perceived as credible, and to collectively organize, institutionalize, and sustain prevention.

## Collective Agency and Violence Prevention

Community leaders cannot credibly negotiate neutrality with armed groups and bargain for non-violent spaces without having previously established social control over the community. They cannot establish this without persuading residents to follow their leadership, agreeing on common rules or the application of existing institutions and rule frameworks, and establishing a sense of a common identity beyond the conflict cleavage to motivate people to resist violence. I argue that it is important to understand the causal logic of civilian mobilization for non-violence as a step-by-step process in order to explain the strength and limitations of civilian self-protection efforts, and identify entry points for international support. To do this, I develop a process-oriented theoretical framework. In Table 2.1, I list the social processes of escalation as discussed in Chapter 1 and the social processes of non-escalation as discussed here.

### Depolarization of Social Identities

In Chapter 1, I identified the polarization of social identities as one key process of escalation. This process was actively countered and reversed in non-violent communities. Depolarization was based on '*meaning-making*' that did not endorse interpretation of communal violence as a 'religious conflict', and on alternative narratives of the conflict situation. Community leaders rejected simplistic conflict narratives and one-sided blame and supported proactive 'we-thinking' and alternative identities as 'people of Wayame' in Ambon and 'people of Dadin Kowa' in Jos, as opposed to 'Muslim' versus 'Christian' communities.

Resilience and trauma researchers have drawn attention to the significance of identity, perception, and narratives for coping and positive

Table 2.1 *The social processes of non-escalation*

| Social Process | Mechanisms |
| --- | --- |
| Depolarization of Social Identities | *Meaning-Making* and alternative conflict narrative formation<br>*We-Thinking* and Cross-Cleavage Social Identity Formation |
| Consolidation of Civilian Social Control | *Persuasion* of Community Members<br>*Rule Making* and Institution Building<br>*Repression* of Violence Instigators |
| Engaging Armed Groups for Prevention | *Negotiation* with Armed Groups<br>*Refusal of Collaboration* in Attacks<br>Strategic *Information Gathering/ Dissemination* |

adaptation.[109] When people engage actively with adversity, anticipate challenges, and reframe situations, they are more likely to counter conflict dynamics. Meaning-making has been shown to be a critical component of adaptation to loss and trauma, which helps humans to cope as individuals and as a collective.[110] For example, ethnographic research into resilience strategies among American Indian families showed that a focus on the strengths of a community, or a strength-based perspective, can act as a protective factor and provide people both with the confidence to face challenges and the ability to be proactive. A 'strength-based perspective' emphasized 'overcoming difficulties and remaining strong in the face of traumatic circumstances', which support individuals and communities in dealing with upheaval.[111] Narratives can order, situate, and provide meaning, as well as supply a sense of mastery over adversity that enables agency. This research demonstrates that social trauma does not automatically lead to dysfunction and social distress.[112] Resilience research on war-affected families in Afghanistan further argued that cultural values are

---

[109] Almedom, Brensinger, and Adam 2010.
[110] Almedom, Brensinger, and Adam 2010, p. 128; Eggerman and Panter-Brick 2010.
[111] Denham 2008.    [112] Denham 2008.

an important part of meaning-making resilience strategies. Collective meaning-making can shape and transform individuals' mental health in the context of war and adversity.[113] For civilians living with the threat of violence and oppression, resilience is linked to a sense of sustained hope[114] and the production of a coherent narrative that explains personal and collective experiences.[115] Meaning-making orders the world and gives coherence to the past, present, and future.[116] The acts of interpretation and imagination, meaning-making, and ordering are expressions of agency and ability and strengthen people's confidence and proactive behaviour.

In non-violent communities of Ambon and Jos, community leaders consistently provided interpretations of the conflict situation that rejected apocalyptic understandings of religious violence and narratives that solely blamed the other religious group for the conflict. Leaders and ordinary people developed elaborate we-identities that integrated values of openness, religious tolerance, peace, patience, and understanding into their social identities. These we-identities stood in stark contrast to the deeply polarized and exclusive social identities that affected many people of the conflict region and led them to tolerate or to actively support armed groups. In sum, the depolarization of social identities relies on the mechanisms of a meaning-making that rejects an emerging conflict narrative and produces social hope, and 'we-thinking', i.e. identity formation across the conflict cleavage.

### Consolidation of Civilian Social Control

An important component of escalation to communal war, as discussed in Chapter 1, was the militarization of local communities. The emergence and transformation of gangs and militias and the militarization of local order was based on the mobilization of everyday violence networks of vigilantes, criminals, and gangs. In some of the most violence-prone neighbourhoods of Ambon and Jos, gangs already had a strong presence before violence networks were mobilized and communal violence broke out. These neighbourhoods were particularly vulnerable to violence because

---

[113] Panter-Brick 2015, p. 238.
[114] Almedom, Brensinger, and Adam 2010; Eggerman and Panter-Brick 2010.
[115] Panter-Brick 2015, p. 240.    [116] Eggerman and Panter-Brick 2010.

community leaders were often unable to influence or to confront their local gang leaders. In non-violent communities, this process did not take place. Instead, leaders established social control over youth who wanted to fight within their own community or in other parts of the city. They were able to do so in part because these communities did not host well-established gangs that needed to be dismantled first. Establishing social control was based on *persuading* community members to follow the leadership and prevent violence; *rule making* and informal institution building for conflict resolution; and *repression* of individuals who did not support the prevention efforts and wanted to instigate fighting.

Community leaders primarily used persuasion to consolidate civilian control over those who wanted to mobilize and fight. Persuasion was linked to meaning-making, the interpretation of the conflict as 'not a religious conflict', and 'we-thinking' efforts. Leaders engaged youth and vigilantes, as well as those who supported mobilization, in arguments, trying to persuade them that non-violence would be an outcome beneficial to all of them. Leaders often used their own experience of having lived through previous conflict situations, explaining in detail the painful long-term consequences of killings, destruction, and displacement to those who wanted to mobilize and fight. Leaders used persuasion to convince young men not to give in to peer group pressure and collaborate in attacks on their neighbours. They undertook much effort to persuade community members that preserving local peace was possible, in everyone's interest, and the most effective method of self-protection.

An important precondition for establishing civilian control was the formulation of rules, procedures, and informal institutions for conflict management among community leaders. Institutions were not pregiven, but emerged through meetings in which rumours, threats, and challenges were discussed and decisions were made on how to deal with them. Over time, institutions and procedures for quick and effective decision-making emerged. The establishment of rules and procedures for conflict management was crucial for the maintenance of social control. Informal institutions and procedures built trust, facilitated communication and information exchange, and signalled the credibility of violence prevention efforts to the community. A set of rules also helped leaders to agree on the punishment of those who tried to instigate fighting and who could have joined gangs and militias and carried fighting into the community.

Both non-violent communities had a significant at-risk youth population and residents who wanted to mobilize and join fighting with other groups. In other neighbourhoods without strong gang networks, youth who were organized into vigilante, ethnic, or religious networks joined gangs and militia groups elsewhere to partake in the fighting once the conflicts had started. These were often unemployed young men who had friends in other neighbourhoods. Thus, they were in contact with those who had already fought and could potentially provide information for targeted attacks.

Based on newly established rules and procedures, community leaders were able to co-opt and/or repress youth who wanted to fight. They forbade the acquisition of weapons and their public display, as well as joining the fighting in other parts of the conflict region. In the community of Wayame in Ambon, these rules were enforced by violent means and in Dadin Kowa in Jos, verbal threats of violence were used against potential dissidents. In Wayame, individuals found guilty of having tried to facilitate fighting were publicly beaten, and those trying to collaborate with outside armed groups were threatened with death. In sum, establishing civilian social control, rather than allowing armed actors to control the community, results from persuasion of community members to support violence prevention; rule making, establishment, and/or maintenance of institutions for local conflict resolution; and the repression of those who opposed the leadership and wished to instigate fighting.

### Engagement with External Armed Groups for Prevention

In Chapter 1, we have seen that the formation of militias and their mobility and training was a key explanatory factor for the escalation of communal conflicts into communal wars. Research on non-violent communities in civil war has shown that in some cases, civilian leaders negotiated neutrality with armed groups, for example in Colombia[117] and in Mindanao, the Philippines.[118] Since the literature tends to equate communal conflicts with sporadic riots and not with war dynamics and the interaction of armed and unarmed civilians, negotiation with armed groups in communal conflicts has remained virtually

---

[117] Kaplan 2013.     [118] Hancock and Mitchell 2007.

ignored. However, in and around Ambon and Jos, much violence was produced through the interaction of some civilians from vulnerable mixed communities with outside armed groups. Therefore, refusal to collaborate and negotiations for neutrality were indispensable for preserving local peace. Community leaders internally forbade residents to collaborate and enforced these rules. Only when they had consolidated their authority over youth groups and potential fighters were they able to credibly negotiate with external militias and expect trust and allegiance from the residents under their leadership.

Externally, community leaders continuously engaged with armed groups. In contrast to terms such as non-collaboration, engagement entails proactive and assertive interaction with armed groups. Individual community leaders who displayed rescue behaviour in Wayame in Ambon and Dadin Kowa in Jos emphasized that they engaged with leaders and members of armed groups on the basis of recognizing human needs and desires, while avoiding the dehumanization of perpetrators. Engagement with armed groups fundamentally builds on the recognition that their members need to be addressed as human beings with whom to negotiate despite the atrocities committed.

Engagement as a social process consists of three mechanisms: negotiations, refusal to collaborate in violence, and strategic gathering and dissemination of information. Information gathering refers to regular contact with the leaders of external armed groups, as well as with ethnic, religious, and community leaders from neighbouring communities. In addition, community leaders also often gathered information through their extended family or business networks. Information gathering established and maintained social networks for violence prevention outside the community. This involved regular contact and networking with security forces, who often proved unprofessional and overwhelmed. Furthermore, police and military units at times had incentives to contribute to further violence in the region. These network building efforts served the strategic dissemination of information on neutrality and the refusal to collaborate with armed groups from both sides. Strategic dissemination of the message that the community would refuse to facilitate violence and would not collaborate in it served to deter attacks. By withholding information relevant for an attack and not providing support, non-violent communities were able to raise the stakes for an armed group and deter attacks. Furthermore, through strategic gathering and dissemination of information, community leaders could adapt prevention efforts to the changing strategies of armed groups and persuade leaders from other neighbourhoods and villages to tolerate their refusal to facilitate or participate in killings.

## Conclusion

This chapter presented an analytical framework of non-escalation and community adaptation to explain the outcome of non-violence in mixed and *vulnerable* communities in the context of communal war. Using a resilience lens to understand community adaptation to a hostile environment, I have discussed the role of altruistic forms of rescue agency in the form of community leadership and the ability to build trust and persuade residents in favour of non-violence, and collective agency for violence prevention. More specifically, I have distinguished three social processes of civilian mobilization and non-escalation: depolarization, including the formation of new cross-cleavage identities; the consolidation of civilian social control within the community based on persuasion, rule making, and institution building, as well as the repression of violence instigators; and engagement with external armed groups to negotiate neutrality, refuse collaboration, and strategically gather information on conflict dynamics that informs prevention and supports dissemination of the community's resolve to deter violence. I have further argued in Chapter 1 and in this chapter that escalation and non-escalation are processes that can slow down, halt, or reverse. They consist of sequenced processes that are path-dependent and condition one another. Continuous efforts at depolarization and trust building will not remain credible without established internal control over potential fighters. Maintaining control requires constant appeals to a cross-cleavage collective identity and credible negotiation with external armed groups. Effective engagement with armed groups, negotiations over neutrality, and refusal to collaborate in attacks can only be achieved if community leaders can rely on broad support from their own community.

These processes may not simply emerge in vulnerable and threatened communities but rather depend on individual high-risk rescue agency of leaders who initiate prevention efforts. Sustaining depolarized communal relations and trust, maintaining social control over potential fighters, and continuously negotiating neutrality and non-collaboration with external armed groups required social knowledge and learning among the leadership to adapt to changing conflict dynamics. Anticipation, imagination, and scenario-building of potential risks and challenges informed and sustained prevention efforts. Social knowledge, learning, anticipation, and imagination are generic social dynamics that the climate change literature has identified as facilitators of positive adaptation. I use the term 'social knowledge' generically to mean knowledge held by a specific group of people, or individuals within this group, namely knowledge derived from interaction with the social environment.[119]

In the following chapters, we see how the social processes of civilian mobilization and escalation/non-escalation unfolded in Ambon and Jos.

---

[119] Turiel 1983, p. 1; Berkes 2001.

# 3 | Fieldwork in the Context of Communal Conflicts

In July 2015, during my fourth and last visit to Jos in central Nigeria, my driver and I parked on a street in the commercial centre, a part of town that had become almost exclusively Muslim. I awaited a Muslim woman leader and peace activist whom I had previously met in 2010 for another interview. The city centre had not changed much since then, and I was looking forward to discussing the political developments with my very knowledgeable respondent. I did not remember the exact location of her house, so we agreed to meet in front of the church building on her street. The church, however, had been burned down just a couple of days earlier by Muslim youth. 'It was just a criminal act, nothing to worry about,' my respondent said on the mobile phone when telling me to meet at the burned church. She was late and while my driver – a Christian – and I waited for her in the car, I watched some men on the street noticing us as people who did not belong there. As the minutes went by, I began to wonder whether my respondent, my driver, and I had judged the security situation correctly. How did my driver feel about parking in front of a church burned down just days earlier, waiting for a senior Muslim leader to appear for the scheduled interview? I trusted my drivers to be intimately familiar with the changing conflict landscape of Jos. When discussing routes and meeting plans, they would warn me when protests or strikes were announced that could potentially turn into riots, where (not) to go or park to meet respondents, and when best to return to the capital, Abuja. A few days earlier, two bombs had gone off at a mosque and at a restaurant not far from my interview location, as part of Boko Haram's 2015 string of bombings during Ramadan.[1] The attacks had targeted primarily Muslims, among them a Muslim cleric who had openly preached against Boko Haram. But Christians from Jos I spoke to at this time continued to express their worry that Muslim residents would target them with bomb attacks. Finally, my

[1] BBC News, Nigeria's Boko Haram crisis: Jos blasts kill scores. 7 July 2015.

interview partner appeared and guided me to her house while my driver calmly parked the car and assured me that he was not worried about waiting outside for an hour or so. He found himself a seat in the shade and I noticed him having a lively chat with some of the men who had watched our meeting, a calm scene of light-hearted, everyday interaction as if this part of town had not previously been one of the 'no-go areas' for him after sectarian violence.

In this chapter, I discuss the context of my field research in Jos and in Ambon in eastern Indonesia. I first focus on the research and interview process, including the identification of respondents. Next, I discuss the challenges of conducting fieldwork in the context of communal conflict and strong tensions, as in Jos, and years after an official peace agreement, as in Ambon. I further reflect on the ethical dilemmas that arise from these contexts, particularly with regard to researching non-violent communities, and to interviewing perpetrators who remain embedded within their families and neighbourhoods. Lastly, I focus on the contributions and limitations of my ethnographic observations to the research process, the interpretation of interview narratives, and triangulation of my findings.

## Research Process

During my fieldwork in Ambon and Jos, the security situation was generally volatile. In Jos, the year 2010, when I first arrived, was one of the worst on record. In Ambon, a risk remained of renewed rioting, as exemplified by the sudden outburst of a two-day riot in September 2011. More than once was I called on my mobile phone and warned not to visit particular places in Ambon, such as the bus terminal or the university, for fear of violent protests. The strong military presence in both regions was a constant reminder of the state of insecurity. The political constellations within the communities and the traumatization of residents, particularly in Jos, also affected interviews and at times limited the information I could collect.

The purpose of my field research was to analyse the organization of communal violence and non-violence in the two cities. During my first trips to both Ambon and Jos, I identified and verified that in each city, one ethnically, religiously, and socio-economically mixed and *vulnerable* community had prevented killings: the communities of Wayame in Ambon and Dadin Kowa in Jos. In order to investigate non-violence,

Table 3.1 *Case study communities*

|  |  | Ambon | Jos |
|---|---|---|---|
| Conflict Outcome | *Violence* (Despite prevention efforts) | Poka–Rumahtiga | Anglo Jos |
|  | *Non-Violence* | Wayame | Dadin Kowa |

I conducted interviews in these two communities and collected accounts from community leaders and residents from other areas of the city for potential alternative explanations. I further focused on how people responded to conflict dynamics and protected themselves in Wayame and in Dadin Kowa, in comparison to the residents of two similarly mixed and almost adjacent communities that had unsuccessfully tried to prevent killings: the communities of Poka–Rumahtiga in Ambon and Anglo Jos in Jos. The rationale of this within-case paired comparison[2] of violence and non-violence was to investigate civilian collective action and (non-)escalation under similar circumstances in vulnerable neighbourhoods. My objective was to understand why people were able to prevent fighting in Wayame and Dadin Kowa, but not in Poka–Rumahtiga and Anglo Jos. The paired comparison did not only allow me to rule out alternative explanations, such as geographic or demographic conditions. Perhaps even more importantly, listening to community leaders from Wayame and Dadin Kowa about how they prevented killings, I learned how communal violence was organized. With this knowledge, I was then able to repeatedly interview residents, leaders, and perpetrators from Anglo Jos and Poka–Rumahtiga, and from other violence-prone neighbourhoods, and verify processes of conflict escalation and the organization of violence in communal war.

## Indonesia

Between the years 2009 and 2015, I spent a total of ten months in Indonesia. I was based in Yogyakarta, where I was affiliated with the Centre for Security and Peace Studies at Gadjah Mada University. During my time in Yogyakarta, I completed an Indonesian language

---

[2]  Tarrow 2010.

course. Discussions with academic colleagues at the university and some of the former students from Ambon prepared me for my departure to Ambon and established contacts at the local Pattimura University. Scholars who had previously worked in Ambon also generously supported me with information and advice.[3] After a first round of interviews with local journalists, religious leaders, and NGO staff members, I developed a more nuanced and contextualized understanding of the conflict environment years after the peace agreement. I then collected recommendations for whom to contact among residents from neighbourhoods that suffered most of the violence and those that were less affected. Local NGO workers and scholars at Pattimura University, which is located in Poka, introduced me to residents from the communities of Poka–Rumahtiga and Wayame. From then on, I relied on snowball sampling. Through (former) religious leaders, I was introduced to former leaders and members of militias and was able to conduct interviews on the organization of violence, as well as to verify why militias never attacked the non-violent community Wayame. I conducted eighty-three interviews with fifty-two community and religious leaders, residents, journalists, NGO representatives, university lecturers, and militia leaders and members in Ambon. In addition, I interviewed researchers and civil society practitioners in Jakarta and Yogyakarta who had worked in peacebuilding and mediation efforts in Ambon and Maluku Province.

Maluku Province remained one of Indonesia's post-conflict areas with high numbers of small-scale conflict incidents.[4] In this context, many people were careful about where they were seen with a foreign researcher. Initially, respondents were often curious to meet the foreign student but reluctant to discuss the conflict beyond the basic established facts. I revisited Ambon in 2010 and 2011 to repeatedly meet with respondents and establish rapport. This allowed me to probe deeper into narratives about conflict dynamics and violence prevention efforts. In September 2011, a small riot broke out again in Ambon and eight people were killed.[5] The heavy military presence contained the fighting, but the city remained tense and volatile. I returned to Ambon in December 2011 and met again with a number of former respondents,

---

[3] I thank Jeroen Adams and Gerry van Klinken for very helpful advice and discussions of research challenges.
[4] Barron, Jaffrey, and Varshney 2016.
[5] See International Crisis Group 2011 for further details.

who this time were particularly eager to discuss the conflict in light of the new threats and challenges. This development allowed me to deepen and triangulate my findings.

I conducted most of my interviews in Indonesian, and most of my respondents agreed to a recording of our conversation under conditions of anonymity, provided that the recorder remained covered in public places and out of view. An Indonesian student in Yogyakarta who had never been to Ambon and did not have any ties to the region transcribed my interview recordings. No recording included the name of the respondent, and the student deleted the recordings after transcription.

In late 2014, I arrived in Ambon for my last research trip together with research partners from Gadjah Mada University conducting a research project on the gender dimensions of peacebuilding. Some of the interviews conducted for this research project also took place in the neighbourhoods of Wayame and Poka–Rumahtiga, and the findings of the research team provided me with additional confidence in the accuracy of my findings.[6]

## Nigeria

In Nigeria, I conducted research in Jos in November and December 2010, June 2011, November and December 2012, and July 2015. I initially worked as a consultant for the Geneva-based Small Arms Survey and produced a report about the conflict and local peacebuilding initiatives.[7] My first research took place at a time when the violence in Jos had received much media attention but limited scholarly interest.[8] When I arrived in November 2010, one of the most violent years for the city and surrounding rural areas came to an end with the 2010 Christmas Eve bombings, which were among the very first bombings perpetrated by Boko Haram.[9] My meeting requests were generally met with much openness and willingness to

---

[6] I have noted in footnotes in Chapters 4 and 5 when I cite from interviews conducted by Arifah Rahmawati and her colleagues, and thank her for their excellent collaboration.

[7] Krause 2011b.

[8] I thank Adam Higazi for a very helpful discussion and assessment of the security situation prior to my first trip.

[9] Krause 2011a.

collaborate. People wanted to discuss the evolution of the conflict because they sought to make sense of the compounding tragedy and contribute to analysis of the conflict.[10]

Similarly to my research strategy in Indonesia, my first interviews were conducted with NGO workers, journalists, and academics in Abuja. This helped me to develop a preliminary understanding of the context of the Jos conflict. Subsequently, I interviewed local journalists and NGO workers in Jos before contacting ethnic and religious leaders for meetings. After this first round of interviews and time for reflections, I focused on interviews with residents from the worst-affected neighbourhoods in Jos, and from the non-violent community of Dadin Kowa. I conducted snowball sampling through my initial respondents and relied partly on the personal networks of journalists and community leaders, and on contacts that local NGO peace programmes had developed. Interviews with NGO workers and one government official provided me with contacts to some of the men who had taken part in the fighting, or had been identified as gang leaders. As of late 2012, when Jos had remained calm for about one year, and during my subsequent visit in 2015, when an informal truce among gang leaders and assurances of impunity from security forces had emerged, I was able to interview men who identified themselves as having taken part in the fighting. In total, I carried out 125 semi-structured and narrative interviews with 98 community members and leaders, religious and ethnic group leaders, journalists, NGO workers, politicians, and gang leaders and members. My interview respondents came from the worst-affected neighbourhoods in the centre of Jos, and from Anglo Jos and Dadin Kowa, the two areas of my within-case paired comparison.

I was able to conduct almost all interviews in English. Thankfully, I was always able to work with drivers and assistants who had experience and contacts (often family members) both in Christian and Muslim communities and were able to advise me on safety issues and escort me to interview settings. I conducted all interviews within confidential settings, mostly within people's houses or offices, and sometimes in hotel lobbies. I also learnt much from interviewing grassroots peace activists about their experiences. During my four research stays, I was able to interview many respondents multiple times. Most respondents allowed me to record our conversation under the condition of

---

[10] See also Wood's discussion of this point (2006, p. 377).

anonymity and with the recorder hidden from view, as in Ambon. The recording and subsequent transcription was invaluable for in-depth analysis and the triangulation of my findings.

## Interview Process and Ethnographic Observations

At the beginning of each interview, I introduced myself and my research project to obtain informed consent. All conversations took place under the condition of anonymity, and mostly out of the view of other people. I let respondents choose where to meet. Unless personally introduced by a former respondent, I contacted people through phone calls first to ask for an interview and then confirmed the time and place via text message before meeting in person, which gave respondents an additional opportunity to decline my requests. At the end of an interview, I would ask respondents if they would like to raise any other issues and whether they had any questions for me.

My strategy was to meet many respondents twice or several times. Although my interviews were structured around several key questions on the organization of violence and explanations for non-violence, I let my respondents guide the conversation to learn how they *made sense* of the conflict situation and how they responded to the changing conflict dynamics. Narratives reveal how people construct reality, navigate situations, make decisions, and anticipate consequences.[11] Because respondents' accounts may be influenced by the significant trauma of having participated in or witnessed killings, multiple interviews allowed me to asked probing questions and identify (in)consistencies in explanations of violence and non-violence, which supported triangulation. With some respondents, I needed several meetings until I could probe sensitive topics, such as the recruitment of child fighters in Ambon. I did not pressure respondents on issues they did not seem willing to discuss. Silences and body language often signalled that my interview partner did not consent to the conversational route I suggested, and I let them change direction accordingly.

Moments of 'accidental ethnography'[12] proved vital for understanding the context of conflict dynamics in Ambon and Jos, and the

---

[11]  Monroe 2001b, p. 163.    [12]  Fujii 2015.

prevention of violence in Wayame and Dadin Kowa. These observations greatly enriched my data collection. For example, during my first visit to the non-violent community of Dadin Kowa in Jos, my research assistant – a resident from Dadin Kowa – and I spent some time waiting at the edge of the local marketplace after several interviews, watching people's everyday interaction. We had just completed a focus group discussion with local women about their violence prevention efforts and I scribbled notes. A delivery van stopped near us, blaring out a song in the Hausa language that I did not understand. The noise was deafening and, distracted, I gave up my notes and asked my research assistant what the music was about, and what the lyrics meant. He laughed a little and then explained that it was a Christian song about how Christians would overcome Muslims and triumph, how they would prepare themselves for the fight and not be intimidated by Muslims. I was shocked; this was the only non-violent community in the city of Jos where Muslims and Christians had undertaken extraordinary efforts to prevent killings. Yet such offensive music was played in public, around the marketplace, and no one seemed to intervene. When I asked my research assistant whether the song was indeed as offensive to Muslims as it sounded to my ear (my assistant was Catholic), he agreed that it was. He acknowledged that these things happened regularly, but people decided not to be provoked.

This observation led me to an important insight: non-violent communities are not places of 'communal harmony'. The limited accounts of such communities often imply a notion of harmony and an absence of everyday conflicts. Indeed, when I first conducted research in Wayame, the non-violent community in Ambon, almost ten years after the peace agreement, this place did appear to be an 'island of peace' and was referred to as such. From my first interviews with community leaders about how they prevented killings, it would not have occurred to me that residents may have been deeply affected by tensions and common conflicts across the religious divide. That afternoon at the market in Dadin Kowa, I realized that despite highly effective prevention efforts, significant animosities can prevail. The finding became pivotal in understanding the contingency of civilian prevention work and informed my theorizing of resilient communities.

## Challenges

Conducting interviews in conflict zones raises specific methodological, practical, and ethical challenges.[13] First, the security situation can be difficult to assess, particularly when areas are located in the periphery of a country. Conflicts and tensions tend to be smouldering, no international peacekeepers are present, and large donor programmes with international staff rarely deploy to such areas. The continuity of communal tensions, and the ferocity of atrocities if fighting breaks out, constantly render the security situation difficult to judge. Scholars, journalists, and NGO workers based in capital cities may not have spent time in areas affected by communal violence. This can make information gathering and preparations challenging. Field research contains an almost inevitable learning period during which the ability to judge the security situation and the context increases with greater experience and repeated trips.[14]

Furthermore, the ethical implications of fieldwork in conflict zones, the protection of respondents as well as the safety of the researcher, sometimes do not make field research feasible.[15] The very tense and volatile situation in Jos also impacted my travel plans. I once had to leave the city much earlier than planned because rumours of imminent demonstrations and potential new riots circulated to such an extent that my research assistant and driver judged it best to put my work on hold and no longer enter the city centre until the situation had calmed down.

While these aspects put the researcher at risk, the protection of respondents can be equally challenging. In areas marked by communal tensions, being seen by community members as providing information to a foreign researcher may be harmful for individual respondents. In order to protect interviewees, I let them choose the location of meeting points, whether it was their houses, their offices, or a public café or restaurant. If no such place ensured anonymity, I would meet respondents in my car outside the area in which they lived. I have anonymized my respondents and cite them with pseudonyms, except for individuals, such as militia, community, or religious leaders whose names are known and have been previously published.

---

[13] Nordstrom and Robben 1995; Wood 2006, pp. 373–386; Fujii 2009, 2010, 2015.
[14] Wood 2006, p. 380.    [15] Nordstrom and Robben 1995; Wood 2006.

Whom a foreign researcher visits and interviews during a lull in a communal conflict – and whom she does not speak to – may carry weight and send a message as to whose voices are seen to count. I strove to talk to respondents of mixed ages from all ethnic and religious groups, as well as to both men and women within a community.

Another specific challenge in the context of communal conflict arose from interviewing perpetrators. Discussions of perpetrator research have often focused on demobilized ex-combatants who are approachable through UN and NGO offices and can be interviewed within these premises. By contrast, in communal conflicts, the difficulties of interviewing those who have fought and killed are compounded by the fact that they remain embedded within their families and communities. A foreign researcher is easily spotted. This visibility can lead to co-optation of the researcher or provide the impression that former fighters have a certain degree of social capital that attracts visits by foreigners, international attention, and potentially resources. Furthermore, the notion of 'perpetrator' also takes on multiple meanings. Those who directly participated in killings tend to be men. But while some were thugs and gang leaders before the outbreak of communal violence, others joined to protect themselves and their families or because of social shaming from within their community, in particular from women. Still others were recruited as children, urged on by women and men who celebrated them as brave boys and heroes of their communities. Moreover, behind the front lines of those who fought, unarmed civilians contribute to the killings. Some religious leaders tolerated the gathering of armed men before attacks in their houses of worship; some community leaders collected funds for the purchase of weapons; some women collectively cooked food to provide for large numbers of men before they went into battle. In order to avoid co-optation, I decided to meet gang members and self-identified perpetrators outside their neighbourhoods. In Jos, I would meet them in my car, which had tinted windows, parked in a nearby area, with my driver waiting alongside. This way, these visits would not be visible to local residents who often remained intimidated and at times terrified by the presence of gang or militia leaders in their neighbourhoods. In Ambon, I was able to interview militia members due to the peace agreement and amnesty arrangements for former fighters. In Jos, NGO workers and a local government official facilitated contacts with gang members from the most violence-prone neighbourhoods.

Conducting interviews in non-violent communities also posed ethical challenges. During my first visits to Dadin Kowa in Jos in 2010 and 2011, my research assistant was approached to inform me that I should not spend too much time interviewing local residents in the neighbourhood. Some community leaders felt uneasy about international attention being paid to their prevention work in the context of strong fears of imminent renewed clashes. Youth leaders in Dadin Kowa were repeatedly pressured by external armed groups to facilitate an attack on Muslims in Dadin Kowa and had little interest in contributing to further tensions by drawing attention to their prevention work. Furthermore, some community leaders emphasized that their regular meetings and community engagement to prevent killings cost them much time that they could otherwise invest in their small businesses, and that they had to draw on personal resources to provide food and drinks for meetings. While they provided information to foreign researchers, journalists, and NGO staff, they received no resources in return to support their work. I conducted my interviews in Dadin Kowa over the course of four visits, which limited the time that I spent in the neighbourhood during each visit but allowed me to collect in-depth information.

Scholars who have conducted field research in conflict zones have further discussed the challenge of memory and the impact of traumatic events, suggesting that experiences of violence and killings may form particularly intense memories and may be well remembered.[16] At times, I found that a profound sense of trauma among respondents limited the answers that I could collect on certain questions. For example, as has often been noted in other studies of communal violence, many respondents stressed that they used to live 'in harmony' with Christian or Muslim neighbours before clashes broke out. In fact, one of the most common expressions at the beginning of most interviews, whether it was in Ambon or Jos, were statements that illustrated how Muslims and Christians used to celebrate life events together and maintained friendships, mutual respect, and communal support before the first clashes. I understood such statements primarily as an expression of trauma, a sense of victimhood, and genuine confusion over how conflicts could have escalated to such dramatic lethality. These experiences meant that respondents often

---

[16] Wood 2003, p. 40.

remembered little detail of the inter-communal tensions and conflicts that marked everyday life *before* the clashes begun. Indeed, when asking respondents from religiously mixed areas about mundane conflicts in their neighbourhood prior to killings, they were often unable to recount details, instead referring to inter-communal festivities and the general notion of 'communal harmony'.

This experience was most acute in the two neighbourhoods of my paired comparison that had initially prevented violence: Poka–Rumahtiga in Ambon and Anglo Jos in Jos. In Anglo Jos, I first conducted interviews in December 2010 and then again in June 2011, initially less than a year after devastating clashes. Residents from Anglo Jos seemed unable to recount any details of communal life, or community violence prevention strategies, during the first interviews in 2010. Some could only refer to the 'before violence' state of the community as 'communal harmony'. They expressed deep shock over the clashes and seemed unable to explain why violence broke out. During this period, I limited my meetings to brief visits guided by a research assistant from a neighbouring community who had family members in Anglo Jos and who could provide me with invaluable advice about ethical conduct. Over the next four years, I visited the community again and was slowly able to learn more about communal relations and violence prevention efforts before the clashes, particularly from residents who took part in citywide trauma and peacebuilding workshops. With this support, they were able to reflect on the violent events in their neighbourhood. Clearly, these reconstructions of daily life in the neighbourhood before the outbreak of violence are affected by memory formation after the clashes and the interpretation of clashes conveyed in NGO peacebuilding programmes. The comparison with narratives from non-violent communities offers a helpful contextualization of respondents' explanations of violence and non-violence.

It is to the analysis of violence and non-violence in Ambon and Jos that we now turn.

# 4 | Indonesia

## From Gang Fight to 'Religious War' in Ambon, Maluku Province

*We feel like we have been fooled. Today, the community understands better and people do not respond so easily to provocation. Many people have come to think that we were made a fool. So many killed, so many wounded, so many who lost their property. People who have lost their husband, lost their wife, lost their child. None is replaceable up until this second.*[1]

In January 1999, in the wake of Indonesia's regime change, riots broke out in Ambon, the capital of the small Maluku Province in eastern Indonesia. Within weeks, riots escalated into urban and rural militia fighting between the Christian and Muslim populations, killing at least 1,460 people in 1999.[2] The conflict then accelerated even further and became internationalized in April 2000, when about 3,000 jihadist fighters from all over Indonesia and neighbouring countries arrived in Maluku to 'protect Muslims' and 'wage war' on the Christian population. Between the onset of armed conflict and the February 2002 peace agreement, at least 2,793 casualties were recorded, but it is likely that more people were killed.[3]

The sleepy town of Ambon is set between maritime beauty and lush, steep, mountainous terrain. Traditional villages have merged into a long string of suburban settlements that line the main street around Ambon Bay from the region's airport into the city centre. A gateway to a scattering of tiny and idyllic islands, 'sweet Ambon' was known for its historic spice trade, tranquil beauty, famed singers, and harmonic relations between Muslim and Christian villages. Although Indonesia

---

[1] Eko, former Muslim militia member, Ambon, March 2010.
[2] Estimate based on event data analysis collected by the Indonesian National Violence Monitoring System (Sistem Nasional Pemantauan Kekerasan Indonesia, SNPK).
[3] I assume that local newspapers underreported conflict deaths, particularly in rural areas, because newspaper offices did not fully function during the conflict and the maritime province of Maluku includes a large number of remote villages. This number is therefore a conservative estimate.

is the world's largest Muslim-majority country, in Maluku Province, Christians constitute about half of the population. Ethno-religious tensions rooted in colonial history had been simmering during the last decade of the authoritarian military regime under General Suharto (1966–1998), but Maluku had no history of major communal clashes.

In 1998, at the end of the Suharto regime, Indonesia appeared to be another example of a global trend of 'ethnic' or 'religious' conflict in the post–Cold War era. Anti-Chinese riots erupted in the context of the Asian financial crisis in mid-1997, accompanied by riots and looting in several parts of Indonesia during 1998.[4] The separatist movements in Aceh and Papua gained new momentum during the transition, and East Timor separated from Indonesia after a referendum marked by extreme violence. Communal conflicts ravaged the eastern provinces of Maluku, North Maluku, Sulawesi, and Kalimantan.[5] This clustering of deadly conflicts has been described as a violence-prone 'critical juncture' after regime change and democratization.[6] The majority of the Indonesian archipelago remained largely peaceful,[7] but the afore-mentioned provinces suffered high levels of violence. The Maluku war was one of the worst conflicts during Indonesia's *reformasi* – the period after the end of military rule – and the ferocity of ethnic cleansing has been described as 'the most shocking violence seen in Indonesia since the anti-communist pogroms of 1965/66', except for the violence in East Timor.[8]

Instrumentalist accounts dominate the study of communal violence and explanations of the Maluku war. Scholars of Indonesian politics have analysed how Indonesia's regime change, the weakened and par-tial security forces, and the unravelling of patronage networks between national and local elites contributed to the outbreak of communal violence in Maluku.[9] Micro-level studies have argued that local elites manipulated religious identities for voter mobilization before the first elections after the transition in June 1999.[10] Beyond conflict onset,

---

[4] Sidel 2006.
[5] See van Klinken 2007, Wilson 2006, 2008, and Duncan 2005, 2013 on the conflict in North Maluku; Barron, Azca, and Susdinarjanti 2012 on Maluku; and McRae 2013 on the conflict in Poso, Sulawesi.
[6] Bertrand 2008, p. 427.    [7] Varshney, Tadjoeddin, and Panggabean 2008.
[8] Van Klinken 2007, p. 88.    [9] Bertrand 2004; Sidel 2006.
[10] Goss 2000; van Klinken 2001, 2007.

however, regime change, democratization, and local elite manipulation
do not sufficiently explain *escalation* to communal war. When the
Ambon riots broke out, scholars and observers predominantly interpreted the violence as having been 'provoked' by networks of politicians and military officers close to the former military regime in
Jakarta.[11] This provocateur theme has been common in Indonesian
accounts of collective violence. The idea of the provocateur neutralizes
violent events in public memory by presenting ever-elusive and faceless
perpetrators,[12] in effect denying local people *agency*.

In this chapter, I focus on civilian agency and the organization of
communal war in Ambon and Maluku Province. The men who went
into battle were no faceless 'outsiders', but local men deeply embedded
within their communities as husbands, sons, brothers, friends, and
neighbours. While the political transition and the weakening of security forces created conditions that made a communal war possible, it is
the formation of local militia groups around churches and mosques
that explains the death toll beyond the civil war threshold. A history of
religious polarization and the traumatizing experience of victimization
led to the emergence of a 'religious conflict' narrative. Thugs and
ordinary men emerged as community 'saviours' and militias established
war headquarters at the main mosque and church of Ambon.

I first summarize the national context of Indonesia's regime change
against which the local war unfolded, and the dynamics of violence in
Maluku Province. I then show how communal violence originated
from below as everyday violence networks of *preman* (thugs) and
vigilante groups transformed into well-coordinated mobile militias.
The analysis shows that this ferocious conflict was neither orchestrated
by national political and military elites, nor did the context of regime
change cause the local war.

## National Context: Indonesia's Regime Change

Indonesia's regime change, the national political struggle between the
authoritarian regime and its democratic challengers, the restructuring
of military forces, and the mobilization of Islamist groups shaped the
national context within which the local war in Maluku unfolded.
The Suharto regime crumbled in the wake of the Asian financial crisis,

---

[11] Human Rights Watch 1999.    [12] Purdey 2004, p. 194.

which resulted in a dramatic economic downturn in mid-1997. After a decade of power struggles between a democratic opposition movement and the military–authoritarian regime, the financial crisis turned into a window of opportunity for regime change activists.[13] On 28 May 1998, after several months of demonstrations, General Suharto stepped down from power, marking the beginning of Indonesia's transition to civilian and democratic rule. Vice President Habibie took over the interim government until national elections in June 1999.

General Suharto's survival politics during the 1990s had dramatically shaped nationwide religious polarization, which influenced not only local power struggles in Maluku but also national perceptions of the Maluku conflict. Since the 1980s, a prominent Muslim reform movement had advocated for democratic rule. In reaction to this growing opposition, particularly from the middle class, the Suharto regime had developed new allies among ultraconservative Islamists to prevent Muslim and non-Muslim reformers joining force. This initiative to consolidate support among Muslim activists resulted in the formation of the Association of Indonesian Muslim Intellectuals (ICMI) in 1990. The association became an important vehicle for local and national Muslim political candidates' aspirations. In order to discredit democratic challengers and establish a regime conform Islamic mainstream, opponents to ICMI were frequently labelled as 'Christians' or, less frequently, as 'nationalists', even though the opposition was much more varied, thus deepening religious polarization and political mobilization among Muslim groups.[14]

In response to the founding of ICMI, popular opposition leader and cleric Abdurrahman Wahid founded the Forum Demokrasi in 1991. It developed into a highly respected multi-religious platform of Indonesian intellectuals and members of the political, military, and cultural spheres that opposed the authoritarian regime and successfully undermined its legitimacy. The coalition of moderate Muslims, Christians, secularists, and representatives of other religions laid the foundation for the protest movements that eventually brought down Suharto.[15] This struggle between members of the authoritarian regime

---

[13] Hefner 2000a.
[14] For a more detailed discussion, see Hefner 2000a, p. 141; van Bruinessen 1996, 2002; Sidel 2006; Horowitz 2013.
[15] Hefner 2000a.

and conservative Muslim organizations against pro-democracy activists continued after the fall of Suharto and impacted the local conflict dynamics in Maluku.[16]

Indonesia's June 1999 elections brought Abdurrahman Wahid to power. He represented a democratic and multi-religious Indonesia. His presidency would last until late 2001. Wahid's programme of military reform and disempowerment sparked fierce resistance among military elites in Jakarta.[17] Under Suharto, the military had established a firm position as a centre of power in Indonesian society. The doctrine of *dwingfusi* (dual function) adopted in 1966 had officially granted the military a strong sociopolitical position alongside its defence role. The military and the police were only separated in 1999. Subsequently, the military found itself under increasing pressure to submit itself to civilian control. Military self-financing aggravated human rights abuses because it prolonged violence in conflict areas where the armed forces had access to lucrative natural resources or moneymaking ventures.[18] The destruction of East Timor after the referendum in 1999 triggered calls for investigating human rights violations by army personnel during the reform era.

For Islamist groups and politicians seeking to mobilize voters along religious lines, Habibie's presidency appeared to mark the elevation of Islam to the seat of national state power. As John Sidel wrote, 'never before had forces favouring the so-called Islamisation of Indonesian state and society enjoyed such proximity to power.'[19] Habibie had long served as the chairman of ICMI and had become a patron and promoter of a broad variety of modernist Muslim activists seeking patronage and protection from the state. However, contrary to expectations among supporters of political Islam, the 1999 elections did not result in significant gains for Islamist parties.

Paramilitary Islamist groups emerged during the transition, including Laskar Pembela Islam (Defenders of Islam Force), Laskar Jihad (Holy War Force), and Laskar Mujahidin Indonesia (Indonesian Holy Warriors). They took the demand to implement sharia law to the streets, raiding cafés, nightclubs, and brothels. Ethno-religious violence in the provinces of Maluku and North Maluku turned into catalysts for Islamist mobilization in national politics. The paramilitary group Laskar Jihad formed in direct response to the religiously framed

---

[16] Sidel 2006.    [17] Mietzner 2009; Crouch 2010; Horowitz 2013.
[18] Misol 2006.    [19] Sidel 2006, p. 132.

violence in Maluku and capitalized on the conflict to gain national political momentum. The group recruited thousands of fighters nationally and internationally. On 7 January 2000, more than 100,000 people demonstrated in Jakarta for a jihad in Maluku as a response to the violence – and senior politicians backed their call. According to Noorhaidi Hasan, 'the call for jihad in the Moluccas was part of the politics of recognition pursued by Indonesian Salafis, an attempt to enhance their identity and thereby negotiate a place for themselves on the map of Indonesian Islam.'[20] Even though President Wahid had ordered the military to prevent Laskar Jihad fighters from travelling to Ambon, his orders were ignored, demonstrating the limits of his power over military forces. The arrival of thousands of jihadist fighters in Ambon in April 2000 reignited and transformed the local war. Only when Islamist groups were politically defeated in Jakarta and the military had secured its national political influence did the armed forces bring an end to the jihadists' campaign in Maluku, paving the way for the 2002 peace agreement.

## Summary of the Ambon Conflict

Situated in the eastern periphery of the Indonesian state, Maluku was part of the historic Spice Islands that once provided the world with expensive cloves and nutmeg. Attracted by the profitable spice trade, a strong Dutch colonial presence shaped Maluku's political, social, economic, and legal institutions. Within the contemporary Indonesian state, Maluku's economic development reflected its peripheral status.

At the turn of the millennium, Ambon was a densely populated town of 314,417 people with an almost even religious divide of Muslims (about 40 per cent), Protestants (about 56 per cent), and Catholics (about 3 per cent).[21] Many urban areas and newer settlements were religiously mixed and cultural differences between Muslims and Christians were eroding in urban Ambon. People attended the same state schools and universities, watched the same television programmes and movies, spoke the same lingua franca, and competed for the same opportunities, with religious conversion for marriage or employment opportunities a regular occurrence.[22]

[20] Hasan 2006, p. 187.  [21] Hiariej 2007, p. 15.  [22] Sidel 2006, p. 191.

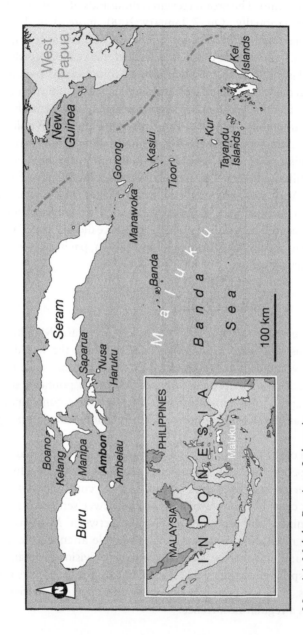

Map 4.1 Maluku Province, Indonesia

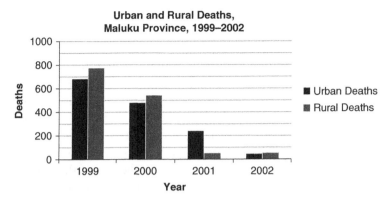

**Figure 4.1** Estimated deaths, Maluku Province, 1999–2002
Source: SNPK Dataset.

Two periods of conflict can be distinguished in Maluku. The 1999 local communal war commenced with the January riots in Ambon. These riots escalated into urban and rural militia fighting, particularly after Indonesia's June 1999 elections. According to newspaper-based event data, the 1999 local war was the deadliest period of the Maluku conflict, accounting for more than half of the casualty numbers. The second conflict period commenced with the arrival of Laskar Jihad troops in April 2000, when the local war took on a radically new and transnational dimension. During the year 2001, the conflict died down, and grassroots peace initiatives emerged.

## Pre-Conflict Maluku

Upon Indonesian independence in 1945, many Christian Malukans feared Muslim religious and Javanese cultural dominance in a unitary Indonesian state. In 1950, some of them proclaimed the Republic Maluku Selatan (RMS, South Maluku Republic) in an effort to break away. Although not exclusively Christian, the independence movement was dominated by South Maluku Protestants. Upon Indonesian independence in 1945 some 12,000 Malukans resettled in the Netherlands, where they held on to the dream of an independent state.[23] By 1999, only a small group of RMS supporters remained in Maluku, but

[23] International Crisis Group 2000.

rumours that Christians wanted to form an independent state came to fuel the communal war from 1999 to 2002.

The legacy of colonial rule continued to impact both urban and rural livelihoods well into the 1990s. It had resulted in a complex landscape of legal pluralism in rural Maluku that made conflicts over landownership extremely difficult to resolve.[24] Historically, colonial resettlement policies had changed the status of clans and families and their ownership of land, and rivalries between villages of the same religion shaped local conflicts as much as tensions between Muslim and Christian villages.[25] By the end of the authoritarian regime, traditional regulations had largely failed to address numerous land disputes,[26] and conflicts between villages over land rights were an important factor that fed rural violence during the 'religious' war.[27]

Maluku's local economy was based mainly on subsistence horticulture and fishing. The village populations relied on a mix of sources for income, including subsistence agriculture and the production of spices for the national and international markets, fishing, petty trade, miscellaneous state projects, and small businesses set up by migrants who settled in Java and the Netherlands.[28] A sizeable and predominantly Muslim migrant population from Sulawesi and Java, including the ethnic Butonese, Bugis, and Makassere (BBM), had significantly shifted religious demographics and opportunities within the local economy. The percentage of Muslim migrants rose steadily, from 5 per cent of the total Malukan population in 1971 to more than 14 per cent in 1995.[29] Migrants were often socially and economically disadvantaged. As 'second-class citizens', they were exempted from elections for the village head, lacked local political representation, and were not allowed to own land or participate in the historically profitable spice trade. Being barred from positions in the local administration, they developed a strong presence within the private economic sector. Migrant communities were also excluded from local *adat*, the customary law system. *Adat* includes regulations for landownership and inheritance rights, as well as for village heads (*rajas*), relationships

---

[24] Von Benda-Beckmann and Taale 1996, p. 38.
[25] Von Benda-Beckmann 2004, p. 226.     [26] Mearns and Healey 1996.
[27] Adam 2010, p. 25.
[28] Von Benda-Beckmann and von Benda-Beckmann 2007, p. 199.
[29] Sukma 2005, p. 2.

**Figure 4.2** View over Ambon City[31]

between villages (*pela*), and conflict management. *Adat* is specific to the eastern Indonesian islands, but its forms and rules somewhat differ from island to island.[30]

In urban Ambon, the colonial legacy had led to Christian dominance over the local bureaucracy until well into the mid-1980s. Suharto's alignment with conservative Muslim groups and the subsequent campaign to Islamize government offices impacted social and economic structures and increased religious polarization. From 1992 onwards, members of ICMI were systematically appointed to vacant positions within the local bureaucracy, limiting opportunities for Christians. During the 1990s, General Suharto twice appointed a local Muslim as governor instead of a military officer, as had been standard practice during the previous two decades.[32] Both times, the alternative candidate for the position was a Protestant, thus heightening frustration and anxiety among Ambon's Protestant population. Public sector

---

[30] For an excellent discussion of *adat* and community development from colonialism to contemporary Indonesia, see Davidson and Henley 2007.
[31] Photo credit: Jana Krause.    [32] Sukma 2005, p. 2.

employment decreased in Maluku and in other Indonesian provinces as the impact of the financial crisis reduced the government budget.[33] Besides fearing political marginalization, Christians faced increasing difficulties in securing employment in the state sector upon graduation. Furthermore, turning to the private sector, they found themselves in dire competition with Muslim migrants, who were well established in business and trade.

In October 1998, an anonymous pamphlet emerged, claiming that Maluku's governor, Saleh Latuconsina, had replaced 'all 38' top civil servants in the province with Muslims.[34] Although the governor vehemently affirmed the importance of a 'balance' between Protestant Christians and Muslims, he had indeed appointed a Muslim deputy governor and a Muslim provincial secretary. Thus, the Christian elite was removed from the three most powerful positions in the province,[35] hardening their impression of a loss of political and economic power. In December 1998, during a meeting with Ambon's senior religious leaders, the governor encouraged guarding against rumours of violence and provocations along religious fault lines. However, according to a report on the first riot from March 1999, 'the atmosphere was so tense ... that the Muslims left convinced that the Christians had decided that the only way to address the problem was to rid the province of Muslim migrants.'[36] Religious leaders established communication posts among churches and mosques, connected by cellular and landline phones, to guard against rumours.[37] Thus, the Ambon riots broke out in a context of strong religious polarization and fears of violence.

## The 1999 Local War

Youth fights in Ambon and in the villages around the city were common, but on 19 January 1999, on Lebaran (Eid al-Fitr), the celebration of the end of the Muslim holy month of Ramadan, such a fight at the bus terminal sparked a riot that triggered three years of heavy fighting. An argument between a Christian public transport driver and at least one Muslim passenger deteriorated into a wide-ranging brawl. Within

[33]  Van Klinken 2007.    [34]  Van Klinken 2001, p. 2.
[35]  Van Klinken 2001, p. 2.    [36]  Human Rights Watch 1999, p. 7.
[37]  Spyer 2002.

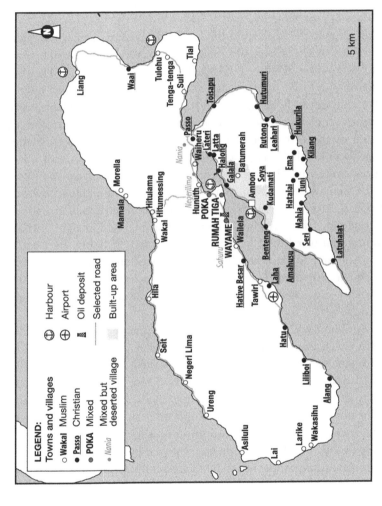

Map 4.2 Religious segregation on Ambon Island

hours of the incident, Christian (red) and Muslim (white) fighters were attacking neighbourhoods using traditional or homemade weapons such as knives, spears, machetes, bows and arrows, and Molotov cocktails. By the end of the day, numerous houses, stores, offices, churches, and mosques had been destroyed or burned, scores of people had been displaced, and many wounded or killed. The confrontation escalated into days of mob violence.

According to the first report on the conflict, as early as the first night (19 January) white and red headbands were handed out at mosques and churches so that fighters could tell one another apart.[38] Hearing rumours of attacks on churches and mosques, hundreds of people had mobilized to fight by the end of January. One incident many residents remembered was the mobilization of a large crowd of Muslim villagers from the Leihitu area in the north of Ambon Island, which includes the villages of Hila and Wakal. These north coast villages were one of the Muslim strongholds during the war. On 20 January, this group marched down the mountains towards Ambon to attack Christian villages and neighbourhoods, provoked by rumours that Ambon's main mosque had been burned. A traditional war leader led the crowd. However, before they could reach Ambon and clash with mobilizing Christians there, the military was able to stop them. Community and religious leaders on both sides reportedly prevented mobs from launching attacks in several other instances.[39]

In Ambon City, churches and mosques emerged as central nodes within violence networks, serving simultaneously as meeting places to coordinate the organization of aid for victims, the formation of riot groups, and the storage of looted goods. Those who had to flee their homes often found refuge at mosques and churches, where their pitiful situation aroused anger and fuelled desire for revenge. Due to recruitment patterns within the military and police – the military dominated by Muslims and the local police by Christians – security forces were drawn into the conflict and felt obligated to protect their religious kin.

Leaders of armed groups reportedly coordinated attacks in several waves to facilitate looting. Houses were marked and their owners attacked before goods were looted and stored in houses of worship,

---

[38]  Human Rights Watch 1999, p. 17.    [39]  Human Rights Watch 1999.

**Figure 4.3** The bus terminal in Ambon, Maluku[40]

some of which, it had previously been falsely claimed, burned down.[41] Religious terms were employed to distinguish between Muslim and Christian areas. The city's main dividing line became known as the 'Gaza Strip' and the fighters as 'Israelis' (Christian) and 'Palestinians' (Muslims). Graffiti desecrated walls and buildings with insults against Jesus and the Prophet Muhammad, references to Jews, Israel, Muslim Power, Muslim pigs, Stars of David, and the phrase 'Allahu Akbar' in Arabic writing.[42]

According to event data, at least 340 people were killed between January and March 1999. Although the urban Ambon clashes received the most attention, rural clashes were significantly more deadly during this period: approximately 236 people were killed in rural Maluku between January and March 1999, compared to 82 recorded casualties in Ambon City. Rural violence resulted in ethnic cleansing on Ambon Island and the islands of Aru, Kei Besar, Haruku,

---

[40] Photo credit: Jana Krause.    [41] Human Rights Watch 1999.
[42] Spyer 2002.

and Saparua. In April, killings continued in rural areas of the small islands Banda and Kei Kecil, while Ambon remained largely quiet.

National and local government efforts to bring the clashes under control had little impact on the conflict. In January 1999, Maluku's governor called senior religious leaders together for a public pledge for peace, but the violence continued unabated. In February, President Habibie sent a fact-finding team to Ambon to report on the situation and provide recommendations for the settlement of the conflict. In March, the Indonesian government formed a special armed forces team to improve the security situation and the response of military and police forces. In May 1999, religious, community, traditional, and youth leaders signed another peace declaration in Ambon. A nineteen-member team formed by the Indonesian military was sent to Maluku to support the local administration, but no investigations took place into the causes of the violence or the allegations about provocation from outside the community.[43]

Calm returned to Ambon in May, a few weeks before Indonesia's first free national and regional elections in forty-four years took place in June 1999. Due to the destruction, voting did not take place in some districts in Maluku.[44] Furthermore, many Muslim migrants who had fled the province were unable to participate in the elections. Despite heavy lobbying, Muslim party leaders failed to achieve their voter registration targets.[45] The election results favoured the Indonesian Democratic Party – Struggle (PDI-P) led by Megawati Soekarnoputri, the party most Christians in Maluku had voted for. Shocked by an unexpected local election loss, Muslim politicians accused Christians of having planned and instigated the clashes to influence the vote. Even though Christian leaders agreed they had profited from the displace-ment of Muslim communities prior to the elections, they denied having instigated any violence for the purpose of influencing the election results.[46] According to van Klinken, Muslim party leaders likely mis-judged their prospects of winning a large share of the vote in the election given their major disadvantage in organizational capacity compared to the PDI-P, a party that relied on the very effective Protestant organizational network in Maluku Province.[47]

---

[43] Sukma 2005, p. 7.    [44] International Crisis Group 2000, p. 5.
[45] Van Klinken 2007.    [46] Tanamal and Trijono 2004.
[47] Van Klinken 2007.

Ambon did not remain calm for long. In July 1999, stone-throwing incidents in the city reignited the clashes. Violence began in the neighbourhoods of Poka and Rumahtiga on the other side of Ambon Bay. This location was significant because the area was the most pluralistic and modern settlement on Ambon Island. Predominantly a middle-class neighbourhood, the area included the university and the homes of many government officials. According to residents of Ambon and Poka–Rumahtiga, the clashes came as a shock. Until then, the killings had been confined to some of the poorest neighbourhoods of Ambon, which were known for regular gang fights, and to villages where inter-ethnic tensions were ripe. Furthermore, community leaders in Poka–Rumahtiga had tried to prevent violence in their area. The fall of this modern settlement and the rise of religious segregation marked the beginning of the deadliest period of this communal war, when local militias consolidated. Between August and December 1999, an estimated 907 people were killed.

In August 1999, ethno-religious violence also erupted in the newly formed province of North Maluku. In the 'Bloody Christmas' massacre on Christmas Day, about 500 Muslims were killed in North Maluku. According to an account by the International Crisis Group, local Christians went on the offensive against the local Muslim minority in Tobelo.[48] Christians denied the charges, arguing that the massacres were committed by military troops.[49] According to eyewitnesses, trucks carrying men armed with automatic weapons made their way to Muslim settlements in an overwhelmingly Christian area.[50] The residents were butchered with machetes, shot, or burned alive in their houses. About 250 people, mostly women and children, were burned to death in the nearby mosque. Even by the standards of the final years of the Suharto regime, the Bloody Christmas killings represented brutality on an almost unthinkable scale. This incident was widely covered in the Indonesian press and became pivotal to the conflicts in both Maluku and North Maluku. Nationally, jihadists mobilized to protect Muslims in Maluku and North Maluku, thereby gaining a national stage.

[48] International Crisis Group 2000, p. 6.   [49] Aditjondro 2001.
[50] Hefner 2000b.

*Laskar Jihad and the Transnationalization of the Conflict,*
*2000–2002*

Laskar Jihad emerged on Java Island and attracted thousands of volunteer fighters from all over Indonesia and neighbouring countries.
In January 2000, it staged a rally in Jakarta with more than 10,000
followers in attendance, and by April 2000 the group had trained and
dispatched about 3,000 jihadi fighters to war-torn Maluku Province.[51]
Their arrival significantly changed the dynamics of the local war, which
took on a new, national dimension in the context of power struggles
between the reform government under President Wahid and senior
military officers in Jakarta.

Laskar Jihad was the paramilitary division of the Sunni
Communication Forum (FKAWJ), an organization formed by
a group of hard-line Muslim leaders in 1998 to distinguish itself from
the mainstream Indonesian Islamic organizations Nahdlatul Ulama
and Muhammadiyah, which they accused of corruption. FKAWJ
rejected a democratic system as incompatible with Islam and refused
to support any political party. It accused the Wahid government of
siding with religious minorities and 'nominal' Muslims, thwarting the
application of Islamic law.[52] The group's commander-in-chief, Ustad
Jaffar Umar Thalib, had formative experience fighting with the Afghan
Mujahidin in 1988–1989 and had studied Islamic law in Lahore,
Pakistan. Although the fatwas that declared jihad in Ambon were
issued from Yemen, the jihadist movement was essentially an
Indonesian organization and formed part of the established Islamic
conservative opposition against Wahid's presidency and his prospec-
tive successor, Vice President Megawati.[53] Thalib claimed that
a FKAWJ team had been sent to Maluku in late 1999 to gather information on the conflict and falsely accused Protestant churches of planning to form a breakaway Christian state comprising Maluku, West
Papua, and North Sulawesi, with the support of remnants of the former
Republic of South Maluku based in the Netherlands. Based on these
accusations, he declared Christians in Maluku were 'belligerent
infidels'.[54] At the end of January 2000, the Laskar Jihad registration
post in Jakarta had signed up more than 2,000 local Muslims who
declared themselves ready to go to Maluku. The group set up a training

---

[51]  Schulze 2002; Hasan 2006; Sidel 2006.    [52]  Fealy 2001.
[53]  Schulze 2002; Hasan 2006.    [54]  Fealy 2001.

camp in Bogor, near Jakarta, where some 3,000 men received training from members of university student regiments, veterans from the Afghan, Kashmir, and Mindanao wars, and military personnel.[55]

Under the umbrella of FKAWJ, Laskar Jihad was well organized. FKAWJ remained responsible for organizing and financing the dispatch of volunteer jihadist fighters and for providing financial support to the families of recruits. Money was raised from members and sympathizers, and also through public donations. In April 2000, just before the first jihadist fighters set out for Maluku, young men standing at intersections and holding boxes labelled 'Contributions for jihad in the Moluccas' became a common sight in cities where FKAWJ branches had been established.[56] Hasan wrote that the bulk of financial support came from 'secret donors', most likely high-ranking military officers and members of the former Suharto elite who did not want their names publicized, and an FKAWJ spokesperson admitted to having raised significant funds from the transnational Salafi network in Malaysia, Singapore, Japan, Australia, the United States, and the Gulf States.[57] The Indonesian military did not stop the jihadists from entering Maluku despite a decree from President Wahid. As the Crisis Group reported, these orders were relayed directly to Armed Forces Chief Widodo and through Civilian Minister Sudarsono.[58]

In Ambon, many Muslims initially enthusiastically welcomed the jihadists, and celebrations took place in front of the Al-Fatah Mosque, Ambon's main mosque.[59] With their arrival, the number of violent incidents and the death toll rose again as of April 2000. Local Muslim militias and jihadists with modern weaponry drew the Laskar Kristus, the Christian troops, back into battle for what was perceived as an all-out 'religious war'. The summer and fall of the year 2000 saw a second spike in casualties after the deadly clashes in late 1999. The conflict continued with low intensity in 2001, killing 294 people, compared to 1,460 in 1999 and 1,025 in 2000.

About 3,000 Laskar Jihad fighters were stationed on Ambon Island in July 2000.[60] The jihadists openly pursued an agenda of religious cleansing. Apart from Laskar Jihad, about 300 Laskar Mujahidin fighters had also arrived in Ambon, operating largely as a secret but

[55] Hasan 2006, p. 186.   [56] Hasan, 2006, p. 124.   [57] Hasan 2006, p. 125.
[58] International Crisis Group 2000, p. 3.   [59] Hasan 2006.   [60] Hasan 2006.

highly effective fighting force.[61] The jihadists tried to impose their own version of society on Muslims, including Islamic law.[62] In June 2000, President Wahid declared a civil emergency for Maluku. A military spokesman admitted that a significant proportion of the soldiers in Maluku were 'emotionally involved' in the conflict.[63] In an effort to ease tensions, a Balinese Hindu took over command from a Christian; it was hoped that he would appear neutral to both sides. The civil emergency and a large troop exchange did not provide immediate improvement. Some militia leaders were arrested during this period, but most were later released.[64]

However, in the aftermath of the 9/11 attacks and the subsequent 'war on terror', jihadi networks in Ambon briefly caught international attention. The restructured military forces eventually expelled the jihadists from the islands, and in late 2001, peace talks between the warring parties commenced. Starting as a secret movement among the younger generation of religious leaders and the governor, these talks paved the way for the 2002 Malino Peace Agreement mediated by Vice President Jusuf Kalla. After a small women's movement re-established communications across the religious dividing line, some religious leaders within the main church and mosque started to denounce the violence and – in concert with security forces and local politicians – brought militia leaders under control. Negotiations proceeded from the understanding that the violence in Maluku was 'provoked' from 'outside', a narrative that ignored local leaders' responsibilities and foreclosed truth seeking. Laskar Jihad's presence in Ambon cemented the provocateur narrative and led many community leaders to argue that the entire conflict was externally provoked. However, as the event data demonstrate, the local war in 1999 – before the arrival of Laskar Jihad – was the deadliest period of the conflict. After the communal war, Ambon and many rural villages remained religiously segregated and very few streets counted as neutral areas.

## Communal Violence from Below: Mobilization and Conflict Escalation

The existence of everyday violence networks and the perception of a 'religious' conflict among religious and community leaders made

---

[61]  Hasan 2006.    [62]  Schulze 2002, p. 58.
[63]  International Crisis Group 2000, p. 10.    [64]  International Crisis Group 2000.

militia formation possible. The emergence of mobile militias explains how the Ambon riots could escalate into a communal war that engulfed the entire province. From January to June 1999, an estimated 464 people were killed, compared to 996 people who lost their lives between July and December 1999 when militias had consolidated. At Maranatha Church, Ambon's main church, a communication office connected every church and logistical unit of Christians through radio communication. The Al-Fatah Mosque just a few hundred meters away established the task force for 'Coping with Bloody Idul Fitri', led first by retired general Rustam Kastor and later by former naval officer Yusuf Ely, a local businessman. Both crisis centres were 'collecting and disseminating battlefield intelligence'.[65] Where did these militia fighters come from, and why were they willing to fight a 'religious war'?

## Political Mobilization and Everyday Violence Networks

In Indonesia, everyday networks of violence have long existed under the term *preman* (literally 'free man') and have a complicated history rooted in Dutch colonial rule.[66] *Preman* were essentially thugs for hire. Suharto's New Order regime normalized violence and extortion as state practice,[67] and *preman* 'were allowed to operate protection rackets with virtual legal impunity on the condition that a proportion of their profits made its way through the state bureaucracy, and that they were available to be mobilized when the state felt its hegemony under threat'.[68] *Preman* is a grey-zone category that captures a wide range of actors with different networks and opportunities, ranging from local criminals to gang leaders with ties to key national politicians and military officers. After the fall of Suharto, 'many people turned to local *preman*, paramilitary, and vigilante groups for security', and 'a new decentralized intersection between criminal and political interests established itself.'[69] *Preman* broadened their networks along ethnic and religious lines and expanded control over neighbourhoods and public places for exploitation, such as markets and bus terminals, food stalls, cinemas, gambling facilities, and shopping malls.

---

[65] Van Klinken 2007, p. 97.    [66] Ryter 1998.    [67] Lindsey 2001.
[68] Wilson 2008, p. 193.    [69] Wilson 2006, p. 269.

Research has consistently linked the outbreak of riots in Ambon to the role of *preman*.[70] One conspiracy theory that community and religious leaders in Ambon referred to claimed that Ambonese *preman* based in Jakarta were deliberately sent back to Ambon at the end of 1998 to spark communal clashes. Several reports discussed allegations that, after a gang fight that involved Ambonese *preman* escalated into a riot in Jakarta in November 1998, up to 600 gang members were sent back to Maluku during December 1998.[71] Indonesian human rights investigators claimed to have evidence that the Jakarta riots were partly perpetrated by youth who were trucked in and paid to take part in violence.[72] The perception that thugs were deliberately sent back to Ambon to 'provoke' trouble made sense in the context of the regime change. However, with Christmas and the Muslim fasting month of Ramadan approaching and explicit threats against the Ambonese *preman* in Jakarta, other reasonable explanations exist for their return to Ambon.

The broad and shadowy *preman* category has often played into the prominence of the instrumental 'provocateur' narrative in Ambon. The first report on the conflict published by Human Rights Watch in March 1999 traced the origin of the provocateur theme to the fact that some of Ambon's *preman* groups had strong links to politicians in Jakarta. However, the report also noted that 'local leaders in Ambon tended to see the violence as locally instigated for narrow communal goals.'[73] Van Klinken similarly argued that rather than external actors, local elites were responsible for the onset of fighting.[74] While instrumentalist approaches account well for potential elite motivation they do not explain how communal violence was organized and why so many ordinary people fought, or supported the fighters, in a 'religious war'.

Interview respondents from Ambon confirmed that those who rose to become militia leaders and fighters were local men who were 'nothing' before the conflict,[75] and there were many of them. Anthropological research by David Mearns documented that by the late 1990s, the city had 'a chronic unemployment problem, especially for senior high school and university graduates'.[76] Mearns noted that people worried over the

---

[70]  Human Rights Watch 1999; Goss 2000, pp. 11–12; van Klinken 2001, 2007.
[71]  Human Rights Watch 1999; Aditjondro 2001, p. 112.
[72]  Human Rights Watch 1999, p. 9.     [73]  Human Rights Watch 1999, p. 2.
[74]  Van Klinken 2001, 2007.     [75]  Barron, Azca, and Susdinarjanti 2012.
[76]  Mearns 1996, p. 97.

number of young Christian men without work and the prospect of finding any:

'There is already a feeling that these youths are spending too much time hanging around the Kampong [neighbourhood] drinking and wasting their lives.'[77]

Particularly among Christians, growing unemployment, the rise of Muslims to positions within public administration, and the dominance of migrant Muslims in the informal economy resulted in swelling ranks of local *preman*. Joining *preman* groups became an alternative means of generating an income when government positions became unattainable. According to Christian respondents from Ambon, many Christian young men saw a career as *preman* as more attractive then joining the informal economy because traditional jobs as merchants or traders were seen as 'dirty' and as 'Muslim occupations'.

## Social Polarization and 'Religious War'

In January 1999, no one expected a communal war to unfold. Many residents and religious leaders stated that they did not worry when clashes broke out on 19 January because youth fights between the Mardika and Batumerah neighbourhoods in central Ambon, where the first clashes took place, were very common. When clashes continued, the conflict was primarily perceived as an 'ethnic conflict' between Ambonese Christians and Muslim immigrants. The violence led to an exodus of the migrant population and disproved any clear-cut 'religious conflict' narrative.[78] Even as people assembled in churches and mosques to coordinate fighting from the first days of clashes, religious leaders remembered the start of the conflict differently. One senior pastor at the Maranatha Church – I name her Natalia – stated that the conflict was very quickly perceived as a 'religious struggle':

At the beginning, people did not see this as a religious conflict. They saw it as ethnic [*suku*], because there were writings on the walls of houses in many places: 'Drive out the BBM.' But within a few days only, it changed and became religious. Initially, I saw many such writings against BBM on the walls during the first days.[79]

---

[77] Mearns 1996, p. 100.     [78] Van Klinken 2007; Adam 2010.
[79] Natalia, 2009.

By contrast, Salem, a Muslim religious leader from Batumerah, stated that the conflict was only perceived as 'religious' after about three months of fighting:

Only after three months or so did we consider this a conflict between Muslims and Christians. ... At the time, all our people were concentrated at the mosque. Our code was that with the sound of the drum everyone had to come to the mosque to be informed what was happening.[80]

Some residents recalled that they were unsure whom they were fighting when they first mobilized to protect their neighbourhoods. Eko, a former Muslim militia member who had lived in the Christian-dominated neighbourhood of Passo all his life, explained that during the first weeks he fought alongside his Christian neighbours to protect the area against outsiders. When the 'religious conflict' narrative solidified and Christian militias consolidated their positions of power in local communities, fighters went from house to house to expel all remaining Muslim residents from Passo. Eko had to flee and cross the makeshift boundaries erected to mark dividing lines between 'Muslim' and 'Christian' areas. He found refuge in the predominantly Muslim neighbourhood of Waihaong, where he did not know anyone because he had had few Muslim friends. Having lost his house, his job, and his livelihood in his early twenties, he joined the Muslim fighters and went into battle against Christians in other neighbourhoods and villages.[81]

Nuri, a Muslim resident who had lived in the Christian-dominated area of Soya, recounted how she first discussed the clashes with her Christian neighbours when everyone was confused about the violence, until the 'religious conflict' narrative emerged and all Muslim families had to flee for safety:

*Q: When the conflict broke out in 1999, you were still living in Kayu Putih, Soya. Where did you evacuate to?*
At the time, it was Eid. Tuesday afternoon at 3 o'clock, the conflict started. We defended ourselves in the complex. The Christians, in the upper areas, they were also panicking, so we often stood guard at night together. We looked after each other to ensure that nobody would attack, because they did not know either what would happen. Only on the third day of the

---

[80]  Salem, interviewed by Arifah Rahmawati, December 2014.
[81]  Eko, Ambon, December 2009.

conflict did we evacuate the *kampung*. The one who told us to leave was the pastor. We left because they worried that somebody would come from elsewhere, and that they [the Christians] would not be able to handle them. If it was only them, our neighbours, they could perhaps deal with it. But if outsiders would attack, then they could not guarantee anything. Then we were taken away in a truck to the provincial police headquarters. When we left the *kampung*, there were already people on the streets with machetes and spears. By then, our neighbouring *dusun* of Batu Bulan, where some Muslims had lived, had been razed to the ground.[82]

Within the context of Indonesia's regime change, a history of inter-religious tensions and the visible destruction of mosques and churches, the perception of a conflict with a decisively religious dimension resonated among religious leaders and many ordinary people. Local political actors reinforced such perceptions with their interventions. According to John Titaley, the former head of the Protestant Synod, during the first days and weeks of the clashes, politicians publicly urged Ambon's religious leaders to 'stop the fighting' and bring the situation under control in an effort to display political leadership. Meetings between the most senior religious leaders, John Titaley and Ali Fauzy from the Al-Fatah Mosque, took place almost daily. But their appeals to stop the violence only reinforced a 'religious conflict' narrative, instead of holding *preman* and weak security forces to account. Ambon's religious leaders met in public, renounced the violence, and conducted reconciliation ceremonies, yet clashes continued unabated. Emang, a senior Christian militia leader, stated that these public peace pledges and reconciliation ceremonies only contributed to cementing the perception of a religious conflict:

Religious leaders first came out to the city's main square on 26 January 1999 to pledge peace, even though the problem was not a religious problem. But when religious leaders became involved like this, the situation was made a religious problem.[83]

Discourses and conflict narratives have constitutive power and activate group boundaries. Politicians urging religious leaders to 'stop the fighting' effectively evoked religious communities. Furthermore, when state institutions failed, religious institutions filled a vacuum and came to monopolize discursive space at a time when ordinary people lacked cell

---

[82] Nuri, interviewed by Arifah Rahmawati, Ambon, December 2014.
[83] Emang, senior Christian militia leader, March 2010.

116                    *Indonesia: From Gang Fight to 'Religious War'*

phones and Internet access to facilitate independent information gathering. Under pressure from their congregations to lead and to provide information, advice, and protection, religious leaders allowed or actively encouraged militia mobilization for community protection.

Rapid escalation despite public peace statements from senior religious leaders further undermined inter-communal trust. The experience of being targeted and victimized based on religious identity, and witnessing killings and the visible destruction of churches and mosques, contributed to collective traumatization and cemented the 'religious violence' narrative.

Anthropological research provided evidence of people's sense of traumatization and anxiety, documenting numerous accounts of exceptional sightings of Jesus and the Prophet Muhammad that circulated within religious communities. These end-time visions reinforced the perception of a 'religious war' and fuelled mobilization for self-protection. Among Christians, a narrative of an 'apocalyptic battle between Muslims and Christians' in which 'America' was expected to intervene on the side of the Christians emerged.[84] Prophecies circulated that interpreted the violence as preceding Jesus' second coming and assured followers that all Christians who had died in fighting were safe in heaven.[85] Salem recounted one such incident:

At the time, we heard that someone saw a white horse at the gateway to Batumerah, together with some troops who resembled Prince Diponegoro [a Javanese prince who rebelled against the Dutch]. We did not start this rumour, but people from outside Batumerah spread it. Maybe the ancestors came out to protect Batumerah.[86]

Jopy, a former protestant pastor at Ambon's well-known Bethel Church, remembered:

People said that they saw a tall, large white man, with long hair, as if Jesus became a war hero, leading people into battle.[87]

These discourses reflect people's need to make meaning out of mundane things under crisis conditions where they had very limited access to information.[88] Millenarian understandings of an epic religious war were particularly strong among the urban population. Within rural

---

[84] Bubandt 2000, 2004.   [85] Bubandt 2004, p. 102.
[86] Salem, December 2014.   [87] Jopy, a former pastor, March 2010.
[88] Spyer 2002, pp. 35–36.

communities, ethnic identities and communal belonging were some-times prioritized over polarized religious identity.[89] The traumatic wit-nessing of violence and destruction in the context of a 'religious conflict' narrative triggered emotional motives to support fighting or directly participate in it. Several Muslim women and men stated that they did not prohibit their sons from joining the fighting because they were living 'in a time of jihad'.[90] Christian groups sang traditional hymns such as 'Onward, Christian Soldier' when going into battle.[91] Natalia and Sister Brigitta, a Catholic nun who worked with her, stated that opposing the militia leaders and questioning their mobilization and recruitment of ordinary men and young children came to be seen as treason.[92]

'We did not know what to do' and 'we did not understand the situation' were sentiments religious leaders repeatedly expressed dur-ing interviews I conducted in Ambon. In 1999, the city had no institu-tions that could have facilitated communication and exchange among religious leaders outside the local government. According to Abidin Wakarno and Jacky Manuputty, who established the interfaith institu-tion Lembaga antar Imam Maluku after the war, communication channels only emerged during the 2002 peace negotiations. Religious leaders had no training in conflict mediation and no knowledge of violence prevention strategies that could have informed them how to counter rumours and polarization. Instead, many perceived the conflict as a 'religious' confrontation rather than as the result of fights within a well-established violence network of *preman*, exacerbated by politi-cal mobilization around the elections and weak security forces. John Titaley recalled:

I did not understand the situation. Before the riot, conflicts happened in villages here and there. But we could stop it. And before the riot, in the Moluccas, when villages fought each other, it would be finished after one week. They would live in harmony again. And never did they fight in the name of religion. You would not hear a Muslim shout 'Allahu Akbar!' We did not understand what was going on.[93]

[89]  Bubandt 2004; Adam 2010.
[90]  Muslim women from the village of Hila, northern Ambon Island, conducted by Arifah Rahmawati, 2014.
[91]  George, a former Christian youth leader, August 2009.
[92]  Natalia and Sister Brigitta, Ambon, November 2009 and Jakarta, April 2015.
[93]  John Titaley, former head of the Protestant Synod, November 2009.

The religious conflict narrative further justified extreme dehumanization of the opponent religious group, as Emang recounted:

We saw Muslims no longer as humankind and they no longer saw us as
humankind; we saw them as chickens that had to be killed. Human life no
longer had value. In fact, the chicken was more valuable than a human
being.[94]

## Militia Formation and Militarization of Local Communities

According to militia leaders and members, many religious leaders on
both sides were quick to understand the first clashes in January 1999 as
a 'religious conflict'. Emang stated:

When the fighting broke out, all the religious leaders were intoxicated and
understood this as a religious conflict. When their churches were burned
down, they could not remain calm; they saw this as a religious conflict.[95]

Jakub, a reverend who was among the small group of Christian and
Muslim representatives who conducted the pre-Malino peace negotiations, remembered:

At the beginning of the conflict, we were convinced that this is religious war,
religious conflict. So we looked for text from scripture to legitimize it.[96]

Natalia added that religious leaders had no communication channels or
knowledge of how to verify rumours and gather independent
information:

Q: *What kind of rumours or stories did you hear that caused mobilization
and fighting?*
Oh, for example, they would say, 'Your graveyard in Batumerah has been
opened and the earth has been taken out.' And we got very angry. How can
they do such things to us! And we were thinking, 'We are trying to keep them
[Muslims] safe, and look at what they are doing.' But now I think the
Muslims heard similar rumours and felt the same things.

Q: *Did you ever check the graveyards? Did they really do these things?*
No! No, they did not. But we heard this and we believed it. But now, in peace
time . . . it is so shocking to remember what happened.[97]

---

[94] Emang, March 2010.     [95] Emang, March 2010.
[96] Jakub, a Christian senior pastor, Ambon, December 2009.
[97] Natalia, March 2010.

The March 1999 Human Rights Watch report noted that the fighting crowds were often initially led by men not familiar to people in the neighbourhood,[98] an observation that led many to believe that the riots were instigated and 'provoked' by shadowy elites who somehow controlled violence in Ambon and were able to turn fighting 'on' and 'off'. At the same time, many people from different neighbourhoods explained that they did not feel endangered by their own Muslim or Christian neighbours, but primarily by Christian or Muslim groups from *outside* the neighbourhood coming to attack. People knew that their own neighbours were unlikely to take up arms against them because they knew each other, but that anonymity could embolden people and overcome such hesitations. Faisal, a Muslim resident of Ambon, explained:

We did not understand what was going on, but the fighting looked like scoring a point. ... It always means you don't have to burn the house in your area, because then other people will hate you regardless if they are Christian or Muslim. You only burn houses in other *kampungs* so that you don't have to take responsibility for that, because people don't know you.[99]

Based on these accounts, I argue that the spread of fighting that local leaders and residents so often described as engineered and 'provoked' resulted from *preman* and ordinary men who mobilized and fought in different neighbourhoods, in collaboration with residents from the targeted mixed areas, but avoided killing their own neighbours.

The perception of a religious conflict allowed fighters and militia leaders to perform the roles of 'saviours' for their neighbourhood-based religiously defined communities. The names of militia leaders on the Christian side have been well known at least since the 2002 peace agreement. These so-called grassroots leaders led hierarchically coordinated militias from Ambon City. Most militia leaders later received immunity for supporting or tolerating the peace agreement. The Protestant Church had an established hierarchical structure throughout Maluku, which helped militias coordinate their activities. By contrast, Muslim groups were less hierarchically organized. Although the Al-Fatah Mosque took over leadership, Muslims in rural areas were locally organized. Muslim militias did not establish a top-down hierarchy coordinated by regional militia leaders, but had

[98] Human Rights Watch 1999.    [99] Faisal, March 2010.

several urban and rural strongholds. On the Christian side, Berty Loupatty led the Coker ('handsome boy'), which had been a well-known *preman* group before the conflict. Agus Wattimena coordinated the Laskar Kristus, the Christian militias, and Emang Nikijuluw emerged as leader under Wattimena and took over command after the former's death in 2001. Several other local leaders coordinated the fighters within different neighbourhoods.[100] Emas, a Christian journalist, recalled:

There were groups in every neighbourhood. Emang's group was a grassroots group. They formed the group to defend the Christian neighbourhoods. He assembled young children and collected funds to buy sulphur to make bombs. They collected funds to maintain themselves.[101]

Christian militias were based within the town of Ambon and they were well integrated into church communities. For example, in a filmed interview, John Ruhulessin, a senior Christian pastor, acknowledged and defended the integration of *preman* and fighters into church structures. A filmed sequence showed him praying with members of the Coker, and Ruhulessin stated: 'They [*preman*] are part of the congregation and as a priest, I must take responsibility for them; all priests must recognize that they are part of the congregation.'[102]

A number of religious leaders and residents further explained that they did not support militias because they were threatened from within their communities or by thugs, but rather out of fear and desire for protection. Natalia explained the role of religious leaders as follows:

We were trying to defend ourselves and our congregation. People thought that Agus Wattimena could help to protect us. He had a lot of followers and he had shown that he could frighten the Muslims. Early in the conflict, people thought that he would frighten the Muslims ... because he was very powerful and he had a lot of followers.[103]

Paul, a former child fighter who joined the militias when he was ten years old, recounted:

During the war, I was separated from my parents and I joined the Cicak. In Ambon, the famous child groups were the Cicak under Agus Wattimena,

---

[100] Schulze 2002.   [101] Emas, December 2009.
[102] A statement made by John Ruhulessin, a leading pastor during the Ambon conflict, to an Australian journalist in January 2000. ABC Australia 2000.
[103] Natalia, March 2010.

and the Agas under Berty, with the Coker. The adult fighters ordered us what to do. We were in the Maranatha Church, and in the Batu Gantung Church. Our lives were in the church. We all ate there. We had weapons and people were thankful.[104]

The local Muslim militias had three strongholds. One group was based in the urban neighbourhood of Batumerah in Ambon. A second group was recruited from the Muslim Leihitu villages on the north coast of Ambon Island. A third group was led by *preman* from politically influential families from the villages of Pelau and Kailolo, on the neighbouring island of Haruku. In addition to the central command post at the Al-Fatah Mosque, Muslims established several smaller command posts around Ambon Island to connect urban and rural forces.

The emergence of militia groups united ethnically diverse groups of indigenous and migrant Muslims under the umbrella of religious identity, even though tensions between both groups had long existed in urban and rural areas. The number of migrant Muslim refugees sheltering at mosques fuelled anger and a sense of solidarity among indigenous Muslims early in the conflict. This practice, particularly at Ambon's Al-Fatah, strongly contributed to socializing the Muslim community into a perception of 'religious violence'. Eko stated:

We stood together on our religious identity, and these [ethnic] differences did not matter. Yes, one group was from Ambon, one from rural areas in Maluku, then one from Saparua [Island], from Haruku [Island]. But based on our religious identity, we were all the same.[105]

Salem explained how 'Muslim solidarity' formed among ethnically diverse groups:

Q: *Whose initiative was it to use the sound of the drum to convey commands?*
It came from the mosque leaders. The drum would sound if there was an attack on Batumerah, like if we thought that Soya or Karpan [Christian neighbourhoods] would attack. People would then come with their weapons to the mosque. . . . In the upper areas of Batumerah, there are a lot of ethnic groups from other villages and from Southeast Maluku. If they heard the

---

[104] Paul, interviewed by Arifah Rahmawati, December 2014.
[105] Eko, March 2010.

sound of the drum, they all came down to the central part of Batumerah. What we had then was Islamic solidarity.

*Q: Were any people responsible for stopping the spread of rumours?*
If there were rumours, we would pass them on to Al-Fatah Mosque. In Batumerah, nobody took a central role in controlling rumours.

*Q: What about rumours that Batumerah would be attacked?*
Yes, then we would receive commands and orders from Al-Fatah. Nobody in Batumerah at the time was willing to take command. There was only a group to guard. We were not thinking of attacking the Christians, we just defended ourselves. ... At the time, we leaders at the mosque would go around the *kampung* and pray so that God would protect Batumerah. We religious leaders could not do much.[106]

The transformation of local gangs into militia groups and the segregation of the population severely altered daily life. Public offices closed down because employees could no longer get to work. Newspaper offices split into the Christian *Suara Maluku* and the Muslim *Ambon Express* when communication between journalists broke down. Market and trade connections were disrupted and resulted in shortages of goods and high prices. Former fighters, both Christian and Muslim, recounted how the conflict engulfed entire communities: while men fought, women would watch street battles and cheer their men into fighting. Every time an attack was planned and carried out, women would cook food for the fighters who moved through the neighbourhoods in preparations for attacks.

As religious leaders aligned with thugs and criminals, social networks reconfigured and made militia formation, recruitment through religious neighbourhood-based networks, and communal war possible. Event data provide evidence of interacting urban and rural dynamics of violence. As Figure 4.4 shows, fighting was often concentrated either in urban or in rural areas, suggesting that violence occurred according to concerted militia movement. The most striking disparity is the low fatality rate in urban areas between January and March 2000 compared to the high rural fatalities during this same period. For example, in late 1999 and early 2000, major battles took place on remote Buru Island. These involved not only local village fighters but also militia

[106] Salem, December 2014.

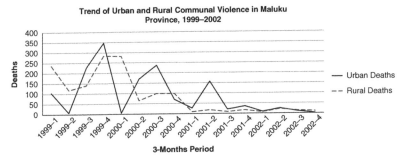

**Figure 4.4** Urban versus rural deaths in Maluku, 1999–2002
Source: SNPK Dataset.

groups from Ambon. Emang Nikijuluw said at that time his troops had developed into mobile combat unit that fought in various places:

*Q: Did Christians from Ambon also protect Christians in other areas, on the other islands?*
Yes, we were mobile. We were based in Ambon, but we would go to Seram and we would go to Buru. During the conflict, we were like troops, like a militia.

Newspaper articles often recorded that several hundred or even more than 1,000 people were involved in attacks on rural villages, further providing evidence that mobile militias organized and supported fighting in various rural areas. Mobile militias thoroughly planned attacks on urban and rural communities in collaboration with residents of the targeted areas (Chapter 6 provides a more detailed analysis of the production of violence for the case of Poka–Rumahtiga). Mobilization to 'protect' resulted in combat units moving into battle across town or even across islands. Preparations for attacks were wrapped into narratives of self-defence. George, a former Christian youth pastor, said that the rationale that prevailed at Maranatha Church was 'in order to be safe, it is better that we strike first.'[107]

The narrative of a religious war of apocalyptic proportions allowed militia leaders and members to perform a 'saviour' role and changed moral boundaries. The breach of social norms, exemplified by the recruitment of young children into battle, was justified in the name of religious defence. Children were organized into child militia groups,

---

[107] George, Ambon, December 2011.

the Agas[108] and its subgroups on the Christian side and the Linggis[109] among the Muslims. During attacks on villages and urban neighbourhoods, children would squeeze through narrow pathways, sent in first to torch houses and create panic among the fleeing population before adult fighters moved into a targeted area. This open recruitment of young children within the mosques and churches further fostered the militarization of social order and militia leaders' positions of authority as religious 'saviours'. Natalia explained how she was silenced when trying to prevent the recruitment of children in the church:

'Aren't you willing to give your children to defend Jesus?' That's what the militia leaders were saying. Many pastors believed Agus Wattimena. They thought that he was saving us, that he was our saviour.[110]

Militia recruitment was partly coerced through social pressure and partly voluntary. Many men who fought and women who supported them referred to religious motives and defence of the religious community, as well as revenge for previous atrocities, to explain their participation. Other important motives included social and economic benefits and the pleasure of playing the 'game', as some respondents would call their participation in fighting and killing. Latu, a former Muslim fighter, said:

The fiercest fighters were the children. Those who went and attacked first were the children. It was a time when going to heaven was guaranteed, and all of us, including the children, seemed to be in a race to die.[111]

Participation in militia fighting further provided unemployed young men with a significant rise in social status as protectors of their communities. Militia members explained that local communities would prepare food before men went into battle, and that as militia members they could 'ask' for money from local politicians. Thus, joining the militias resulted in significant economic benefits. Although the local population suffered from serious food shortages, the disruption of transportation links, and the breakdown of the local economy, militia fighters would have access to food and drink in abundance before going into battle. Furthermore, being part of a militia group raised young

---

[108] Indonesian terms for a tiny biting insect in Maluku.
[109] Indonesian for sand flies.   [110] Natalia, Ambon, March 2010.
[111] Latu, a Muslim militia fighter, interviewed by Arifah Rahmawati, December 2014.

men's social status within their neighbourhood communities. Eko admitted that his motives for participating in militia fighting had nothing to do with religious identity or even revenge for the killings of friends and family members, but with the pleasure of partaking in killing.[112]

Other important emotional motivations were a sense of obligation to protect one's religious community, as well as feelings of shame. Some former fighters explained that men could not stay in their houses knowing that other men went into battle. Even if fighters were not directly coerced, 'you would be ashamed of yourself if you stayed at home watching others go into battle.'[113]

The arrival of Laskar Jihad fighters dramatically changed the power dynamics between local Christian and Muslim militias and further cemented the perception of a religious war. Ambon Island had remained relatively calm between January and May 2000, even though heavy clashes took place on the islands of Seram, Saparua, Haruku, and Buru. The jihadists reignited the local war. According to Eko, the jihadi fighters 'came in the name of religion, and in the name of religion we were to be protected; they won the heart of the community'.[114] According to Noorhaidi Hasan, 'Moluccan Muslims played a crucial role in facilitating the arrival of Laskar Jihad's fighters ... support was provided by people attached to the Al-Fatah Mosque ... and at least fourteen officials ... signed a letter supporting the arrival of Laskar Jihad's fighters.'[115] The jihadist fighters rapidly initiated new waves of attacks on Christians.

Apart from attacking Christian villages, Laskar Jihad also established a broad education, health, and welfare network. Its entry into Ambon was through sending teachers and doctors and providing social services that had stopped functioning, such as garbage removal.[116] According to Ali Fauzy, the presence of the jihadists confirmed to local Muslims that the conflict was a jihad, leaving those who would not join the fighting 'ashamed to keep silent while their Muslim brothers who had come from far away put their lives at risk by traveling to Ambon'.[117] Rustam Kastor, who had led the Muslim war headquarters at the Al-Fatah Mosque, recounted how a 'crazed mass of people

---

[112] Eko, March 2010.   [113] Latu, December 2014.   [114] Eko, March 2010.
[115] Hasan 2006, p. 191.   [116] Schulze 2002, p. 60.
[117] Cited in Hasan 2006, p. 194.

bestowed blessings upon their fighters after Laskar Jihad's leader, Thalib, preached a sermon at the mosque'.[118]

Many Muslims initially welcomed the Laskar Jihad paramilitaries as 'saviours' of the Muslim community. Their support eventually declined when they discovered that the fighters lacked the required tactical and strategic skills for combat, which frequently nullified the tactics and strategies deployed by local Muslim militias.[119] The only skilled external jihadi fighters were the Laskar Mujahidin, who 'played an important role in teaching Muslim militias the technology of assembling bombs'.[120] The presence of the jihadists strongly restricted daily life for many Muslims. Some Muslims also feared them for their modern weapons and radical agenda. Muhammad, a former youth leader from Batumerah, one of the Muslim strongholds, explained:

During the conflict our lives were ruined. We could not earn money anywhere and the economic situation was terrible. It was all destroyed and we did not think that we would ever have peace. There were so many interests at play, and there were the Laskar Jihad. Here, we were afraid of the Laskar Jihad. Especially after they attacked the Yongab [Batalyon Gabungan; joint battalion of elites forces from the military, the police, and the navy]. And the women had to wear the hijab.[121]

Jihadist radio broadcasts warned Muslims they would be killed for doing business with Christians. Although many people were frightened by the presence of the jihadists, these rules were increasingly disregarded. By late 2001, small markets where Christians and Muslims intermingled had sprung up in areas declared as neutral. With political changes in Jakarta, a military crackdown on the jihadists, and peace negotiations under way, a significant part of the war-weary Muslim population came to no longer approve of the jihadists' presence. When prospects for a peace agreement became realistic and secret negotiations started among and between both sides, part of the Muslim leadership renounced their support for Laskar Jihad and publicly denounced their activities.[122]

---

[118] Kastor 2000a.    [119] Hasan 2006.    [120] Hasan 2006.
[121] Muhammad, interviewed by Arifah Rahmawati, Ambon, December 2014.
[122] Ely, 2000.

## Conclusion

This chapter has analysed how in the context of Indonesia's regime change and democratization, gang fights in Ambon escalated to a communal war in Maluku Province. It traced how communal violence emerged from below and focused on the mobilization of armed and unarmed civilians. The political mobilization of everyday violence networks, which existed before the conflict, and the polarization of social identities and traumatization, facilitated the formation of militias. Militia formation and the militarization of local order explain the dramatic conflict escalation to a communal war. This analysis found that the patterns of violence were dominated by militia attacks, which were often coordinated with residents from around the targeted area. Residents provided vital information to militias on the strength and preparation of opposing armed groups and state security forces, and of whom to target and whom to spare. The term 'riot' holds little explanatory value for these violence patterns and the high casualty numbers in rural areas. State security forces were evidently unable to contain the fighting. Event data confirm that the deadliest period of the conflict was the local war in 1999, which resulted in more than half of all casualty numbers of the conflict before Laskar Jihad and other jihadist groups arrived in Ambon with heavy weaponry in April 2000.

The chapter further examines people's responses to the first clashes and the emergence of a perception of a 'religious war'. A recurrent theme among my interview partners was that community and religious leaders 'did not know what to do' and felt overwhelmed by the rumours, the tensions, and the dramatic escalation of violence. Ambon did not have institutions for conflict management among ethnic and religious groups independent of the structures of the authoritarian Suharto regime, and few informal communication networks existed between religious leaders of different faiths that could have facilitated conflict management. Exclusive religious identities and emotional motivations of hatred, revenge, and support of militias were hardly pregiven. They emerged in a climate of fear and unprofessional security forces, and through the traumatic witnessing of the killings and destruction. Political actors who demanded that religious leaders 'stop the violence' rather then that security forces stop gang fights, and the perception among religious leaders that they were in a religious war, greatly contributed to the emergence of the conflict narrative and the consolidation of militia groups that recruited through religious networks.

These findings have important implications for the prevention of conflict escalation and communal war. This analysis shows that the men who fought and killed were no faceless provocateurs or outsiders, but first and foremost husbands, brothers, sons, friends, and colleagues deeply embedded within their communities, even if they only killed in neighbourhoods *other* than their own and were not necessarily identified by their victims. Recognizing that large-scale communal violence is ultimately rooted in the mundane violence networks that threaten and undermine people's security in the homes and on the streets even before major clashes break out is important for understanding prevention. The next chapter focuses on conflict escalation and non-escalation within two neighbouring mixed communities in Ambon: Poka–Rumahtiga and Wayame.

# 5 | (Non-)Violence and Civilian Agency in Ambon, Indonesia

*We would have been ashamed of ourselves if we had killed our own neighbours. I don't think that the Muslims of Poka–Rumahtiga and the Christians of Poka–Rumahtiga fought and killed each other directly. It was outsiders coming in.*[1]

In Poka–Rumahtiga and Wayame, two ethnically, religiously, and socio-economically mixed and almost contiguous suburban neighbourhoods of Ambon, many residents and community leaders did not expect – nor were they likely to have wished – to see their neighbours killed. Until July 1999, many people in Ambon assumed that the fighting concerned some villages and predominantly poor and violence-prone city neighbourhoods, which had a reputation for gang fights. However, as discussed in the previous chapter, Ambon's riots and gang fights escalated into a communal war when militias formed around the region's church and mosque networks. Given the mobility of these combat units, no religiously mixed area in and around Ambon was saved merely by demographic composition or geographic location. Contrary to local people's expectations, the deadliest period of the Maluku war commenced with clashes in the most cosmopolitan and pluralistic area of Ambon: the neighbourhood of Poka–Rumahtiga.

Poka and Rumahtiga, two administratively different areas, had practically merged into one community around Ambon's university. Unlike other religiously mixed urban areas, there was no internal segregation into 'Muslim' and 'Christian' streets, and family houses followed no particular religious pattern. This was a place where people intermingled and religious identity was not of primary concern. Many students, lecturers, and civil servants lived there in close proximity to the university. A thirty-minute drive or a ten-minute boat ride from

---

[1] Kristina, resident from Poka–Rumahtiga, interviewed by Arifah Rahmawati, December 2014.

Ambon's central market and bus station, the neighbourhood was well situated outside the bustling city centre. The adjacent urban village of Wayame was smaller in population size but equally mixed. In contrast to the lively area of Poka–Rumahtiga with its student population, Wayame was a calm neighbourhood with both modest and middle-class houses. During the year 2000, when Laskar Jihad dominated the Maluku war, heavy militia battles took place in Poka–Rumahtiga. I visited the area repeatedly between 2009 and 2014, and streets remained dotted with the ruins of burned-down houses, a few of them almost completely covered in heavy grass. Narrow lanes behind the main road lay completely in ruins, a ghost village behind the university campus, hidden from view. The scale of destruction was ample testimony to the ferocity of the fighting.

In this chapter, I show that although tensions were very high in both communities, people did not so much fear their own neighbours taking up arms against them but external Christian or Muslim armed groups entering the neighbourhood for an attack. Community and religious leaders publicly spoke out against violence and tried to prevent fighting. Yet, in Poka–Rumahtiga, youth groups mobilized for self-defence and fighting began when outside armed groups entered. By contrast, in Wayame, community leaders prevented youth mobilization and repeatedly averted external militia attacks. I first examine the local geography of violence on Ambon Island. I then discuss violence prevention efforts in Poka–Rumahtiga and the eventual clashes in this cosmopolitan neighbourhood. In the second half of the chapter, I focus on how people in Wayame mobilized to counter the regional escalation dynamics and prevent fighting. In the wake of the conflict, a new social order and institutions for conflict management and prevention emerged in Wayame, driven to a significant extent by the extraordinary leadership of one religious leader. My analysis demonstrates that civilian prevention efforts and community adaptation to the conflict zone explain the outcome of non-violence in Wayame, and that these efforts took place within a specific context of conflict dynamics and geographic conditions. I triangulate my findings with statements collected from militia leaders and members, who explained in interviews why Wayame was not attacked. Their accounts confirm that people's efforts to depolarize group relations, establish civilian control and rules for conflict management, and engage with external armed groups in negotiations prevented killings in Wayame.

## Local Geography of Violence

In the previous chapter, which summarized the Maluku conflict and analysed event data, we saw that the first period of communal fighting in and around Ambon died down in May 1999. After the elections in June had taken place in an atmosphere of relative calm, many families who had fled the area returned to Ambon in the belief that the clashes were over. Local newspapers reported minor clashes in several rural villages on Ambon and on Saparua Islands, and stone-throwing incidents in Ambon in July. Fighting broke out again with dramatic intensity on 23 July 1999 in Poka–Rumahtiga. With the burning of a religiously mixed housing complex in Poka the deadliest period of the Maluku conflict commenced, which lasted well into January 2000.

During the January to April 1999 Ambon clashes, armed groups had used houses of worship to assemble, recruit, and coordinate fighters and to store looted goods, while religious institutions organized care for refugees and distributed aid to the victims. The clashes in Poka–Rumahtiga had a traumatizing impact beyond the immediate neighbourhood and sparked renewed mobilization for self-defence within multiple areas of Ambon and surrounding villages, which allowed militias to consolidate. As the previous chapter has shown, a pattern of communal violence emerged in which civilians and militias coordinated attacks. Residents collaborated with mobile militias, often asking them for 'protection', and providing them with information on settlement patterns and the strength and strategies of security forces in the neighbourhood. The request for protection and provision of war-relevant information facilitated attacks on the Christian or Muslim population within a mixed area.

The strongest Christian militias were based in the city of Ambon, in the neighbourhoods of Kudamati, Benteng, and Mardika. Other large Christian villages, such as Hative Besar, which bordered Wayame, and Passo, located between Ambon City and Poka, also hosted a large population of mobile Christian fighters. Muslim militias had their strongholds in both urban and rural areas. One of the strongest groups recruited its members from the villages of Seit, Wakal, Hitu, Hila, and Mamala, which together were also referred to as the 'Leihitu area', on the north coast of Ambon Island. The large neighbourhood of Batumerah, in the centre of Ambon City, hosted another Muslim militia group. A third Muslim group came from the islands of Haruku and Saparua close to Ambon Island, and fought on Ambon and Seram Islands (see Map 4.2, page 101).

Poka–Rumahtiga and Wayame were both located in close proximity to Christian and Muslim strongholds. In 1999, Christian militias were the stronger fighting force because they coordinated through the highly centralized structures of the Protestant Church in Maluku with its command centre at Maranatha Church in Ambon City. Muslim militias remained loosely coordinated and had several strongholds and commanders, but also established a war headquarters at the Al-Fatah Mosque, Ambon's main mosque in close proximity to the Maranatha Church. With the arrival of Laskar Jihad in April 2000, the balance of power changed dramatically, and Muslim militias came to far out-number and outgun Christian groups.

## Communal Violence in Poka–Rumahtiga: Failed Prevention Efforts

The urban village of Poka–Rumahtiga is located opposite the city of Ambon, across the narrowest passage of Ambon Bay. The area is an important speedboat harbour and the car ferry from Ambon City is docked at the shore of Rumahtiga. To the south, across the bay, lies Ambon City. To the east, Poka bordered the mixed villages of Durian Pata, Hunuth, and Nania. To the west, Rumahtiga bordered the Muslim migrant settlement of Kota Jawa, the region's oil deposit, and the village of Wayame. From the northeast, Poka–Rumahtiga was accessible by street for fighters from the northern Leihitu villages.

Historically a Christian village with an important *adat* house,[2] Poka–Rumahtiga had developed into a modern, pluralistic, and mixed community. Rumahtiga is the oldest village in the area and an *adat* village. In 1979, Rumahtiga (literally 'three houses') was divided into the villages of Poka, Rumahtiga, and Wayame. Poka was a newer settlement around the state university. Due to population growth in the area, Poka and Rumahtiga merged into one settlement and were usually referred to as such, while Wayame grew into a village separated from Rumahtiga by the Pertamina oil deposit.

---

[2] *Adat* refers to customary law. See Davidson and Henley 2007 for an overview.

Demographic statistics on the size and composition of the population before the violence are not available. According to the village
administrator in Poka, fighters burned down the village office during
the conflict and the files were lost. Community leaders estimated that
60 per cent of Poka–Rumahtiga's population was Muslim and the
remaining 40 per cent Christian. Residents said there was no identifi-
able 'Muslim' or 'Christian' community within the area. At the heart of
the   neighbourhood   lay   the   Pattimura   University   campus.
The government had developed large modern housing complexes in
this area that housed civil servants, students, and university lecturers.
The majority of the local population was ethnically Ambonese.
Poka–Rumahtiga included several Muslim migrant settlements, such
as Kota Jawa, on the border with Wayame, and Taeno, in the north of
Rumahtiga. These settlements were considerably poorer than the core
of the village. Taeno was located a five-minute car drive up the steep
mountain behind the neighbourhood of Wailele (see Map 5.1).
The people in Taeno were mostly farmers who were afraid to be
drawn into the conflict. The government had allocated them land to
live on and farm but the land continued to belong to the village of
Rumahtiga.

## Violence Prevention Efforts

When violence broke out in Ambon, the killings had a direct psychological impact on people in Poka–Rumahtiga. Rumours circulated, and
tensions and suspicion were on the rise. Respondents recalled that they
were terrified by the atrocities that took place, the displacement of
entire communities, and the sounds of bombs nearby. During the first
days of the conflict, people in Poka–Rumahtiga learnt that the fights in
Mardika and Batumerah – two central Ambon neighbourhoods that
regularly had gang fights – had taken on a religious dimension. Some
former youth leaders and university students I spoke with, who had
lived in Poka–Rumahtiga during the conflict, said that they were frightened when hearing of armed groups going into battle in the name of
religion.

During the first days of the conflict, people in Poka–Rumahtiga
witnessed how community leaders and residents courageously prevented killings, protected the neighbourhood, and supported victims
from other areas. On 20 January 1999 – one day after riots broke out in

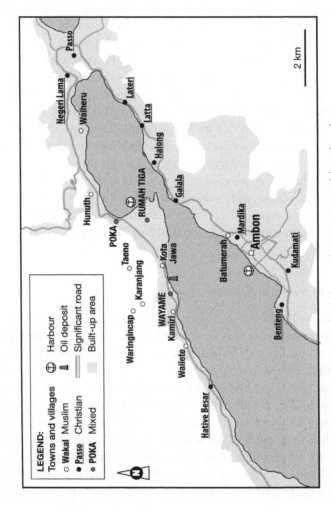

Map 5.1  Ambon City, Poka–Rumahtiga, and Wayame neighbourhoods

Ambon City – upon hearing the false rumour that the Al-Fatah Mosque in the city had been burned, hundreds of armed men from the Leihitu villages, led by a traditional war leader, marched down the mountains along the main road towards Ambon for a revenge attack. A former Muslim lecturer at Pattimura University recounted how the armed group from Leihitu first intended to march into Poka to attack the Christian population. The imam Ali Fauzy, who was a senior leader at the Al-Fatah Mosque but lived in Poka, convinced them not to attack. The crowd marched on towards Ambon and was stopped near Passo by military forces. Ali Fauzy continued negotiations with the traditional war leaders and eventually convinced the mob to return to their villages. On their return march, however, the men torched several Christian houses in the small villages of Negeri Lama, Nania, and Benteng Karang, along the main road that led from the Leihitu villages to Passo and further into Ambon City. In Benteng Karang, they hacked sixteen people to death with machetes, among them a Protestant minister.[3] The entire Christian community from Benteng Karang fled that day and relocated. Leia, a Muslim resident and community activist from Poka, remembered how, on that day after the Eid celebrations at the end of Ramadan, Muslims from Poka provided the fleeing Christians with food and clothing:

It was the women who had prepared for Eid who took out the food and cakes and put them on tables along the streets. They [the people of Benteng Karang] fled to the military base on foot, leaving their *kampung* (area) behind because people from Leihitu area attacked. Some had broken arms or crippled legs. Others had been cut from behind. We knew a lot of them because they often sold things around here. We also gave them clothing. This just happened spontaneously. At the time, we did not know what the future would bring.[4]

This direct exposure to the threat of killings perpetrated by external armed groups at the very beginning of the communal war led community and religious leaders in Poka–Rumahtiga to meet and assure each other of their peaceful intentions. Both Christians and Muslims feared being attacked by militias from other neighbourhoods and villages, and potentially by their own neighbours. Muslim militias from Leihitu could enter the settlement from the main street, and a significant

---

[3] Muslim and Christian residents of Poka–Rumahtiga, March 2010. This account is also detailed in Human Rights Watch 1999.
[4] Leia, interviewed by Arifah Rahmawati, December 2014.

number of young men from the Leihitu villages had studied at Pattimura University and knew the neighbourhood well. Christians could potentially be supported in fighting by coreligionists from the surrounding villages of Hative Besar, Passo, and Galala, where many Christians had access to speedboats. Given this geography of potential violence, both sides needed each other's protection and support.

Religious and traditional leaders met to discuss the situation and tried to calm the population. The *raja* of Rumahtiga, the traditional leader, played an important role in gathering religious leaders for meetings. The imam based at Pattimura University, Yunus Rehawarin, and the Protestant pastor from Poka, Ferry Nahusona, celebrated an oath of peace for the community of Poka–Rumahtiga in the presence of community members and soldiers stationed in the area. Most respondents from Poka–Rumahtiga remembered that an oath had been given to prevent violence and to remind each other not to be provoked. Fadhlan, a Muslim resident and former university student from Poka, recalled, 'the oath was that whoever attacked would be banished from the community.'[5] An influential Christian pastor from Poka, whom I call Eric, talked about the violence prevention efforts in early 1999 as follows:

When the unrest began in 1999, we were still working to build a sense of togetherness. We got to the point where we were forming joint teams; groups from the two communities were established in January. On 23 July 1999, the unrest first reached Poka. Before, we had still been able to build a sense of togetherness.[6]

Reportedly, there was much goodwill between leaders and neighbours. Community leaders held meetings in an ad hoc manner according to threat perceptions and the information they had received. These meetings did not result in the establishment of specific procedures to address tensions, handle refugees, or approach fighters from other neighbourhoods to deter attacks. Ahmed, who was a university lecturer during the conflict, explained:

I think that at that time, the characteristics of these meetings were of an emergency. So they [community leaders] were just *reacting*, but they were not prepared. No one thought that such a conflict would happen. I think what was carried out was instinctive – the management of religious groups, for

---

[5]   Fadhlan, December 2009.    [6]   Eric, December 2010.

example. Religious leaders would meet and when something happened we would communicate, we would discuss: 'Don't be easily provoked.' But the characteristics of the meetings were informal.[7]

Religious leaders from Ambon's Maranatha Church and the Al-Fatah Mosque had made several joint public peace statements as early as January and February 1999. These statements did not prevent further violence. On the contrary, as Emang Nikijuluw, a senior Christian militia leader explained (see previous chapter), such statements contributed to the perception of a religious conflict and fuelled escalation. People in Poka–Rumahtiga had good reason to doubt that the oath and other peace declarations would keep them safe after atrocities had taken place elsewhere in the city and in rural villages.

Community leaders further established mixed vigilante teams in coordination with the youth leaders on both sides to verify information and guard against outside fighters entering the neighbourhood. Although youth leaders had regarded these efforts as important and sincere, they also recalled a profound sense of fear. Tony, a former Christian youth leader from Poka–Rumahtiga, acknowledged:

At first, all our religious and community leaders were communicating and we were all standing watch together. But we did not really know if this would work.[8]

Fadhlan stated that collaboration between youth groups was not enough to put people at ease.

*Q: I heard that there was a mixed vigilante group in Poka–Rumahtiga to prevent violence.*
Yes, the youth united so that fighting would not happen. But then there was violence. I think many people had good intentions, but some people did not. So in the end, we could not do anything to prevent it from happening. We were attacked [by the Christians]. Then we evacuated.[9]

Ahmed further explained that community and religious leaders did not have much expertise in violence prevention and did not know how to stop people from assembling arms in self-defence:

---

[7] Ahmed, August 2009.
[8] Tony, interviewed by Arifah Rahmawati, December 2014.
[9] Fadhlan, December 2009.

If there is no problem, no conflict, no fighting, no clashes, no war, everyone can talk about peace and how to stop violence. But if people have already been killed, then this is very ineffective. In fact, talking about prevention and peace, they could even be threatened by their own group. You can imagine the crowds with sharp weapons, and you say peace. This is counterproductive. People were already very emotional. There were huge demonstrations. People were already on the streets throwing Molotov cocktails, and if then one leader arrives and says stop, we have peace with the police. . . . I think this is very ineffective at that point. But when everyone has retreated and it is still for a while, then again it is effective. So at the core during the beginning, all this was not effective.[10]

Community leaders in Poka–Rumahtiga would repeatedly state that they did not want conflict, but they did not convince people and maintain their trust. In particular, community leaders did not prevent youth groups from joining the fighting in other areas prior to the July 1999 clashes, which undermined internal prevention efforts. Fighting alongside their Christian or Muslim brethren in other places, some men from Poka–Rumahtiga came into direct contact with militia networks and gained experience in killing. Poka–Rumahtiga did not host strong gangs or vigilante groups like violence-prone Ambon neighbourhoods did, but the community had its fair share of problems with thugs. With the outbreak of the conflict, both Christians and Muslims prepared themselves for self-defence. Poka's former pastor, Eric, admitted how tense the situation was among Christians:

Not all of the men were good here. There were some thugs, and they caused problems. Every *kampung* (area) in Ambon had its boys, [and] Poka too. When the conflict broke out, those men were depended on as key figures. Some of them later became part of the church council. . . . When the situation got tense, church members and the youth came to me with questions. They bombarded me, asking, 'What should we do, Father? Tell us how to protect ourselves!'[11]

Anxieties among residents further heightened with the influx of displaced families in the neighbourhood. Prior to the outbreak of fighting, many refugees entered the area because Poka–Rumahtiga was regarded as one of the safest places in Ambon. With the diversity of the population and its high level of education, a fairly large number of middle-class families, and the presence of the university and many government

[10] Ahmed, August 2009.    [11] Eric, March 2010.

offices, communal clashes seemed unlikely. However, the large number
of refugees, particularly Christians, destabilized community relations
and heightened tensions. Muslims in Rumahtiga became a minority
when Christians took in significant numbers of refugees, and they felt
acutely threatened, as Said, a former Muslim youth leader from the
area, explained:

*Q: Was there any communication between religious leaders and youth lea-
ders to prevent violence within your neighbourhood?*
The situation here was safe, but then so many refugees came here because
their *kampungs* had been destroyed, and they wanted to take revenge on the
Muslims here. Then things changed. They caused the destruction here.
The Christians negotiated protection with the security forces stationed in
Rumahtiga. Some of them also wanted to protect us because we were
a minority, but others disagreed. But our community was not always like
this. The tensions only started when all these refugees came here to
Rumahtiga. ... With the refugees, our Christian neighbours became the
majority here in Rumahtiga. Some of us evacuated, and others stayed to
guard our houses. If they had not accepted refugees, no conflict would have
happened. The Christians of Wailela and Hative Besar wanted the Christians
in Rumahtiga to attack us, and then our people from other areas wanted us to
attack them as well.[12]

A Christian and a Muslim youth leader from Poka explained in a joint
interview that both sides were mobilizing in self-defence because in
Poka, Christians were a minority and felt threatened and in Rumahtiga,
Muslims, as the minority there, similarly felt under threat.

## The 1999 Clashes in Poka–Rumahtiga

The first clashes in Poka lasted from Friday to Monday, 23–27
July 1999, but reportedly only killed one person. However, there was
extensive damage to property and businesses. A mixed housing complex and government buildings were burned down and the local market, which had been dominated by Muslim migrants, was destroyed.
Part of the student housing development was also burned down. Both
Christian and Muslim families evacuated the area. Muslims were driven out of the entire area because Christian armed groups were stronger. Some Christian families also fled because they did not want to be

---

[12] Said, December 2014.

involved in the fighting. Two days later, 27–29 July 1999, fighting continued in Rumahtiga, where the reported death toll was much higher. According to a report by the Protestant Church of Maluku, thirty-one Christians died and eighty were wounded during clashes in Wailela, which is part of Rumahtiga. George, a former Christian youth leader, recounted how people did not know how to handle the tensions and prevent violence:

*Q: Can you tell me a bit about the situation in Poka and Rumahtiga during the conflict?*
We did not know what was happening. Suddenly, there was fighting on all sides. There were people who would say that the mosque had been burned or the church had been burned. Nobody knew what was happening.

*Q: When you heard all this, how did you react?*
We called together all of the religious leaders and the youth leaders and we made a commitment that even though fighting took place elsewhere, it could not happen in our neighbourhood.

*Q: And you were one of the youth leaders?*
Yes. But then in 1999 many outsiders came in.

*Q: Do you know where these people came from?*
No, I don't know. When they came in, there were gunshots everywhere and the local people panicked. I, as a Christian, I brought my Muslim neighbours to the ferry dock so that they could evacuate to the other side, to Galala, and then I went with them all the way to Halong [a navy base and refugee shelter]. We did not want this fighting.

*Q: How did you defend yourself at the time?*
As youth leaders, we had a role in the conflict. We defended and protected our neighbourhood from outside provocation. We checked the rumours and everything that happened between Christians and Muslims. . . . We defended ourselves with machetes, bows, and arrows. Some of us even put together guns. And we faced our Muslim neighbours because we could not be sure if they wanted to attack, and vice versa. But we never attacked our Muslim neighbours. We were only there with our weapons when there was contact [fighting].[13]

Both Muslim and Christian respondents explained that there was no joint coordinated effort among community leaders to handle the

---

[13] George, interviewed with Arifah Rahmawati, December 2014.

refugees' situation or the tensions their presence brought up. George stated that community leaders did not show enough foresight and did not realistically anticipate the problems that an influx of refugees would bring:

I think there was fighting here in Poka because they did not really understand the influence of outsiders. They were fine with their neighbours, but when outsiders came in, then it started and they did not know how to handle the situation.[14]

An interview with Ruben, a former Muslim resident from Poka, confirmed that thugs were involved in the first clashes and equally maintained that residents did not kill their neighbours:

The people who fought here, the Christians, they were very cruel. *Even before the conflict they often beat people.* Like, if they got drunk, they would ask for money from passers-by, and if they didn't receive it, they would beat them. Our houses were completely destroyed. They burned the houses, but those people who burned them came from outside. It was not our neighbours. People from outside came and took over control.[15]

Many residents from Poka–Rumahtiga insisted that clashes did not break out because neighbours took up arms against each other. Christian residents and the Christian pastor from Poka accused faceless 'provocateurs' of stirring up the unrest in Poka, which is a familiar narrative of the Ambon conflict that hides local agency. Muslim neighbours accused Christian refugees who had temporarily settled in Poka of being responsible for the violence, which they said was organized with support from militia groups from Ambon City and the large Christian villages of Hative Besar and Passo.[16] The fact that only one person was killed during four days of fighting in Poka suggests that Muslim neighbours were warned about the imminent attack and evacuated in time to save themselves. Leia, a Muslim woman who lived in Poka with her family when the first clashes happened, could not believe that people would kill their neighbours:

When the first clashes happened in Poka, in July 1999, people came from outside to attack, from elsewhere. I think some of our neighbours were influenced by people from outside. They [Christians] would not have done

[14] George, December 2014.
[15] Ruben, interviewed with Arifah Rahmawati, December 2014.
[16] Muslim university lecturers who lived in the area during and after the conflict, March 2010.

it on their own, because people at the market were warned. They would say, 'You should leave.' They only attacked when the market was empty. I think they did not want to face their neighbours because they could not kill them. Maybe strangers they did not know, they could kill them. But I think they could not kill their own neighbours, because there was a warning at the market.[17]

Ruben also stated that he did not fear his Christian neighbours as much as he did the Christian armed groups from other neighbourhoods entering his area:

*Q: Who were you most afraid of during the conflict? The Christians?*
The ones [Christians] who were from Poka and from Rumahtiga were not so bad. But outsiders came in here by crossing over from Halong. They already had control of the beach, so if we wanted to go to Ambon by speedboat, we would have to watch out and lie down because they would fire at us when we passed the peninsula. From Galala, they would fire on us.[18]

However, others explained that local people from Poka–Rumahtiga were also involved in the fighting because youth groups on both sides had mobilized for self-protection, as the former traditional leader of Poka said:

Honestly, we were all trying to protect ourselves. We Muslims tried to protect ourselves. The conflict here in Poka was first between us, the Muslims, and the Christians. The Christians were joined by others from outside. They accused us, saying that people from Hitu were coming to support us. But nobody came down from there. Only in 2000, the outsiders, Laskar Jihad, came in.[19]

Respondents also stated that factors such as religious identity, religious pride, and peer group pressure were important drivers of mobilization and willingness to fight. After a week of fighting in June 1999, smaller clashes continued in Poka–Rumahtiga throughout the year and further destroyed family homes and market stalls. According to local newspaper reports, nineteen violent clashes took place in Poka–Rumahtiga between July and December 1999, killing at least sixty-two people.

Reactions among Christian and Muslim neighbours to the violence in Poka–Rumahtiga in 1999 were mixed. Some residents explained that

---

[17] Leia, December 2014.     [18] Ruben, December 2014.
[19] Former traditional leader of Poka–Rumahtiga, interviewed by Arifah Rahmawati, December 2014.

relations broke down completely, while others insisted that they remained in friendly contact despite the conflict. Rather than fearing Christian or Muslim neighbours, many were afraid of militia groups from both sides. Other respondents explained that some Christian and Muslim families evacuated together because they neither wanted to take part in the fighting nor be victimized. Both Muslim and Christian refugees sheltered at the navy base in Halong, which was one of the few religiously mixed refugee camps in Ambon. Other respondents stated that they avoided each other after the June 1999 clashes. The community segregated along religious lines and communication between religious leaders broke down. Most Muslim families fled to other areas, and Muslim students could no longer reach Pattimura University because the entire university area had become a Christian stronghold. Kristina, a Christian resident from Poka and university lecturer, explained:

We did not really understand the situation at the time. After the first clashes we just avoided each other. Muslims went to the mosque; Christians went to the church. Everybody just wanted to save themselves.[20]

## Laskar Jihad and the Clashes in Poka–Rumahtiga in the Year 2000

By January 2000, fighting on Ambon Island had died down and some of the families returned to their homes and started reconstruction. However, some of the Muslim families had evacuated to Hila and other Muslim villages of the Leihitu area, where they were influenced by one of the strongest Muslim militia groups. The breakdown of peaceful relations in Poka–Rumahtiga, under the influence of Christian refugees and the displacement of Muslim residents and university students, had deepened the religious cleavage and triggered calls for revenge. The arrival of Laskar Jihad fighters in Ambon in April 2000 drove the region into a second year of war. For some of the Muslims who had fled Poka–Rumahtiga, the jihadis provided an opportunity for revenge. Laskar Jihad and Laskar Mujahidin fighters collaborated with local Muslim militias from the Leihitu villages and from Kota Jawa. Poka–Rumahtiga was a strategic location from where

---

[20] Kristina, March 2010.

all of Ambon Bay's speedboat travel and market access could be controlled.

In June 2000, Muslim militias and jihadists launched an attack on Poka–Rumahtiga and fought the Christian militias in heavy battles that lasted for several days. The entire Christian population of Poka–Rumahtiga fled the area, most of them to the large village of Passo on the other side of the bay.[21] According to Emang, a former militia leader, Christian militias were outnumbered and outgunned by Muslim militias with heavy weaponry provided by Laskar Jihad. The remaining Christian population of about 2,000 people was driven out of the neighbourhood, and the university campus was destroyed. Due to the colonial legacy, some Muslim students from the poor villages in the Leihitu area saw Pattimura University as a symbol of Christian oppression. The majority of the teaching staff were Christians. The university campus was burned and looted, which provided not only an opportunity to plunder valuable equipment but also a symbolic victory over the history of Christian domination. Poka–Rumahtiga turned into a Muslim stronghold from where Muslim groups controlled speedboat traffic in the bay and further disrupted supply channels for the Christian populations in Passo and Ambon. Several Christian university lecturers who had lived in Poka–Rumahtiga recalled that Muslim neighbours warned them of the imminent attack. Kristina, who still lived with her family in Poka when the attack happened, recounted how she escaped with the help of her Muslim neighbours:

*Q: Did people in Poka and Rumahtiga try to prevent fighting again in the neighbourhood?*
I think the outsiders came in and razed everything to the ground. They came from the Leihitu villages. It was too many people and we could not do anything.

*Q: Did the people from Poka and Rumahtiga join the fighting?*
The Leihitu people fought. My family was still in Poka when this happened. Our Muslim neighbour helped us when the people from Leihitu wanted to attack our house. There were people who did not want their families, their colleagues, and their friends to be killed. We could jump out of the window and save ourselves, and escape.[22]

---

[21] Boehm 2005.     [22] Kristina, March 2010.

## Summary

In sum, community leaders in Poka–Rumahtiga did not actively depolarize communal relations and failed to manage the situation of refugees in a manner that would have prevented mobilization for revenge killings. The presence of victimized families at mosques and churches raised both feelings of religious solidarity and fear among residents. Leaders further did not establish social control, procedures for conflict management, or hierarchies of command. They did not prevent youth groups from their community joining the fighting in other areas. This provided some of the men with both first-hand experience in killing and contacts among external militias. Community leaders did not openly discuss the organization of violence in Maluku through the churches and mosques. They did not engage external militias in negotiations to prevent an attack on their community. The lack of publicly visible negotiations with militias from other neighbourhoods did not allow them to convincingly counter rumours and stop internal mobilization for self-defence. Some of them actively encouraged mobilization for violence in the churches and mosques, as happened in other areas of Ambon Island. The Protestant minister from Wayame, John Sahalessy, who had played a crucial role in preventing fighting, as is further explained later, stated that he had repeatedly met with religious leaders in Poka–Rumahtiga to facilitate prevention, but found that some of the leaders actively preached war:

I forbade the priest in Poka to stir up the people and told him not to call people into war with the Muslims. He said, 'we are ready, ready with weapons.' I said, 'ready for what?' In the end, they caused trouble; they fought and were destroyed. It was terrible, and people swam through the sea to escape, but they were shot at.[23]

## Non-Violence in Wayame

Wayame remained the only religiously mixed neighbourhood on Ambon Island that was not devastated by clashes. Beyond the region, the community became well known for its prevention efforts. A number of brief reports on Wayame's Team 20, a team of community leaders that established new institutions for conflict management and

---

[23] John, April 2015.

negotiated neutrality, have been published since the conflict,[24] and one detailed study about the community is available in Indonesian.[25]

## Local Geography and Composition of the Neighbourhood

Wayame was located at the urban periphery of Ambon, along the shore, a thirty-minute drive from the city centre. It was also conveniently accessible by car ferry and speedboat from Ambon. Wayame was a relatively new settlement. Historically, it was under the village administration of neighbouring Rumahtiga. In 1993, Wayame became an administrative entity of its own. According to Pariella, Wayame had a population of 4,607 people in 2007, which was almost evenly split between Muslims and Christians.[26] The neighbourhood was smaller than Poka–Rumahtiga and had no significant university student population. Residents worked as farmers, civil servants, merchants, and school and university teachers.[27] The core village of Wayame was religiously mixed. Settlements around its borders were predominantly Christian on the western side towards the Christian village of Hative Besar, and predominantly Muslim along the shore and on the eastern side towards the Muslim settlement of Kota Jawa in Rumahtiga. Behind the village centre and up the hills, two Muslim migrant settlements, Waringincap and Karanjang, were located. There, migrants had settled since the 1970s. Over the years, some migrant families had also moved into the newer housing complex in the core of Wayame.

The geography of threat and potential violence for Wayame's population was similar to the situation in neighbouring Poka–Rumahtiga. Christians feared the Muslim Leihitu militias from the north coast coordinating an attack together with the migrant Muslim population from Kota Jawa. Muslims feared Wayame's Christians would collaborate with Christians from Hative Besar, Passo, Galala, and other Christian strongholds in Ambon City. On the border with Hative

---

[24] Tempo 2001; Pamudji, Akiko Horiba, Miqdad, Gogali, and Sipasulta 2008; Indonesian Institute of Sciences, Centre for Humanitarian Dialogue 2011.

[25] Pariella 2008. The author has been a professor at Pattimura University and lived in Wayame during the conflict. In 2002, he was head of the Christian delegation during peace negotiations. In his doctoral dissertation, he provided interviews and conversations with his neighbours to describe in detail how community leaders met regularly, negotiated together with armed groups, and established rules and regulations guiding everyday life in Wayame.

[26] Pariella 2008, p. 129.    [27] Pariella 2008.

Besar, the Muslim migrant settlement of Kamiri Wailete bordered Wayame. There, clashes took place in January 1999. To the east, in Kota Jawa, another large Muslim migrant settlement, fighting also took place. Both Christian and Muslim residents of Wayame had reason to fear attacks.

In 1999, Wayame arguably found itself in a more vulnerable position than Poka–Rumahtiga because Christians from the large village of Hative Besar had already attacked the Muslim minority in Kamiri Wailete, a settlement directly on the border with Wayame. This Christian armed group could have marched into Wayame and attacked Muslims. The majority of Wayame's population along the border with Christian Hative Besar was also Christian.[28] Furthermore, in Poka–Rumahtiga, the respected imam Ali Fauzy, who was a senior leader at the main mosque in Ambon, had prevented an attack by the Muslim Leihitu militia at the start of the conflict, on 20 January 1999, an action that should have inspired confidence in preventing killings in Poka–Rumahtiga. In the following, I analyse civilian agency and non-escalation in Wayame according to the theoretical framework presented in Chapter 2.

## Collective Agency and Violence Prevention

### Depolarization

Wayame's residents shared stories about the preconflict situation that were similar to those of people from neighbourhoods affected by communal violence. They spoke of 'harmonious' relations between Muslims and Christians, joint festivities, and support in constructing and maintaining houses of worship. When fighting broke out in Ambon and turned into a 'religious' confrontation, people in Wayame were as shocked and frightened as in Poka–Rumahtiga. During the first days of the Ambon riots, they could see the smoke over the city from the other side of the bay. Many people had connections to Ambon, whether through relatives, friends, or business partners. Thus, tensions and fears of violence were high. People in Wayame were also directly exposed to violence from the first days of the local war because of the fighting in Wailete, when the Muslim minority was attacked and the houses of Muslim migrants were burned. Muslims from Wailete fled

[28] Pariella 2008, p. 134.

into Wayame, where people helped them to escape to the army barracks, as Lina, a Christian resident from Wayame, recounted.[29]

The mobilization of armed men from the Muslim villages of the Leihitu area on 20 January 1999, which almost led to an attack on Christians in Poka–Rumahtiga, further showed people in Wayame how vulnerable they were to outside attacks. The Leihitu militia killed several Christians, including a pastor, in Benteng Karang, and they destroyed houses in Negeri Lama, a village where the protestant pastor from Wayame, John Sahalessy had lived. His house was burnt on 20 January 1999. Sahalessy moved to Wayame and immediately started prevention work. The former head of the Protestant synod in Ambon, John Titaley, remembered that Sahalessy had a very good understanding of the conflict dynamics and that he initiated prevention efforts very early.[30] Wayame's former Muslim leader of Team 20, Hanafi Marhum, was also exposed to the dangers of communal violence during the first days of unrest in Ambon because he had celebrated the end of Ramadan with his family in Passo. This area was majority Christian and later became a Christian stronghold. His family had to evacuate. With the support of Christian friends, he safely returned to Wayame.[31]

People in Wayame were so frightened that families sent women and children to the military base guarding the oil deposit for temporary shelter while men remained in their houses to protect their possessions. One Muslim man from Wayame recounted that when the killings happened in Hative Besar, he assembled machetes in order to be prepared to defend himself and his family because everyone was frightened.[32] In this climate of fear, Sahalessy went to Wayame's mosque and assured his Muslim neighbours that he would prevent any preparations for attacks by Christians on Muslims in Wayame, and that he wanted to jointly protect the neighbourhood. Sahalessy explained:

I was not afraid because I believed in myself, and believed that I was clean. My mind was never influenced by any of the thoughts about fighting and killings. I did not only blame the Muslims, I also blamed the Christians. Muslims and Christians were equally wrong. They all wanted to defend themselves and yet they were all wrong. So I took the middle road and

[29] Lina, November 2009.     [30] John Titaley, December 2009.
[31] Hanafi, December 2011.     [32] Muslim resident of Wayame, December 2009.

went to the mosque and told them that I would guarantee that the Christians of Wayame would not trouble them. At the main church in Ambon, they were angry and said that I accepted bribes from the Muslims. At the time, everyone was very afraid, even the leaders at the main church.[33]

According to numbers of internally displaced people (IDPs) collected by an investigation team from several mosques, part of the Muslim migrant population from Wayame fled their houses during the first half of 1999. About 1,000 people from Rumahtiga, Wayame, and Poka sheltered temporarily at the military complex in Wayame for fear of attacks. However, residents of the main part of Wayame village did not completely evacuate their houses during any stage of the conflict.[34] In order to demonstrate the sincerity of his prevention efforts, on the first day of fighting, John Sahalessy went into the neighbouring Christian village of Hative Besar to retrieve the dead bodies of Muslims killed there for a proper burial:

I went and recovered the bodies of the victims, all eighteen, with a pick-up truck that I borrowed from a Chinese. Everybody else was too afraid to come. I brought out the bodies for a proper burial.[35]

In Wayame, community leaders could not draw on strong inter-religious institutions or traditional institutions that could have been used to collectively organize and prevent violence. Instead, rules and institutions had to be newly established. A first step towards institutionalizing conflict management and violence prevention was the depolarization of communal relations. Community leaders encouraged the formation of an inclusive social identity as 'people of Wayame' that would contrast with the collective identities of 'Muslims' and 'Christians' caught in a 'religious conflict'. They discouraged the public discussion of conflict developments and the circulation of rumours outside of community meetings, where these issues could be properly addressed. At a time when most people did not have telephone connections, ordinary people had to rely primarily on information gathered through religious and community leaders and their regional networks.

Religious leaders in Wayame reiterated that the violence was not an apocalyptic confrontation or 'final war', as the conflict was

---

[33] John Sahalessy, April 2015.
[34] Lina, a Christian woman from Wayame, March 2010.
[35] John Sahalessy, April 2015.

increasingly perceived among people in Ambon (see Chapter 4 for a more detailed discussion of the religious war narrative). Sahalessy went to the mosque to deliver a sermon and the imam preached at Wayame's church. Community leaders discouraged the use of provocative religious language and specific terms that emerged during the conflict, such as '*Acang*' to refer to Muslims and '*Obet*' to refer to Christians.[36] People were forbidden to wear religious symbols in public. Cica, a Muslim woman from Wayame, explained:

We had to ensure our safety together. If the Christians had to go to church, then the Muslims would secure the area. If the Muslims had to go to the mosque, then the Christians would secure the area. We had to watch out for each other and make sure nobody sparked conflict between us, because we had been united since the times of our ancestors.[37]

A crucial point in shielding the village against the dynamics of revenge killings was the joint decision not to allow displaced persons to take refuge at the church or mosque in Wayame, as people did in religious buildings in the city and in neighbouring Poka–Rumahtiga. Refugees were often traumatized, and some wanted revenge. They were thus seen as a danger to communal relations. The decision not to receive refugees in Wayame was tolerated in Ambon and in the neighbouring villages. The only place where refugees were allowed to stay temporarily was the military compound in Wayame. Hanafi, Wayame's former youth leader, explained that community leaders jointly organized the integration of refugees into the community to prevent tensions:

When the conflict first broke out, the Muslim victims from Hative Besar and the Christian victims from Talake came here and took refuge with the C-Company [military compound]. We held a meeting with them and told them that they could only stay if they followed our rules. We wanted to keep Wayame safe. I think they wanted peace so they followed all of the rules.[38]

Wayame was no place of harmony, as several respondents explained. During the conflict, fear and mistrust were common features of life and needed to be constantly addressed. John Sahalessy's wife explained that many residents collectively supported the sense of a common identity of 'people of Wayame' and continuous prevention efforts. She also

[36] Pamudji, Akiko Horiba, Miqdad, Gogali, and Sipasulta 2008; Pariella 2008.
[37] Cica, interviewed by Arifah Rahmawati, December 2014.
[38] Hanafi, December 2011.

emphasized that people were terrified but gradually started to support community leaders in keeping their area safe:

We were very afraid when we saw what happened in Wailete. All the time, there was the sound of gunfire and bomb explosions. It was terrible. Then we agreed with our Muslim neighbours to guard our area together, and we cooked food for each other. We women would stand watch during the night. We would be positioned at the watch posts while the men went on night patrol around the villages. We could not sleep during the night because we had to do the watch. We supported the men with the night watches.[39]

Countering polarization, and mobilizing residents for collective prevention rather than fighting, enabled community leaders to subsequently establish control over the neighbourhood and those who wanted to instigate violence.

### Consolidating Civilian Control

Community leaders met for the first time on 24 January at the village office to discuss the tensions after refugees from Wailete had entered Wayame.[40] At this time, Sahalessy had already individually met with Muslim leaders to assure them of his protection, and had recovered the dead bodies of Muslim victims in Wailete for a proper burial. Thus, the first meetings took place against this demonstration of leadership and sincerity in prevention efforts. The village head formally presided over a meeting between religious and youth leaders, elders, and soldiers from the battalion stationed next to the oil deposit. They all agreed to take care of the refugees and to make efforts to depolarize the situation. Wayame's Team 20 emerged from these meetings and became the decision-making body that established rules and regulations to protect the village. Consisting of ten Muslims and ten Christians, the team met regularly to discuss tensions, address rumours, and reaffirm commitment to peace and non-violence.

Every settlement in Wayame had at least one representative within Team 20. All team members were men between forty and sixty years old. Six of the Muslim men were traders, three worked for local companies, and one was a soldier. Although all were born and raised in Maluku, only two of them were indigenous Ambonese. The other eight were originally from Sulawesi, Java, and from the neighbouring

---

[39] John Sahalessy's wife, Palu, April 2015.   [40] Pariella 2008, p. 184.

island of Seram. On the Christian side, most men worked for the local government, one was a soldier and one a Protestant minister. Eight out of the ten were born and raised in Ambon, one was from Toraja in Sulawesi, and one was a Chinese Catholic.[41] According to Hanafi, the youth were linked to Team 20 and involved in the coordination of violence prevention efforts. His account indicates awareness of imminent threats and the social knowledge to proactively guard against them:

We were aware of the tensions and of the dangers. Wayame could also be destroyed like other places around here. We had to anticipate things well and work hard to develop communication with all villages that could have threatened peace in Wayame.[42]

Team 20 agreed on procedures to handle conflicts and gather information to address rumours and tensions. Their rules focused on preventing men from joining the fighting outside Wayame. Furthermore, the sale and consumption of alcohol became forbidden, so as to provide no reason for resentment among the Muslim community, as well as to prevent youths fighting. People reported for drinking alcohol were publicly beaten. Christian team members dealt with cases involving Christians and Muslim team members dealt with cases involving their own faith. Wayame had its own problems with youth fights, as did most other neighbourhoods in Ambon. Residents stated that the young people of Wayame were 'known as drunks' and they 'used to fight regularly', although there were no serious casualties. Team 20 also set up a rotation system of mixed night watches to guard entry points into the village. These night vigils became a meeting point. Women provided food and drink to the watchmen and also took part in the night watches.

Sahalessy emphasized that he used persuasion and appeals to a common identity as much as threats to maintain control over the youth, and occasionally violent punishments:

I told the youth, 'don't you dare try to go to war.' During the war, the Christians in Ambon wore a red headband and the Muslims a white one. I told them that I did not want to see anyone in Wayame with such headbands. In Wayame, there are no Muslims and no Christians. We are Indonesians. In the church you can be a Christian and in the mosque you

[41] Pariella 2008, p. 190.    [42] Hanafi, December 2011.

can be a Muslim, but outside you are Indonesian. Some people would write names in Arabic on their houses, and Christians would hang crosses near their terrace. I told them to get rid of it, that it's not permissible. I kept an eye on this so that there was no space for those who wanted to provoke people and organize an attack.[43]

An important factor that strengthened Wayame's position of neutrality, and that exemplifies community adaption to a changing conflict zone, was the establishment of the 'Pasar Damai', a peace market and neutral trading ground within Wayame, in October 1999. During a time when all markets in the city and surrounding villages became religiously segregated and people suffered from major food shortages, Wayame's market was a neutral area where both Muslims and Christian could trade. The interruption of trade and business resulted in a sharp rise in food prices and a scarcity of products. Wayame's market eased the hardship on all sides and allowed farmers and fishers to sell their produce. The market was located close to the shore and accessible via speedboat from Ambon City. Separate stands for Christian and Muslim speedboats were maintained to prevent people from being transported to the wrong speedboat point in Ambon, where they would likely be massacred.

Wayame's Team 20 came to an arrangement with the fishers from the Leihitu villages and arranged for their catch to be sold in Wayame to Christian traders. The Butonese, a Muslim migrant group and the main vegetable producers, were also able to sell their produce at the market. The products sold in Wayame were cheaper than goods at segregated markets in Ambon City, which went through several middlemen before being sold. The military was paid to guarantee safe transactions in Wayame and maintained easy access to food. Thus, the military stationed in Wayame developed an interest in safeguarding its neutrality. The 'peace market' integrated Wayame into the political economy of the conflict. Militias on Ambon Island developed an interest in respecting Wayame as a neutral area to secure access to products. While most communities suffered daily from the breakdown of trade, Wayame's residents reaped the benefits of their laborious violence prevention efforts.

The formulation of rules and informal institutions to mitigate daily conflict, avoid provocations, and keep potential instigators under

---

[43] John Sahalessy, April 2015.

control, together with the establishment of the peace market, demonstrate a profound level of social learning about conflict dynamics and
community organization in order to adapt and to resist escalation.

**Engaging Armed Groups**
Respondents from many neighbourhoods of Ambon, including
Wayame and Poka–Rumahtiga, explained that they primarily feared
'the outsiders coming in' – the provocateurs (who were always
understood to be outsiders) – rather than their own neighbours
taking up arms against them. Communal violence on Ambon Island
often resulted from militias attacking the Muslim or Christian population of another settlement, with the help of collaborators from the
targeted area. These collaborators could be either long-term residents
or refugees who had only recently entered the neighbourhood.
Consequently, Wayame's Team 20 worked to prevent their own
youth from collaborating with armed groups from other areas of
Ambon Island. Community leaders and members of Team 20
explained that Christian youth from Hative Besar and Muslim
youth from Kota Jawa tried to stir up the youth in Wayame multiple
times, calling them cowards for not joining in the fighting. Cica,
a Muslim woman from Wayame, remembered that, as early
as January 1999, Team 20 had enforced non-collaboration with
external fighters:

The village chief announced that we should not deal with outsiders.
We should stand together and be united, and whatever happened outside
of Wayame, we should ignore it. There was a lot of fear. And when we heard
that a family member or a friend was killed, we were very hurt. But what
could we do? We stayed here in Wayame and we remained united.[44]

Community leaders announced that anyone found participating in
violent clashes would not be allowed back into the village. Even the
corpses of those who fought in the neighbouring villages had to be
buried outside the neighbourhood. Christians who were killed in the
clashes had to be buried in neighbouring Hative Besar and Muslims in
Kota Jawa, Rumahtiga. Weapons were also banned in the territory of
Wayame. Lina, a Christian woman from Wayame, recounted how
Team 20 enforced non-collaboration:

[44] Cica, December 2014.

The leaders explained at a village meeting that people should not be involved in fighting. Nobody should do anyone wrong so that no one would have reason to attack us. Whoever chose to get involved in the conflict, maybe in neighbouring Rumahtiga, would not be allowed back into Wayame, and if he died the body would not be buried here. We feared that if people would get involved in the fighting elsewhere, and if people would die, this would cause revenge.[45]

According to Cica, these rules were generally followed:

For instance, there was a person from Hative who got married and lived in Wayame. When the village of Hative was attacked, he wanted to help out in Hative, but the village chief told him to come back to Wayame. He could not fight in Hative. But he still went and was struck by a machete. They took him to Kudamati Hospital in the city, but he died. His body was not brought back to Wayame even though his wife and children were here. He was buried in Kudamati. If it had been brought back to Wayame, maybe another of his brothers could have been carried away by emotions or vengeance, causing conflict and unrest in the village.[46]

Hanafi, expressed the rationale of preventing youth from Wayame fighting in other neighbourhoods as follows:

If we did not mobilize to fight, then outsiders would not be able to attack and come in. I told them [the Muslim youth in Wayame] that whoever went to war and was found out could not come back to Wayame. That was my promise to them and to the Christians. We forbade people to carry weapons or to make bombs, machetes, knives, or guns. We strongly forbade them. If someone was caught walking with a machete we punished him and beat him badly.[47]

Negotiating non-collaboration and neutrality included safeguarding the community from any form of entry by militia groups. Members of Team 20 explained that they did not allow militias to march through Wayame to reach a village that they wanted to attack, such as Hative Besar or Kota Jawa, because they feared that fighting would results in chaos and people would feel obliged to fight alongside their religious group. Team 20 members maintained regular communication with neighbouring militia groups and with the command posts at Maranatha Church and Al-Fatah Mosque in Ambon. They received

---

[45] Lina, December 2010.   [46] Cica, December 2014.
[47] Hanafi, December 2011.

information on plans of attacks and assured religious and militia leaders that they did not need 'protection'. They actively deterred militia leaders from planning attacks. Community leaders did not rely only on the information from the command centres at Ambon's Maranatha Church and the Al-Fatah Mosque but also filtered and verified information through their social networks. The former Muslim youth leader, who led Team 20 during the time that Laskar Jihad dominated the conflict in Ambon, explained how he accessed war intelligence through religious networks to prevent an attack on his neighbourhood:

We expected our Christian team members to inform us when there were rumours of a planned attack against Muslims in Wayame. And when Muslim militias gained regional control, the Christians asked me if I was willing to warn them. I was a member of the Joint Secretariat for the Muslim Ummah, so I knew whether or not Muslim groups would attack, and I assured them that I would warn them.[48]

Community leaders repeatedly negotiated Wayame's neutrality with all sides involved in the conflict, using contacts developed through trade with the establishment of the neutral market, traditional ties of inter-village friendship, and family contacts through religiously mixed families. Traditional *adat* relations did not contribute to maintaining peace among the Christians and Muslims of Wayame because most Muslims were not indigenous Malukans and thus were excluded from the *adat* system. However, indigenous Christian community leaders of Wayame could appeal to a *pela* relationship with the Muslim village of Wakal and a *gandong* relationship with Hitumessing, two of the Muslim militia strongholds from the Leihitu area on the north coast of Ambon Island. *Pela* and *gandong* are ceremonial alliances between villages, which establish mutual obligations to assist in times of crisis and in communal projects, such as the construction and repair of the church and mosque.[49] Many neighbourhoods and villages on Ambon Island with traditional *pela* or *gandong* relations still fought. After the conflict, the inter-village alliances became a source of peacebuilding efforts.[50]

---

[48]  Hanafi, December 2011.

[49]  Bartels 1977. *Pela* is often based on an incident in the past that established the alliance, while *gandong* marks a kinship relation based on common descent and ancestry and is thus an even stronger relation than *pela*.

[50]  Bräuchler 2015.

Negotiations for neutrality to discourage attacks were undertaken by a mixed group of members from Team 20 to assure each other of the sincerity of their prevention efforts. For instance, a Christian member of Wayame's Team 20 who took part in negotiations for neutrality in Kota Jawa recounted:

We were on alert when we met with the community in Kota Jawa because many people were not from this *kampung.* . . . The people of Kota Jawa were not worried about Wayame as a potential threat to them; who they were afraid of were the people from Hative Besar.[51]

One of the Muslim members who participated in joint negotiations for neutrality with people in Hative Besar stated:

When we arrived, we shook hands with each other. Then we were introduced to the traditional leader by the team leader. My impression was that people looked on cynically and maybe hated me.[52]

Both Muslim and Christian leaders convinced the militias not to attack because they and their people had neither been attacked nor threatened others. In the context of recurrent rumours of attacks, suspicion remained high. Christian members of the team once almost killed one of the Muslim residents because of rumours about an imminent attack from the Muslim Leihitu villages.[53] Interview accounts by residents and members of Team 20 confirm that Wayame was repeatedly under threat of attack. Wayame's imam explained that the geography of violence and the positioning of militia groups made residents fearful:

*Q: Did militias from outside Wayame try to attack you, attack Wayame?*
Yes, both Christian and Muslim groups tried to attack. The Christians from Hative Besar were always a danger. Once, a group of Muslims from Batumerah came to Wayame by speedboat, but the Muslim members of Team 20 negotiated with them so that they returned to Batumerah. They came by speedboat. The first one carried people and the second one carried weapons. That was in the year 2000. Once, the people from Kailolo [on Haruku Island] wanted to attack, and wanted me to facilitate this.

*Q: Is Wayame easy to attack?*
It is easy to access for groups from both sides.[54]

---

[51] Cited in Pariella 2008, p. 211, author's translation.
[52] Cited in Pariella 2008, p. 210, author's translation.   [53] Pariella 2008, p. 201.
[54] Wayame's imam, August 2009.

With the arrival of Laskar Jihad on Ambon Island, the power balance changed dramatically. In 1999, the Protestant pastor, John Sahalessy, led Team 20. After Laskar Jihad arrived, Muslim members took over more leadership functions. The jihadists imposed restrictions on Muslims' interactions with Christians, but Muslims in Wayame claim to have defied them. The Muslim leadership's line of defence towards the task force at Al-Fatah and to Laskar Jihad was:

We in Wayame live in mutual respect with one another. They [the Christians] do not hinder our religious duties and they did not damage our religious symbols that we hold in high esteem. We cooperate and protect each other; therefore, there is no reason not to communicate or economically interact with them [the Christians].[55]

In order to ensure their safety, Wayame's leadership provided the Leihitu forces, which later received support from Laskar Jihad, with sophisticated communication equipment that supported the strategic gathering of information about potential threats to Wayame, but also enabled the Leihitu war leaders to better coordinate their attacks on other areas. Pastor Sahalessy explained that his team systematically gathered and disseminated information to judge the security situation and reiterate non-collaboration:

Usually, people from Hitu and Wakal came to Wayame every two weeks with their militia leaders to receive information. ... We from Team 20 provided them with a telephone for better communication and cooperation.[56]

Community leaders in Wayame came under increasing pressure when they refused to become involved in the conflict. They were accused of timidity and a lack of solidarity, and met much resistance from their religious communities. Some were threatened or accused of treason.

After Laskar Jihad attacked Poka–Rumahtiga in July 2000, the paramilitaries established a command post in Kota Jawa. Aware of the dangers of Muslim attacks in revenge for atrocities committed by Christians from Hative Besar and Poka–Rumahtiga, Sahalessy negotiated with Muslims in Kota Jawa to prevent an attack on the Christians of Wayame and Hative Besar. Sinda, a Christian woman from Wayame, recounted:

[55] John Sahalessy, April 2015.     [56] John Sahalessy, cited in Pariella 2008.

The Christians from Hative Besar attacked Muslims in Wailete. Then the Muslims and the Laskar Jihad entered Hative Besar through the main street along Wayame for an attack. But people in Wayame were left at peace because there had already been attempts to resolve the conflict, spearheaded by Father Sahalessy after Hative Besar attacked Wailete. The pastor held a meeting with the Muslims from Kota Jawa and tried to find a solution, but there was no success. Then the Muslims attacked and the jihad troops walked down the main street and the soldiers did not intervene. But they did not attack people in Wayame.[57]

John Sahalessy's wife gave a similar account, stressing that his reputation in protecting Muslims in Wayame kept Sahalessy safe when negotiating with Muslim militias and jihadi commanders:

It's because he looked after the Muslims in Wayame. They were safe, and so the relatives of the Muslims who lived outside Wayame recognized that he was a priest who could protect their relatives in Wayame.[58]

Pastor Sahalessy also understood the need to maintain regular communication with the security forces stationed around Wayame in order to ensure their support. Given the location of the Pertamina oil depot next to Wayame, he persuaded staff members of Pertamina to provide money for food and cigarettes for the soldiers. He did not believe that the soldiers who were tasked to protect the oil depot would also protect the people of Wayame, as discussed further below.[59]

## Rescue Agency and Leadership

At the onset of violent conflict, Wayame's residents were frightened and the community did not have pre-existing institutions to manage the conflict situation. Nor did clear procedures for decision-making or a sense of unity exist when the communal war broke out. Instead, Wayame had to develop a new institutional framework, decision-making procedures, and a hierarchy of command to adapt and mitigate its vulnerability to internal mobilization for killings and attacks from external militias. Given the very early witnessing of the killings of Muslims in the neighbouring settlement of Wailete to one side, and the near massacre of Christians in Poka and Rumahtiga to the other,

---

[57] Sinda, interviewed by Arifah Rahmawati, December 2014.
[58] John Sahalessy's wife, April 2015.   [59] John Sahalessy, April 2015.

why did residents in Wayame not become paralysed by a pervasive sense of fear, but instead choose to collectively organize and prevent killings? I argue that the extraordinary leadership, or rescue agency, of Pastor Sahalessy built trust and momentum for collective action and enabled the subsequent institutionalization of conflict management and prevention efforts, which established a new social order in Wayame.

How to explain the emergence of such initial leadership? Sahalessy described himself as the 'lone commander' who took action, managed conflicts, and kept the youth under control. He stressed that he had gained experience of conflict situations and escalation dynamics when stationed as a pastor on other islands of Maluku Province, where he had to mediate armed conflict between rivalling Christian communities. Consequently, he had developed a social knowledge of conflict dynamics before the Ambon conflict broke out, had previously been confronted with mobilizing men and killings among Christians, and was therefore less vulnerable to perceiving the Ambon conflict as a 'religious war':

*Q: Before the clashes started in Ambon, had you had experience with violent conflict elsewhere?*
Oh yes, I did. When I was stationed on Saparua Island, back in the 1980s. There was a local war too, but between Christians. I mediated there. That's why I was often entrusted with conflict resolution. The war was between the villages of Porto and Haria and some others, and they used bombs and knives and everything.[60]

Social knowledge of conflict dynamics and the experience of effective prevention played a key role in enabling the community leader to proactively address threats and challenges, and to initiate the establishment of institutions for conflict management. Furthermore, Sahalessy's self-image was one of high confidence and commitment to what he perceived as his mission:

I'm a man who has been entrusted by my God to give a sense of security, comfort, and peace to my people. As such, wherever my people are, like in the Bible, I am the shepherd and they are the sheep I must protect. That's why I remained in Wayame. I told them as long as you are here, I will stay in Wayame. If nobody is left, be they Muslim or Christian, only then will I leave.

---

[60] John Sahalessy, April 2015.

I made this statement, and that's what I did then. I was doing good, so why should I be afraid? I trusted God was there to protect me.[61]

Sahalessy's leadership as the 'lone commander' relied primarily on persuasion and the encouragement of a common identity as 'Indonesians' and as 'people of Wayame'. However, as he acknowledged, he also used repression and violent punishments to keep instigators under control:

I asked people to report to me so that I could handle things. If not, there would have been trouble. I was a commander managing conflicts. All I asked was for honesty. I had to be a little rough because I wanted to protect people so that there would be no killings. So the people were afraid and they did not dare to break my rules.[62]

Thus, social order in a non-violent community was partly based on means of repression and punishment. It was not a democratic social order but a community with a clear hierarchy of command, rules, and punishments for noncompliance. However, as statements from Wayame residents testify, Sahalessy primarily worked with persuasion. His protective actions or *rescue agency* – at times at great personal risk, as when retrieving the bodies of Muslim victims in a neighbouring village for burial, or negotiating with the Laskar Jihad – inspired confidence in his willingness and ability to keep people safe. One Muslim resident from Wayame described the pastor as follows:

*Q: Can you tell me more about the Protestant pastor from Wayame?*
Yes, the old pastor, Reverend Sahalessy. He was not from here. He preached in Wayame. His home was razed in January 1999 in Negeri Lima when Leihitu attacked. But he did not seek vengeance. At the beginning of the violence, we did not know his character. I am one of the people who admire him greatly.

*Q: And on the Muslim side, were there any leaders like this pastor?*
Yes, there was Imam Noho. He has already passed away.

*Q: And what were Noho's sermons like?*
Well, for Muslims, the principle is not to bother them [the Christians], just to stand watch. If the Christians provoked us, only then would we act.[63]

---

[61] John Sahalessy, April 2015.    [62] John Sahalessy, April 2015.
[63] Abubakar, interviewed by Arifah Rahmawati, December 2014.

Reflecting on his course of action, in comparison to other religious leaders, Sahalessy stressed that he *acted* rather than *talked*, and convinced people that he would keep them safe:

At the time, the top religious leaders in Ambon, they only talked. There was no action. But the grassroots, the ones below them, the little people, they didn't reach them. So how could things possibly be safe? They couldn't. Me, I went to the grassroots. I asked, 'what do you need?' Only then could we have an effect. And they didn't. So how could they persuade those at the grassroots? They couldn't. Some of them could only react with tears and crying. But what is the point of crying if you don't take action? ... Me, I fought for the little people. How could they feel safe? How could they eat? They couldn't. So I was forced to act. In the middle of the night I took a speedboat to the port (under Muslim control) and looked for rice, and brought it back for them. That's what I did.[64]

Apart from motivations to keep himself and others safe, religious values and a self-identity of having to protect others strongly feature in John Sahalessy's account of his actions:

I am a priest. I was called to speak for peace. I wasn't called to earn money, or what have you. I was sent to speak for peace. How could I not speak for peace? How could I face God? I have to speak for peace. You must make peace with him. You are Muslim, he is Christian, and you must make peace. I'd ask them in the church and in the mosque, ask my wife, I asked them: 'If the Prophet Muhammad lived at the same time as the Prophet Jesus, would they both go to war?' Everyone answered, 'no.' 'So if they wouldn't go to war, why are you doing that? You believe in them. So why are you going to war? That means you are wrong. That's why we should manage this conflict so that our lives can be lived well again.'

The Christian pastor was not the only community leader who stood out for his prevention work. As has become clear in previous citations, Wayame's Muslim youth leader and the imam were also credited with strong community leadership and the ability to stand up against Muslim militias and refuse to collaborate in attacks. During the year 1999, however, the first and most deadly year of the conflict, and before the external intervention of the Laskar Jihad paramilitaries, Christian militias dominated on Ambon Island. When Sahalessy's house was burned to the ground in January 1999, the pastor could have sought

---

[64] John Sahalessy, April 2015.

revenge, and could have mobilized Christians for attacks, particularly since Christians from Hative Besar had already killed Muslims in Wailete and were ready to continue fighting. Instead, Sahalessy continuously negotiated on all sides and repeatedly warned his Muslim neighbours of rumours of Christian attacks. According to Cica, a Muslim woman from Wayame, the pastor was disliked among some Christians for his protection efforts.

*Q: I heard that this pastor is not liked very much among some Christians.*
Yes, because he helped us Muslims too much. All of the Muslims of Wayame have to recognize that Wayame was safe because of his actions. And the Christians listen to their pastor even if they do not like what he says. A couple of times, he knocked on our door when we were sleeping and said, 'I've heard that my brothers [the Christians] from Benteng are coming here to do something [attack/cause trouble].' And if Christians in Hative considered attacking, he would always let us know. I can imagine that some Christians do not like him.[65]

Other residents confirmed that Sahalessy repeatedly stood up against Christian militias and stated that if they wanted to fight in Wayame, they would have to kill him first. The Muslim youth leader from Wayame explained that he also informed Christians when he heard rumours of an attack on the Christians in Wayame:

If there were rumours that people from Leihitu were going to attack, I would report it right away, and we would stand watch together. The same thing happened if the Christians heard about people from Hative or wherever: they would inform us and stand watch.[66]

As I discussed in Chapter 2, rescue agency links altruistic behaviour and high confidence, based on a belief in the ability to effect change, to social knowledge and social learning. These aspects enabled the imagination of threat scenarios, risk anticipation, and proactive prevention. Sahalessy's leadership, and conflict management by Team 20, were based on a continuous evaluation of attack scenarios and potential collaboration between militias from different locations of Ambon Island and some Wayame residents. This anticipation and social learning about conflict dynamics allowed adaptation, such as regular negotiations with external armed groups and the maintenance of the 'peace market' to sustain Wayame's neutrality.

---

[65] Cica, December 2014.    [66] Hanafi, December 2011.

## Triangulation

Why would militia groups respect Wayame's refusal to collaborate? I have triangulated my findings by interviewing former militia members and youth leaders. The responses from those who fought give me confidence that the absence of violence in Wayame cannot be reduced to geographic or demographic factors. Said, a former youth leader from Rumahtiga, credited Wayame's Team 20 of for non-violence:

*Q: Why was Rumahtiga unable to avoid violence like Wayame?*
There was no conflict in Wayame because Team 20 held together. They had strong and influential leaders.[67]

Eko, a Muslim militia member from Ambon, explained that Wayame's religious leaders prevented attacks on the neighbourhood:

*Q: Why was there no violence in Wayame?*
There was an imam in Wayame who was very good and very brave. When they threatened him, he refused to give in. When they threatened him in the hope he would give in, he was fantastic and stood his ground.[68]

Wayame was located next to the region's oil deposit. One explanation for the absence of violence in Wayame that some residents and community leaders in Ambon referred to holds that the village was not attacked because residents and militias feared that the oil deposit could explode. A report by the International Crisis Group on the Ambon conflict notes in a footnote:

Outside parts of Ambon City, the only neutral village on Ambon Island is Wayame, facing Ambon City from across Ambon Bay, where village leaders – both Muslim and Christian – have firmly resisted involvement in the conflict. Their resolve has no doubt been backed by the government's need to protect a large Pertamina installation through which oil supplies are channelled not only to Maluku but also to Papua.[69]

This explanation is based on the assumption that the military battalion stationed next to the Pertamina oil deposit for its protection would have also protected people in Wayame, and that external armed groups would not have tried to attack Wayame for fear of strong military resistance. Sometimes, such explanations are also linked to conspiracy

[67] Said, December 2014.    [68] Eko, March 2010.
[69] International Crisis Group 2002.

theories that claim the entire conflict was sparked and maintained by military elites in Jakarta. However, the military had proven numerous times that it was unwilling or unable to prevent communal fighting. On both sides, Wayame bordered communities in which fighting had taken place. My interviews show that militias threatened Wayame on several occasions, and that militia leaders did not refer to the oil deposit as a reason for why no armed group attacked. Instead, they explained that community leaders in this area worked together and did not ask militias for protection.

Soldiers stationed at the oil deposit did not keep the civilian population around the area safe from attack. Sahalessy and Team 20 regularly negotiated with the military stationed next to the oil installation, but Sahalessy stressed that he also needed to negotiate protection of Wayame residents from the military forces, and that he used the Pertamina oil deposit to his advantage to keep soldiers content:

*Q: Did Wayame residents need to financially support the military stationed in Wayame?*
Oh yes! Usually, I would meet with people from Pertamina and ask them for money so that I could shop for these soldiers, rather than asking the general populace, because they did not have the money. We would help the soldiers by giving them cigarettes, drinks, what have you. Money. I'd get it from Pertamina. Pertamina knew it was in a dangerous spot. It could easily be razed. That's why they said, 'Alright, we'll help to keep them content.'

*Q: Some people say Wayame was not attacked because it is located next to Pertamina and the military protected the site.*
That's nonsense. Pertamina was used by the military for making money. They had a lot of oil there. The military would protect Pertamina because of that. They had their interests. But me and Team 20, we would make sure that the military did not get involved in Wayame, that they would respect our leadership. Also, the military led to a lot of moral damage. A lot of our daughters became pregnant. I told them not to get involved in Wayame. Because the soldiers, if they would not come to join in a conflict, they would not get any money. Making money was their method.[70]

Given that security forces were involved in the fighting on both sides during the conflict, Sahalessy's account of negotiating non-involvement from the military rather than relying on their protection for the civilian population of Wayame is credible.

[70] John Sahalessy, April 2015.

Lastly, Emang, the second most senior Christian militia leader in Ambon, confirmed that Wayame was not attacked because militias recognized the community's mutual peace efforts and because Christians from Wayame did not ask for 'protection'.

*Q: Do you know about the situation in Poka and Rumahtiga during the conflict?*
I was in Poka and Rumahtiga. I was involved there.

*Q: How was the situation there?*
Well, there were many assets and there was much material wealth.

*Q: Was the conflict there different than here [in Ambon City]?*
It was the same. The conflict spread with the same motives.

*Q: How were inter-religious relations there?*
Just as bad. Religious relations in Maluku were ruined. So, essentially, you could no longer find ties between the Muslims and Christians. They were severed. We viewed them as enemies. We were closed off. Say someone I knew spoke with Muslims. If we found out, we would kill him. So, our communications were severed during the conflict.

*Q: And Wayame?*
In Wayame, there were two leaders who took on a role and secured the area. There was the pastor Sahalessy and the [Muslim] youth leader Hanafi. They were the two main leaders and they played a significant role in keeping things safe. So, nobody from the outside could come in. We just kept an eye on things, so nobody from the outside could come in. They kept an eye on their village together, and so the conditions there remained safe.

*Q: And were there Christians or Muslims who wanted to attack Wayame but were also very close to Rumahtiga and Poka?*
Yes, but in Wayame they were watched by both communities. So, the Muslims protected the village from outside attack. So, pretend we are in Kota Jawa. If we wanted to attack Hative Besar, we could not go through Wayame. The people of Wayame would not allow it. We would have to go across the mountains first. So they built strong communications, such that Wayame became a symbol of peace, as it was the only village in which Christians and Muslims could continue to live together.

*Q: And why could they do that?*
Because of the role of those two leaders. They were quite strong.

*Q: And this was not possible in Rumahtiga and Poka?*
Maybe because there was UNPATTI [Pattimura University], and some rich people's houses. With UNPATTI there was much to loot.[71]

Emang's account acknowledges that Wayame's religious leaders refused to collaborate with militia groups. Although Emang referred to the houses of some rich people in Poka–Rumahtiga, the core village of Wayame was equally a middle-class settlement where there would have been much to loot. The looting of Pattimura University in Poka–Rumahtiga he referred to took place in June 2000, during an attack by the Muslim Leihitu group in collaboration with Laskar Jihad and Muslims previously displaced from Poka–Rumahtiga. Christian residents and university lecturers alleged that the Muslim forces looted the university campus, and that some soldiers took part in, or profited from, the looting. However, John Sahalessy instead stressed that some Christians from Poka–Rumahtiga and their religious leaders wanted to fight in 1999, which led to a revenge attack by Muslims in 2000. He recalled that he had tried to persuade Christians not to attack in 1999, and not to destroy mosques, but they fought and destroyed the mosque of a senior religious leader, Ali Fauzy, and therefore invited a revenge attack.[72]

In sum, Wayame's violence prevention efforts were effective because community leaders engaged with external militias in negotiations and refused to collaborate. They did not provide war-relevant information. With limited access to information, militias would have risked being confronted by armed fighters from the other religious group or by military forces either in Wayame or upon returning to their homes. Another factor that helped Wayame's community leaders to negotiate neutrality was their ability to use the script of 'religious conflict' to their own advantage. 'Religious' militias would have weakened their position of authority within mosques and churches if they had attacked a neighbourhood against the explicit wishes of its religious leaders, and without a pretext of 'protecting' or 'avenging' Christians or Muslims in Wayame.

## Conclusion

This chapter offered a comparative analysis of failed prevention efforts and communal violence in the community of Poka–Rumahtiga and

---

[71] Emang, March 2010.   [72] John Sahalessy, April 2015.

effective prevention efforts and community adaptation in neighbouring Wayame during the communal war. The accounts of community leaders, residents, and militia members give me confidence to argue that it was civilian violence prevention rather than geography, demography, or the strategies of militias that account for non-violence in Wayame. The interview material showed that people in Poka–Rumahtiga and in Wayame similarly feared killings, and were primarily more afraid of attacks by external armed groups then their own neighbours.

In both communities, formal or informal institutions for conflict management were largely absent when fighting commenced, and traditional institutions had eroded. Community leaders tried to establish new procedures to handle rumours and prevent mobilization. While in Wayame, they successfully established social control over instigators and engaged armed groups in negotiations, in Poka–Rumahtiga, leaders did not effectively manage the threats and challenges. Prevention efforts were not perceived as sincere among many in the community. Leaders failed to coordinate the influx of displaced people, which resulted in polarization and calls for revenge killings in the area. Leaders did also not prevent residents from mobilizing and joining the fighting elsewhere. Although many people from Poka–Rumahtiga stressed that external militias attacked and carried out the killings, my interviews also testify to internal mobilization for violence and collaboration in attacks. Even though fighting was not prevented, the peace efforts saved lives, and many helped their neighbours escape the killings.

In Wayame, key leaders demonstrated significant social knowledge of the conflict situation and learning with regard to changing conflict dynamics, which allowed them to anticipate threats and challenges. They jointly managed refugees and prevented mobilization for self-defence or revenge. Without continuous adaption to the socio-economic transformation of the region, including local food provision, Team 20 would have been in a weak position to convince residents of the sincerity of prevention efforts and engage militias to deter attacks. The institutionalization of violence prevention and conflict management procedures allowed leaders to consolidate civilian authority within the village at a time when the entire region was militarizing under the control of militia groups.

After the war, tensions in Wayame remained high despite the successful prevention of killings. When interviewed more than a decade after the formal peace agreement, some respondents hinted at a sense of shame among men from Wayame who did not fight and did not demonstrate 'masculine' attributes, such as bravery, as their peers did during the war. The former Muslim youth leader concluded, 'even though Wayame is peaceful, it is not comfortable today; the youth want to prove their masculinity and their religious identity.'[73]

---

[73] Hanafi, interviewed by Arifah Rahmawati, December 2014.

# 6 | *Nigeria*
## *A Deadly Conflict Cycle in Jos, Plateau State*

*When you see your family slaughtered, all religious values of peace become irrelevant; you cannot be peaceful anymore.*[1]

Nigeria's 1998 transition from a dictatorial military to a civilian regime has been marred by incessant violence. Communal violence has been one of the deadliest forms of political violence and Jos, the capital of Plateau State, and the surrounding rural areas in central Nigeria, rank among the places worst affected. At least 7,175 people were killed in Plateau State between 2001 and 2016.[2] In Jos, more than 2,460 people died in the years 2001 to 2010. Communal clashes sparked by political appointments and election results killed at least 1,000 people in 2001 and 834 in 2008. During the intervening years, mobile militias carried out intermittent 'guerrilla warfare'[3] in small towns and rural areas, killing more than 1,300 people. In 2010, urban and rural clashes as well as bombings by Boko Haram took more than 1,500 lives. Overlapping ethnic, religious, family, and economic networks between urban and rural populations have fuelled killings. Mobile gangs have often carried out urban violence, while in rural areas well-armed militia groups have organized attacks. The geography of violence, displacement, and segregation has reshaped patterns of settlement, business, transportation, and trade.[4]

There is a substantial literature on the Jos conflict,[5] which is rooted in local elite competition over who qualifies as 'indigene' and is

---

[1] NGO leader in Jos, November 2010.
[2] Author's dataset based on comparison and coding of data available from ACLED; Nigeria Watch; newspaper articles through AllAfrica.com; and victim numbers collected by community leaders in Jos. See also Higazi 2011, Krause 2011b, International Crisis Group 2012, and Human Rights Watch 2013 for previous discussions of victim numbers.
[3] Higazi 2008, p. 109.    [4] Onoja 2015.
[5] Tertsakian and Smart 2001; Danfulani and Fwatshak 2002; Best 2007; Ostien 2009; Higazi 2011, 2016; Krause 2011b; International Crisis Group 2012; Milligan 2013; Bonkat 2014.

therefore entitled to political appointments, positions within government offices, access to higher education, and land rights. These tensions date back to colonial rule. Jos lies in the centre of Nigeria and was established around tin-mining activities during the colonial period, when it attracted migrants from all parts of Nigeria. The local populations of Berom, Anaguta, and Afizere farmed in the region, while large numbers of Hausa and Fulani (as well as smaller numbers from other ethnic groups) migrated from northern Nigeria to work in the mines and constituted the most numerous group within nascent Jos.[6]

The colonial legacy of indirect rule initially relied on northern emirate structures. Later, political power was transferred to the 'native' tribes of the Plateau. The Berom were one of the largest tribes among these, and they came to most vocally defend 'indigene' rights. Yet Hausa migrants from the north constituted by far the most numerous group in early Jos. The 'ownership' of the city and claims to 'indigene' status were fiercely contested between descendants of the native tribes and the Hausa and Fulani.[7] The Berom, Anaguta, and Afizere have insisted they are the rightful 'owners of the land', while the Hausa and Fulani have argued that they 'founded Jos and nurtured it into a city'.[8] Indigene certificates ensured access to political representation and positions within the civil service, and they legitimized claims to landownership. Only local governments issued these certificates and therefore decided on indigene status.

Urban conflict dynamics interlinked with tensions in rural areas. The increasing scarcity of land and access to riverbanks resulted in contested claims over land use between indigene farmers and Fulani herders.[9] The politics of labelling and the selective reciting of historical accounts fostered group boundaries and secured political control over local government areas (LGAs). Within a sociopolitical environment characterized by strong patronage networks, the exclusion of one faction of the political elite was widely felt as socio-economic decline among its constituency. Ethnic and religious identities strongly overlapped and reinforced the local political cleavage, pitting the predominantly Muslim Hausa and Fulani against the majority Christian Berom, Anaguta, Afizere, and other ethnic groups. Discrimination against Christians in the Muslim-dominated northern states of Nigeria and

---

[6] Plotnicov 1967.   [7] Plotnicov 1972.   [8] Best 2007.   [9] Blench 2003a.

repeated outbreaks of ethno-religious violence in the cities of Kano and Kaduna further added fuel to tensions in Jos.

These tensions turned violent with the end of military rule. With the onset of communal violence, a once-localized conflict over indigene rights was thoroughly reframed into a religious crisis with regional, national, and transnational dimensions. Religious identities became strongly polarized and one-sided conflict narratives predominant. After the January 2010 clashes, a heavy military presence within the city averted further mass killings, but smaller clashes and so-called silent killings of individuals found in the 'wrong' neighbourhood of the city continued. Rural areas around Jos suffered years of communal clashes, which died down only in 2016. Since 2010, bombings by Boko Haram have repeatedly threatened the fragile peace in Jos. Despite significant casualty numbers, the bombings did not incite renewed clashes as of 2011.

## National Context: Nigeria's Regime Change

Since independence in 1960, Nigeria was ruled by military regimes almost without interruption. The annulment of the presidential elections in 1993 gave rise to a harsh dictatorship under General Sani Abacha. The military regime consolidated its hold on state power, transforming decentralized patrimonial rule into a predatory dictatorship, resulting in a downward spiral of political disorder, social division, and economic decline.[10] Abacha's death in June 1998 marked the end of the military regime. Political violence exploded after Nigeria's transition. In 2011, Human Rights Watch estimated that political violence had cost more than 15,700 Nigerians their lives since the country returned to civilian rule in 1999.[11]

Nigerian scholarship has thoroughly examined ethnic politics and conflicts over 'indigene rights' and citizenship.[12] Ethnic politics are rooted in the structures of the colonial and the early post-colonial regime. Nnoli linked the emergence of the contemporary citizenship-versus-indigene rights crisis to the 1979 and subsequent constitutions, the rising political consciousness and organizational capacity of

---

[10] Lewis 1996; Maier 2000.   [11] Human Rights Watch 2011.
[12] Nnoli 1995, 2003; Institute for Peace and Conflict Resolution 2003, 2008; Ukiwo 2003; Obi 2004; Best 2007.

minority groups – particularly in the 'Middle Belt' region around Jos – and the creation of new states in 1967 and 1976 to accommodate ethnic grievances.[13] The 1979 constitution privileged those citizens who belonged to the 'indigenous' community of the state in which they reside. Democratization exacerbated conflicts over citizenship and indigene rights because it 'entails a radical redistribution of power as well as the acceptance of a political culture of equality'.[14] Nigeria's constitution gives states the right to exclude indigene people of other states if the local government considers such measures necessary for the state to 'develop at its own pace'.[15]

Religion became entrenched in Nigerian politics since the mid-1970s, with politicians and religious leaders urging their followers to vote along religious lines.[16] In 1979, when a new constitution was drawn up, the introduction of sharia law in some northern states had already been a matter of debate.[17] In 1989, during a second drafting of the constitution, the debate gained new intensity. The Christian Association of Nigeria (CAN) protested against the state financing religious courts, particularly because these courts also settled land disputes between Hausa and Fulani Muslims and Christian ethnic groups.[18] Democratization lent the religious factor a new fervour. The introduction of a sharia criminal code in twelve northern states in 2000 and 2001 provoked major protest from Christians. Many objected to what they perceived as a progressive Islamization of public life and discrimination against Christian minorities in northern cities. Sharia courts were introduced in the northern states to handle matters of civil law. Muslims were given a choice of appealing to a sharia court or to a secular one. Disputes over the introduction of sharia law resulted in deadly clashes that killed thousands in Kano and Kaduna between 2000 and 2002. A substantial number of Christians fled the northern states for Plateau State. They brought with them stories of discrimination and atrocities, exacerbating tensions between religious communities in Jos.

The Boko Haram insurgency profoundly aggravated the security situation in Nigeria. In Jos after the 2010 clashes, the movement reinforced local perceptions of 'religious violence', particularly among Christians. Boko Haram's repeated bombings in Jos became

[13] Nnoli 2003, p. 14.   [14] Ake 2000, p. 112.   [15] Nnoli 2003, p. 14.
[16] Falola 1998, pp. 2–3.   [17] Kenny 1996.   [18] Kenny 1996.

intertwined with local conflict narratives. The Islamist insurgency appeared to prove correct those Christian politicians and other spokespersons who blamed the Jos conflict on a 'jihad' by the Muslim Hausa and Fulani from the northern part of Nigeria against the Christian minority ethnic groups in the 'Middle Belt'. In 2012, several churches were bombed. In 2014, twin bombings targeted both Christians and Muslims in crowded central marketplaces but no longer sparked renewed clashes. In 2015, during Ramadan, Boko Haram again bombed a restaurant and a mosque in Jos but no further clashes took place.[19]

## Summary of the Jos Conflict

Plateau State is one of the most diverse federal states, with more than fifty-eight relatively small ethnic groups and more than forty languages.[20] The North–Central Zone of Nigeria (also referred to as the 'Middle Belt'), in which Plateau State is located, has been described as a 'hyperactive conflict zone' plagued with rural conflicts over land and grazing rights and political representation.[21] The main ethnic groups in Jos are the Berom, the Anaguta, the Afizere, the Igbo, the Yoruba, and the Hausa and Fulani.[22] The Berom, Anaguta, and Afizere are recognized as the main indigene groups in Jos and are predominantly Christian. Due to their long residence in Jos, many Hausa and Fulani in the city referred to themselves as 'Jasawa' ('people of Jos'). The name was meant to distinguish them from the large Hausa–Fulani population in the states of northern Nigeria. 'Jasawa' is used for political representation of the Hausa in Jos and as such has been contested. The origins of the Jos conflict are inextricably linked to the legacy of colonialism and the contemporary architecture of the Nigerian federation. The question over who owns Jos has been present in the region since independence.[23]

According to my newspaper-based event dataset,[24] at least 7,175 people were killed in the metropolis of Jos and in small towns and rural

---

[19] BBC News 2015.      [20] Best 2007, p. 4.
[21] Institute for Peace and Conflict Resolution 2008, p. 54.
[22] Other, larger indigene ethnic groups on the Plateau include the Ngas, Goemai, and Tarok.
[23] Plotnicov 1972.
[24] The dataset covers Plateau State for the years 2001–2016 and is based on reporting by the Armed Conflict Location and Event Data Project (ACLED), which I cross-checked with national newspaper reporting, casualty estimates

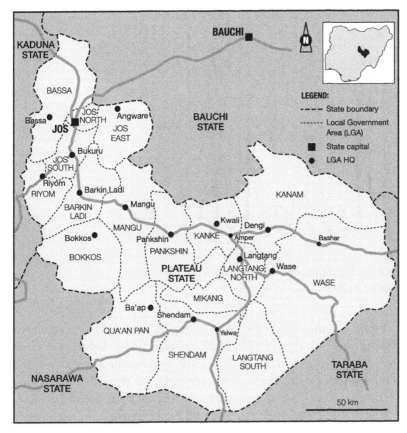

**Map 6.1** Jos and Plateau State, Nigeria

villages of Plateau State between 2001 and 2016 in communal violence. The majority of these deaths, 57 per cent, took place outside Jos City, and I have coded these clashes as 'rural violence'.[25] Killings in Jos account for 36 per cent and bombings for the remaining 6 per cent of casualty numbers. When only focusing on the years 2001 to 2010, the last year with major clashes in Jos, killings in the city amount to 60 per cent and rural clashes to 37 per cent of all deaths, with bombings claiming the remaining 3 per cent.

    reported by Human Rights Watch, and victim numbers collected by community leaders in Jos.

[25]  See Higazi 2008, 2013, 2016 for an excellent analysis of rural violence in Plateau State.

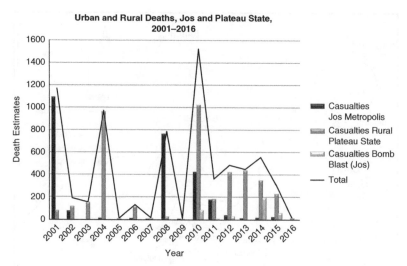

**Figure 6.1** Estimated deaths, Plateau State, 2001–2016
Source: Author's dataset, see note 2.

Figure 6.1 shows that the years 2001, 2008, and 2010 account for conflict periods with very high casualty numbers in Jos. Subsequent to the major Jos clashes in 2001 and in 2010, rural conflicts escalated and resulted in militia fighting and massacres in rural areas. In 2004, a state of emergency for Plateau State eventually brought rural violence to a halt.

The 2010 clashes in Jos were not directly sparked by elections or political appointments, but by tensions lingering on from the 2008 clashes. In response, the federal government deployed a special task force (STF), Operation Safe Haven, composed of military and mobile police brigades that patrolled major street junctions and violence-prone areas. Clashes subsided, but violence continued in the city in the form of 'silent killings' – the murders of people found in the 'wrong' neighbourhood after ethno-religious cleansing. Although clashes continued in January 2011 in and around Jos, and again in late 2011, killing an estimated 175 people, no mass violence took place in the city during April 2011, even though other areas, such as the city of Kaduna, suffered major clashes. The STF temporarily suppressed fighting, but according to a senior officer, its mandate was not to restore 'peace' but 'law and order'.[26] A long and heavy military deployment

[26] Top-level STF officer, cited in Para-Mallam and Hoomlong 2012, p. 26.

was neither financially feasible nor desirable because civilians increasingly suffered abuse and sexual harassment from soldiers.[27] With the escalation of the Boko Haram insurgency, the number of soldiers in Jos was greatly reduced. Rural clashes in areas south of Jos continued until 2016. According to Higazi, the intermittent violence in rural areas between 2010 and 2015 demonstrated that there was no military solution to communal conflicts.[28] Senior military officers in Jos did not even see a military solution for the city beyond a temporary suppression of fighting.

## Pre-Conflict Jos and Plateau State

Jos was officially founded in 1915 with the commencement of tin mining. The indigene population on the Plateau consisted of mostly farmers with little interest in tin mining. The Berom and other indigene groups argue that the city was founded on land that belonged to them as the native people of the Plateau. The Hausa and Fulani contest this claim and hold that the city was established on 'virgin land' that belonged to nobody.[29] The mining industry attracted migrant workers from all over Nigeria. By the mid-1940s, more than 200 mining camps had been built on the Plateau, and the miner population exceeded 40,000.[30] Some indigene groups were hostile to the influx of Nigerian migrants and Europeans. During the 1940s, the Berom attempted to disrupt mining operations to prevent further destruction of farmland. The Hausa constituted the most numerous ethnic group that worked in the mines. Significant numbers of Yoruba and, later, Igbos and members of smaller tribes also migrated to Jos during the mining period. Those who had received a Western education in the south of Nigeria served within the colonial administration. Others worked as craftsmen or in commerce. Due to the mining activities, the city expanded rapidly and the population grew steadily between 1930 and 1960.[31]

British colonial rule initially relied on the political structures of the neighbouring Bauchi Emirate to administer Jos. The Bauchi Emirate was part of the Sokoto Caliphate, which was established in 1804 in contemporary northern Nigeria. It emerged during the Islamic reform

[27] International Crisis Group 2011.   [28] Higazi 2016, p. 381.
[29] Best 2007, p. 17.   [30] Dung-Gwom and Rikko 2009, p. 6.
[31] Plotnicov 1967, p. 36.

movement of Usman dan Fodio (1754–1817).[32] The Caliphate was one of the largest political entities in pre-colonial Africa and comprised around thirty emirates. Fourteen of the thirty-six federal states had direct experience with the emirate system.[33] In contemporary Plateau State, the legacy of the dan Fodio movement remained palpable. Christians remembered that the jihadi expansion was stopped at the mountains of the Jos Plateau.[34] Most of the local ethnic groups remained animist, and later turned to Christianity. Only the lowlands of Plateau State came under the influence of the jihadi movement, and emirs came to reign in Wase and Dengi.[35]

The Hausa settled in self-governing communities in Jos and the surrounding rural area. From 1914 to 1952, they elected one of their members to the position of 'Sarkin Jos' (Chief of Jos) to represent their community. The title originally referred to the 'native town'. Under British rule, the city of Jos was divided into the Government Reserved Areas (GRA) for Europeans and other foreigners, the township for educated southern Nigerian clerks and Europeans, and the native town mainly for Hausa migrant workers.[36] Over the years, ten Sarkin Jos came to manage the everyday affairs of the town. Administrative control remained beyond the reach of the indigenous population until the early 1950s. To many people in the town, it seemed that what the Hausa had not achieved with the dan Fodio jihad, they were allowed to finish through the British colonialists: 'From the indigenous peoples' point of view, their land had been overrun by their former enemies – the Hausa – by means of the superior might of the Europeans, who were now taking more and more of the fertile alluvial plains as mining concessionary leases.'[37]

In 1947, the institution of the traditional paramount ruler of Jos, the Gbong Gwom Jos, was installed. Following the establishment of the Berom Tribal Council and Berom Native Authority, political power was gradually transferred to the Berom. The appointment of a Berom to the Gbong Gwom led to tensions with the local Anaguta and Afizere tribes, but also with the Hausa over the position of the Sarkin Jos. The Hausa claimed the privilege of traditional and political

---

[32] Last 1967.    [33] Paden 2005, p. 70.
[34] Plotnicov 1972, p. 8; Interviews in Jos.
[35] I thank Philip Ostien for pointing this out. For background on the Sokoto Caliphate, see Last 1967; Paden 2005.
[36] Plotnicov 1967.    [37] Plotnicov 1972, p. 8.

representation for their own community. This rendered the Jos town council ineffective during the 1950s. Elected members were selected proportional to tribal representation within each ward, and they fought over preserving their groups' privileges. The colonial administration noted in 1954 that the city 'with its polyglot population must always be considered a potential trouble spot'.[38] Competition between the Berom and the Hausa arose over political control of the city of Jos until both groups reached a stalemate during the 1960s. Political elites on both sides cooperated temporarily during the political domination of the Igbos.[39]

Although Plateau State was long considered more peaceful than neighbouring regions, its history is not free from violent conflict. In 1945, a two-day riot between Hausa and Igbo traders took place in Jos, and the city provided 'the setting for the very first urban riot between ethnic groups in Nigeria'.[40] In 1966, a year before the Biafran War broke out, the Berom joined the Hausa in a temporary alliance against the Igbo in Jos. Although it is not clear how many Igbos were killed, Plotnicov noted in a footnote that 'in Jos the count was large enough to require the excavation of mass graves with bulldozers provided by local tin mining companies.'[41]

From the 1960s to the 1990s, the Nigerian federalist structure emerged, resulting in changes and adjustments to the boundaries of Plateau State. The country's three regions were split into twelve states in 1967. The number of federal states has since increased to thirty-six. Plateau State was carved out of the former Benue–Plateau State in 1976. The creation of neighbouring Nassarawa State in 1996 further reduced the size of Plateau State.[42] When the largest ethnic group, the Tiv, remained mostly in Benue and Nassarawa, the Berom saw political control over Jos finally within reach.[43] The contested history of Jos also finds expression in the contemporary trend among the indigenes to rename areas and streets to erase the Hausa legacy, although most people in Jos speak Hausa fluently.

During the colonial and early post-colonial period, migrants dominated Jos while the indigenes made up less than 2 per cent of the city's

---

[38] Plotnicov 1967, pp. 42–48.    [39] Plotnicov 1972, p. 9.
[40] Plotnicov 1972, p. 6.    [41] Plotnicov 1972, p. 12.
[42] For a comprehensive overview of the history of Nigerian federalism in general, and of Plateau State in particular, see Suberu 2001, pp. 91, 102.
[43] See Plotnicov 1972 on Berom–Tiv competition in Benue–Plateau State.

population.[44] The Igbo, Yoruba, and Hausa were traditionally strong in trade and other commercial activities. Ethnic and religious institutions and associations became significant in providing networks to an urban population with a large number of migrants.[45] Churches and mosques, as well as ethnic associations, served as localities of social exchange and integration.

The Fulani migration into what is now Plateau State commenced in the late nineteenth century, and greatly increased with the end of colonialism. Fulanis have mostly remained cattle herders and their grazing routes often take them beyond Plateau State. The majority of the population in Plateau State is Christian, although accurate religious breakdowns are lacking.[46] In rural areas, a complex clan organization with traditional rulers is present to this day.[47]

Since the closing of the tin mines, Plateau State's economy has largely been based on rural agriculture. The little industry in the region offered limited employment opportunities. The economic crisis of the early 1980s further deteriorated the economic situation in Plateau State. Mining has badly affected parts of the Plateau; about one-third of the land around the mines suffered from significant soil erosion with negative consequences for agricultural production.[48] Large numbers of cattle have caused further degradation and erosion.[49] With the closing of the mines, Jos developed into a 'civil service state' where people mainly sought government employment,[50] thus lending additional leverage to the issue of indigene certificates and ethnic patronage networks. The 'migrant' populations of Igbo, Yoruba, and Hausa were traditionally strong in trade and other commercial activities. Therefore, they came to dominate commerce and trade in Jos North LGA. Another economic transformation over the past three decades has been the emergence of highly profitable vegetable farming due to the expansion of the expatriate population in Jos and the creation of the capital city of Abuja. The Hausa–Fulani were the first to adopt dry-season farming. Some Fulani cattle herders also bought land and began gardening

---

[44] Plotnicov 1967, p. 61.    [45] Last 2007, p. 614.
[46] Tertsakian and Smart 2001, p. 5.
[47] For an overview of traditional rulers in northern Nigeria and their role in conflict prevention, see Blench, Longtau, Hassan, and Walsh 2006.
[48] Pasquini and Alexander 2005; Thapa and Yila 2012. However, Pasquini and Alexander (2005) also point out that farmers in Plateau managed to adapt farming practices in response to soil degradation.
[49] Blench 2003b, p. 2.    [50] Fwatshak 2011, p. 5.

during this period. Dry-season farming is a capital-intensive business because it requires irrigation pumps, fertilizers, and transportation to urban markets.[51] Similar to economic dynamics in urban Jos, the Hausa and Fulanis' vast trade networks placed them at an economic advantage over the indigene population in rural areas; with their extensive commercial networks and capital they became successful dry-season farmers and made substantially higher profits than the Berom population.[52] The Berom and other smaller groups were slow to recognize these developments; some 'indigenous' communities adopted modernized farming practices only in the late 1990s.[53]

The two main competing groups, the Berom Christians and the Jasawa Muslims, both developed extensive networks of ethnic patronage linked to central religious institutions. Berom ethnic associations have historically played a political role in regional 'Middle Belt' politics, i.e. the political mobilization of non-Hausa and Fulanis against Muslim and Hausa–Fulani dominance.[54] Berom associations, particularly the most vocal Berom Educational and Cultural Association (BECO), have always had a strong Christian background.[55] The Jasawa are represented through the Jasawa Development Association (JDA). The JDA won strong support from Hausa and Fulani elders since return to civilian rule.

Ethnic associations sought to consolidate economic advantages with their activities. BECO and JDA consolidated trade and banking networks along ethnic lines and actively defended their shares in the market.[56] Under military rule, both ethnic associations lobbied military rulers for political appointments. By the late 1980s, the competition between BECO and JDA created such tensions that 'civil servants in Plateau State Government were banned from holding offices in ethnic or cultural organizations.'[57] Although confrontation between the political elites of both ethnic groups dominated urban politics in Jos during the 1990s, little was done to bring both groups towards a compromise and reduce the potential for violent escalation.[58] In addition, since 1999,

---

[51] Higazi 2013, p. 34.  [52] Higazi 2013.  [53] Blench 2003a, pp. 2–4.
[54] Tyoden 1993; Egwu 2010.  [55] Adetula 2005, p. 214.
[56] Adetula 2005, p. 224.  [57] Adetula 2005, p. 216.
[58] See, for example, the conference report from 1993 by the Conflict Prevention and Management Centre, in which the uncompromising positions of both side have been reiterated.

agitation for the recognition of the 'Middle Belt' as a geopolitical zone
distinct from northern Nigeria has been on the rise.[59]

The contemporary electoral competition over Jos North LGA is
rooted in the local politics of the 1990s as well as the regime change
in 1999. Under the military administration of Gen. Ibrahim Babangida,
the Jasawa actively lobbied for the establishment of an LGA in which
they would form the majority. In 1991, their request was granted with
the creation of Jos North LGA. The military administration split Jos
LGA into Jos North LGA and Jos South LGA, the latter with headquarters in Berom-dominated Bukuru. Thus, Jos North LGA was
effectively given to the Jasawa, who were the majority group in Jos
North, while Jos South remained dominated by the Berom. The city of
Jos has expanded beyond Jos North LGA and has merged with Bukuru,
which is the headquarters of Jos South LGA, into one urban centre, the
Jos metropolis.

The new boundaries made the Berom, Anaguta, and Afizere minorities within Jos North LGA. The three groups vehemently protested
the creation of Jos North LGA, arguing that they had never been
consulted nor consented to it. Their elites saw the split of the old Jos
LGA into Jos North and South LGAs as a deliberate strategy to give full
political control over one LGA to the Hausa population.[60] Jos North
LGA comprises the commercial centre of Jos as well as the main
political and traditional offices, such as the palace of the indigene
traditional leader, the Gbong Gwom of Jos.

Land conflicts represent a final issue of contention between the
'indigene' Christian and the Muslim Hausa and Fulani and existed in
Plateau State long before the September 2001 crisis. Sporadic violent
confrontations over farming and grazing land were already reported
during colonial times. With the expansion of agricultural production
over the past decades, natural resource conflicts over the use of land –
particularly wetlands – has been on the rise since the 1990s.[61]
The increase of farming reduced the cattle herders' access to water for
their livestock and changed the interaction between farmers and
herders.[62] At the same time, 'very large numbers of cattle have caused
degradation on a massive scale and sheet and gully erosion are
omnipresent.'[63] Before the 2001 crisis, conflicts between farmers and

[59] Ibrahim 2000, p. 54.    [60] Best 2007, pp. 51–53.    [61] Blench 2004.
[62] Blench 2004.    [63] Blench 2004, p. 52.

herders in Plateau State did not reach casualty levels as high as in some neighbouring states. Traditional community leaders settled most tensions without taking recourse to violent means.[64] In some localities, they reached widely respected agreements, whereas in other villages, grievances over the partiality of traditional leaders and bribery were voiced.[65]

Competition over land also fuelled violence in Jos North LGA. Historically, the Hausa and Fulani bought and owned much land in the city centre because they were the most numerous group in early Jos. Since the 2001 clashes, a tacit understanding emerged among indigene groups not to sell further land to the Jasawa.[66] Jos North LGA also had a large number of illegal or semi-legal settlements of Jasawa who either never bought the land legally or never registered the land they bought. The Berom-dominated government had developed the Jos North Master Plan to evict these 'squatter' settlements within the city centre to improve housing and infrastructure.[67] Since inception of the development plan, the Jasawa feared mass expulsion from their settlements within Jos North LGA.

## The September 2001 Clashes

Since the creation of Jos North LGA, elections and political appointments in Jos have always been accompanied by strong tensions between the Jasawa and the Berom. A first minor crisis occurred in 1994 over the appointment of a Hausa candidate as chairman of the Jos North Local Government Council. The Berom and other indigene groups strongly protested and maintained that the position should go to an indigene. Four people were killed during the protests, and parts of several market areas as well as an Islamic school and mosque were destroyed.[68] Although the political elites in Jos were well aware of the long-standing tensions, these remained unaddressed.

After the regime change, rural ethnic clashes erupted in neighbouring states. Several small land clashes occurred between the Tiv and the Hausa and Fulanis over landownership in border areas of Plateau State. The Middle Belt Youth Association condemned the violence against the

---

[64] Blench, Longtau, Hassan, and Walsh 2006.   [65] Blench 2004.
[66] Mustapha, Higazi, Lar, and Chromy 2018.
[67] Muslim journalist from Jos, 2010.   [68] Best 2007, pp. 54–55.

Tiv, blaming 'settlers' and other groups for setting the 'Middle Belt' ethnic groups under pressure:

Some external forces and settlers are behind the problems in Nassarawa, Benue, Taraba, Plateau and parts of southern Bauchi States. Middle Belters are now being laughed at by core Northerners because that is the situation they like to see happen among Middle Belters.[69]

Furthermore, many Christian refugees arrived fleeing the sharia clashes in Kaduna and other northern states.[70] The governor of Plateau State, Joshua Dariye, founded an elders' forum to address the rising level of tensions. The forum was meant to advise the government on issues of peaceful coexistence. However, not much was heard of the forum's work. The governor did not ease the main fault line between the Berom and the Jasawa.

In the 1999 Jos North local government elections, the Hausa and Fulani won six out of fourteen electoral wards, which was the highest number won by one ethnic group.[71] However, a coalition of predominantly Christian ethnic groups elected a Christian chairman to the local government. The Berom and other 'indigene' tribes came to control the local government of Jos and stopped issuing indigene certificates to the Hausa and Fulani population in the city. They strongly protested the loss of their privileges. The Hausa and Fulani were in control of six electoral wards in Jos North while the Yoruba and the Igbo won two wards each. In contrast, the 'indigenes' – the Berom, Afizere, Anaguta, and Irigwe – won only one ward each of the total of fourteen in Jos North LGA.[72] According to Danfulani and Fwatshak, the Muslim Jasawa were frustrated to find that despite winning six electoral wards, they were unable to install a candidate of their own choosing as the executive chairman of Jos North, due to the eight predominantly Christian wards.

Just as in 1994, the 2001 crisis began as a conflict over the appointment of a Jasawa to public office. The federal government in Abuja appointed a Jasawa to the office of poverty eradication coordinator. The Berom strongly opposed the selection of a 'settler' to the position, while the Jasawa demanded the post given their numerical strength in Jos North LGA. Both the Berom youth association and the Jasawa

[69] Obateru 2001.     [70] Danfulani and Fwatshak 2002.
[71] Danfulani and Fwatshak 2002, p. 243.
[72] Danfulani and Fwatshak 2002, p. 247.

youth of JDA voiced their readiness to use violent means.[73] Despite clear indicators and warnings from several NGOs, the government did not undertake any significant preventive measures.

Clashes broke out after Friday prayers on 7 September at a mosque situated at the edge of a majority-Christian neighbourhood within the central part of Jos. Tensions over the blocking of the street into the Christian-dominated neighbourhood during Friday prayers had existed for several years, and had led to small skirmishes weeks before clashes broke out.[74] On that Friday afternoon, a confrontation between a Christian woman passing through the congregation to reach the Christian quarter and Muslim men who tried to stop her escalated into open fighting: Youth groups faced each other along improvised front lines armed with knives, machetes, cutlasses, and a few guns.[75] Pogroms took place in the Muslim-dominated neighbour-hood of Angwan Rogo and the majority Christian area of Angwan Rukuba, and religious minorities were driven out. In the large and central mixed neighbourhood of Nassarawa Gwom, battles took place between Christian and Muslim groups along the frontiers of predominantly Christian and predominantly Muslim areas. On Saturday and Sunday, the clashes spread further through the city. The religiously mixed central neighbourhoods of Jos were affected by killings as some residents and mobile fighters jointly organized attacks. After the fighting had almost died down, the clashes were reignited by the news of the 9/11 attacks in the United States; Muslim groups mobilized for revenge attacks and the killings continued into Wednesday, 12 September.[76] A strong religious dimension underlined the violent clashes from the first day: people were predominantly targeted according to their religious identity, mosques and churches were burned down, loudspeakers spread rumours and encouraged the faithful to fight, and strongholds were identified as the 'sharia line' and the 'new Jerusalem' to mark the religious divide.[77]

Among many NGO representatives, there was consensus that 'the violence could have been foreseen but that government authorities failed to take action to prevent it'.[78] Subsequent peacebuilding efforts yielded little progress because elites on both sides were unwilling to

---

[73] Tertsakian and Smart 2001.  [74] Best 2007, p. 7.
[75] Tertsakian and Smart 2001.  [76] Danfulani and Fwatshak 2002.
[77] Tertsakian and Smart 2001, p. 14; Danfulani and Fwatshak 2002, p. 253.
[78] Tertsakian and Smart 2001, p. 2.

compromise. The Jasawa elite submitted demands for indigene rights, political representation, and the installation of a traditional ruler to the commission of inquiry into the 2001 riot, provoking much resentment among the Berom elite.[79] Mediation efforts were unsuccessful because the political conflict was long-standing and both groups were internally well organized and unable to compromise.[80] Despite the legacies of mass killings of more than 1,000 people, Jos remained relatively peaceful over the subsequent years. Yet inter-communal trust had been deeply shattered; as one resident explained, 'If this can happen in Jos, nowhere is safe anymore.'[81]

## Rural Communal War

One consequence of the Jos 2001 clashes was that in several rural areas of Plateau State, disputes over land rights, cattle rustling, and farmlands became unmanageable, and fighting continued in small towns and villages.[82] The mass killings in Jos along the Christian–Muslim cleavage reverberated among rural communities as information and stories of atrocities spread through family, kin, and religious and trade networks. Especially among Christians, Jos residents buried their dead in their home village, a practice that carried grief and outrage into village communities. Numerous clashes erupted between herders and farmers over landownership, access to water, and grazing rights. Violence affected six LGAs of Plateau State. Militias raided villages and attacked provincial towns. This guerrilla warfare between well-armed militias destroyed more than 100 villages and killed at least 1,300 people until a local state of emergency in spring 2004 brought fighting to a halt.[83]

Conflicts over land are intrinsically linked to the indigene–settler divide and the question of ownership over settlements, towns, and cities. Landownership 'is tied to history, ancestral and traditional rights, religion, traditional power and authority, citizenship, belongingness'.[84] A crisis of ownership sparked by political appointments and decisions similar to the Jos crisis broke out in the town of

---

[79] *Daily Trust*, 'Hausas in Jos Want Own Chief', 28 March 2002.
[80] Former staff member of USAID involved in the peace negotiations in Kaduna and in Jos, 2010.
[81] Interview respondent in Tertsakian and Smart 2001, p. 2.
[82] Higazi 2013, p. 7.     [83] Author's database.     [84] Best 2008, p. 18.

Yelwa in Shendam LGA and the town of Wase in Wase LGA in 2002, and the town of Namu in Qua'an Pan LGA in 2005. In Yelwa, the creation of new districts resulted in open conflict over district boundaries and political control. Similar to the situation in Jos, in Yelwa, the (Christian) Gamai argued that they were the only indigenes in the region and therefore 'owned' the town of Yelwa. The (Muslim) Jarawa countered that they had founded Yelwa. Both communities voiced their exclusive claims to indigene rights and ownership. Ethnic and religious relations became further polarized by the news of violence in Jos City.

After the first clashes in Yelwa in 2002, no mediation took place that would have addressed the conflict dynamics in the region. Isolated attacks on villages occurred in Shendam, Wase, Langtang North and South, and Qua'an Pan LGAs. Many communities initially organized religiously mixed vigilante patrols and meetings to stem the tensions prior to the outbreak of violence,[85] but the lack of action from security forces against the formation of militia groups undermined such efforts. In 2003, the situation was described as 'open warfare between Tarok and Hausa/ Fulani' and the region as a 'no-go zone'.[86] In 2004, the fighting culminated in two well-organized massacres in Yelwa. On 24 February 2004, Muslim militias killed at least seventy-five Christians in Yelwa, many of them within a church compound. The attackers reportedly arrived in pick-up trucks shouting religious slogans, and killings and lootings were well coordinated and proceeded in several steps.[87] Some Christians in the area survived because they found shelter in Muslim houses. These killings sparked many reprisal attacks.

Fierce retaliation for the Yelwa killings hit Muslims in Yelwa in early May 2004 when well-armed Christian militias killed about 700 Muslims in Yelwa within two days. Armed members of the predominantly Christian Tarok ethnic group attacked to revenge the killings of Taroks by the predominantly Muslim Fulanis.[88] The attack was thoroughly planned and coordinated and involved all Christian ethnic groups from Shendam LGA and neighbouring LGAs. Reprisal killings for the Yelwa attack on Muslims further claimed at least 200 Christian lives in the northern city of Kano.[89] A Muslim journalist commented

---

[85]  Higazi 2008, p. 128.    [86]  Blench 2004, p. 56.    [87]  Tertsakian 2005.
[88]  See the detailed investigation by Human Rights Watch 2004; Tertsakian 2005.
[89]  Tertsakian 2005.

that unlike previous outbreaks in Kano, when violence might have been more economically than religiously motivated, this time 'they were just out to kill ... looting was incidental.'[90]

After the Yelwa killings, President Obasanjo declared a six-month state of emergency for Plateau State, describing the situation as 'near mutual genocide'.[91] The killings mostly came to a halt. While the suspension of the civilian administration of Plateau State prevented large-scale attacks, the political conflict over indigene rights and ownership of towns, villages, and farming and grazing land was left unaddressed. The conflict between the Berom and the Jasawa in Jos, and between other 'indigene' and 'settler' groups in small towns and rural areas of Plateau, continued over the following years.

## The November 2008 Clashes

The chairman of Jos North LGA who had been elected in 1999 left office in 2002, but no local government elections took place until November 2008. The Plateau State government suspended elections due to security concerns and fears of more clashes, despite protests by the Jasawa community. The Jasawa elite had been in negotiations about broader political inclusion and political offices with Governor Jonah Jang for several years.[92] During the campaign for the November 2008 local government elections, Jang refused to cooperate with the Jasawa and planned to campaign without Muslim support, and so 'the stage was set ... as a showdown between Jang and the Jasawa' in Jos North LGA.[93] While the indigenes secured the support of churches for their political campaign on the People's Democratic Party (PDP) ticket, the Jasawa allied with the Afizere on the All Nigeria People's Party (ANPP) platform. Many people in Jos, including the Jasawa and Afizere elites, were convinced that Jang could never win Jos North LGA.[94]

As Philip Ostien reported, both sides were prepared to make use of all forms of vote rigging to win Jos North LGA and had youth groups following the stages of vote collection and transportation of ballot boxes to the collation centre to 'guard' their votes. However, the Jos North LGA collation centre had been relocated, and neither side had

---

[90] Tertsakian 2005.     [91] Human Rights Watch 2013, p. 34.     [92] Ostien 2009.
[93] Ostien 2009, p. 28.     [94] Ostien 2009, p. 30.

been properly informed. This fuelled suspicions among the Jasawa that their votes would be lost. Tensions rose when both youth groups waited at the new collation centre for the results. Eventually, the police forcibly dispersed them. Before long, youth gangs started fighting in the central neighbourhoods.[95] According to Human Rights Watch, at least 700 people were killed in two days, and an additional 133 people were documented to have been killed in extra-judicial killings perpetrated by security forces, who gunned down unarmed citizens in their homes, chased and killed men trying to flee to safety, and lined up victims on the ground and summarily executed them.[96] This death toll in only two days marks an even more extreme intensity of violence than the five-day 2001 Jos clashes, which killed at least 1,000 people. At the end of 2008, according to CAN, at least 10,000 people were displaced.[97] A detailed memorandum by the Jos North Muslim Ummah listed how each victim was killed. The number of gunshot fatalities suggests that guns were much more widely used than in the 2001 clashes; almost 90 per cent of Muslim victims died of gunshots.[98]

## January 2010 Clashes

Only a year later, in January 2010, communal violence erupted again within the Jos centre and in the south of Jos, including Bukuru, Anglo Jos, and villages on the outskirts of the city. The fighting spread to some neighbourhoods previously unaffected by killings because joint attacks were organized. Fighting lasted from the morning of Sunday, 17 January until Tuesday, 19 January. The 2010 clashes were sparked by a dispute over the rebuilding of a house in the city centre destroyed during the 2008 riot.[99] Two days later, some of the worst violence of 2010 took place in the south of Jos, including Anglo Jos and Bukuru, and in surrounding rural villages. The context of the outbreak of violence remains disputed. Muslims claimed that a Muslim was attacked while reconstructing his house, which had been burnt down during the 2008 crisis in Dutse Uku, in the city centre. Christians argued that the reconstruction project was just a pretext to stir up trouble in the area. They maintained that the owner of the house

---

[95] Ostien 2009, pp. 31–32.    [96] Human Rights Watch 2009, p. 9.
[97] Dung-Gwom and Rikko 2009, p. 7.    [98] Higazi 2011, p. 23.
[99] Higazi 2011, p. 24.

brought hundreds of armed men to work on his construction site, insulting Christian passers-by and attacking them.[100] The Muslim owner of the house contended that Christians tried to prevent him from finishing the roof of the house and threatened to burn his house down again. According to Adam Higazi's interview with the Muslim house owner, 'Christians mobilised, blowing a whistle and asking people to "come out and fight for Jesus."'[101] Attempts to solve the dispute through the ward head or to call in soldiers to prevent an escalation failed. The fighting was quelled by a heavy military deployment in Jos and Bukuru. Many people believed it was only a matter of time until the next violent outbreak. As a Hausa man in Bukuru noted: 'Most of our people are sharpening their knives for the next crisis.'[102]

The violence in January 2010 did not only hit Jos City. According to a Fulani spokesperson, 'many Fulani herdsmen were killed by Berom youths in the vicinity of Governor Jonah Jang's house in Du District of Jos South Local Government,' resulting in the deaths of about 120 people.[103] Armed Christian and predominantly Berom groups attacked Muslims in numerous villages and settlements of Jos South LGA in 'what appeared to be coordinated attacks',[104] driving out all remaining Muslim residents. Some of the worst massacres took place on 19 January in Kuru Karama, Tim Tim, Sabon Gidan Kanar, Sabon Gidan Forum, and Kaduna Vom, all in Jos South LGA near Bukuru. Furthermore, numerous rural Fulani settlements in Jos South, Barkin Lardi, and Riyom LGAs were also attacked.[105] According to a report by the Jos North Muslim Ummah, 968 Muslims were killed, of whom 242 died in urban Jos and the rest were massacred in villages on the rural outskirts of the city.[106]

In March 2010, a reprisal attack killed at least 164 Berom Christians in the village of Dogo Nahauwa and the neighbouring small villages of Ramsat and Kamang in Jos South LGA.[107] The Dogo Nahauwa massacre started a campaign of revenge attacks by mobile Fulani groups against Berom Christian villages in Jos South, Barkin Ladi, and Riyom LGAs between 2010 and 2013. The massacres traumatized many people in Jos. Both sides often referred to Kuru Karama or Dogo

---

[100] Citizens' Monitoring Group 2010.    [101] Higazi 2011, p. 24.
[102] IRIN News, 2010.    [103] Olaniyi 2010.
[104] Human Rights Watch 2013, p. 49. See also Higazi 2013.
[105] Human Rights Watch 2013, p. 49.
[106] Plateau State Muslim Ummah 2010.    [107] Human Rights Watch 2013.

Nahauwa to underline the extreme cruelty of the killers. Graphic photographs of corpses and mass graves circulated.

Once the military was permanently deployed and suppressed movement by armed groups, patterns of violence changed into 'silent killings' of people discovered in the 'wrong' neighbourhoods of Jos, which further perpetuated the conflict.[108] Both sides reported primarily men going missing since early 2010, and bodies were seldom recovered for burial. The year 2010 ended with the explosion of eight bombs on Christmas Eve. The bombs detonated in predominantly Christian market areas when residents were making final purchases for the festivities. According to Human Rights Watch, 107 people died in the bomb attacks and numerous people were wounded.[109] Boko Haram claimed responsibility for these bombings.

## Communal Violence from Below: Mobilization and Conflict Escalation

Long-standing electoral competition between indigene and settler groups in Jos, conflicts over land rights in rural areas, the historical legacy of religious tensions, and the introduction of sharia law in Nigeria's northern states after the transition all contributed to the escalation of communal violence in and around Jos. Unlike the conflict dynamics in Ambon and Maluku Province in eastern Indonesia, however, neither in the city nor in rural areas did militias with centralized command emerge. Armed groups were not directly attached to 'war headquarters' of mosques and churches in Jos as they were in Ambon. Within the city of Jos, a repeated heavy deployment of security forces eventually contained the fighting. Where did the violence networks that killed at least 1,000 people in 2001 come from, and how did they evolve and transform during the subsequent decade of the Jos conflict?

### Everyday Violence Networks and Political Mobilization

Political mobilization along ethnic and religious cleavages drew on pre-existing networks of vigilantes, thugs, and gangs and their alignment with political actors; further recruitment of men into these violence networks; and an alignment among ethnic and religious leaders with

---

[108] *Daily Trust* 2010.   [109] Human Rights Watch 2011.

politicians for electoral purposes. In Jos, networks of ethnic and religious associations were polarized along lines of political conflict at least since the creation of Jos North LGA in 1991. Furthermore, the weak performance of security forces even before the outbreak of clashes had resulted in vigilante groups forming to protect neighbourhoods against crime and theft. In the areas of Jos that suffered from poor policing, vigilantes were often particularly violent in their execution of 'jungle justice'[110] without police involvement. With ethnic, religious, and everyday violence networks aligned around the main political contestants – the Berom and the Jasawa elites – the organizational potential for mass killings during the 2001 clashes emerged.

In Jos, prior to the first clashes, many neighbourhoods had vigilante groups whose purpose was to protect the neighbourhood from theft and petty crime. Vigilante groups were not initially formed to fight in communal conflicts.[111] They were 'violence specialists' used to executing harsh punishments in everyday life. In the words of one former vigilante leader from one of the most violent city neighbourhoods, 'if you mess up we bring you out of the area and flog you before the eyes of the world.'[112]

In the context of Nigeria's weak statehood, ethnic and religious groups and associations were institutions that performed governance functions, such as offering their members much-needed protection because in many places indigene status was contested and citizenship precarious.[113] Ethno-religious groups provided inter- and intracommunal leadership, security, and conflict management, and were crucial networks for political mobilization.[114] The main protagonist ethnic groups in Jos, the Berom and the Jasawa, both had strong and well-organized associations, BECO and JDA, which also established strong links to religious institutions in Jos.

When the Hausa and Fulani were unable to translate their numerical strength into political leadership of the Jos North Local Government council in the 1999 municipal election, young Muslim men led the

---

[110] 'Jungle justice' is a term often used in reference to the policing by vigilante groups and implies immediate violent punishment without a formal trial. See, for example, Onuoha 2010.

[111] Former vigilantes in the violence-prone Jos neighbourhoods of Angwan Rukuba and Nassarawa, 2012.

[112] Mark, vigilante leader from Angwan Rukuba, 2012.      [113] Idowu 1999.

[114] Ukiwo 2003.

Jasawa to advocate for the formation of a Council of Ulama/Elders in order to unite Muslim ethnic groups.[115] The council drew its members from Muslim politicians, as well as leaders of Muslim movements. The objectives of the Council of Ulama/Elders were 'to defend and safeguard the rights of Muslims religiously and politically in Plateau State; to create a forum whereby Muslims irrespective of their sectarian affiliation or organisation could meet and discuss religious and socio-economic challenges facing them in Jos in particular and Plateau State in general; and to provide a sense of direction to Muslims and Muslim politicians generally'.[116] With the formation of the Council of Ulama/Elders in 2003, the Jasawa Development Association, the most important network of Jasawa Muslims in Jos, received additional backing from religious leaders. The association established itself as the most important political and socio-economic platform for the Jasawa.[117]

Ethnic and religious associations maintained their offices within neighbourhoods dominated by their groups and thus penetrated vigilante and youth groups. The JDA office was located next to the Central Mosque and physically linked ethnic and religious politics, facilitating the mobilization of Muslims for the political agenda of the Jasawa elite. High-level members of the JDA also held top positions in the local branch of the Jama'atu Nasril Islam (JNI), the most important Muslim umbrella network in Nigeria.[118]

On the Christian side, Plateau State's political leadership had been particularly well linked to the Church of Christ in Nigeria (COCIN) since the 1999 transition. Former governors Jonah Jang (2007–2015) and Joshua Dariye (1999–2007) both worshipped at the same COCIN church headquarters in the central part of town, close to the Plateau State government house.[119] Religious teachings became intertwined with ethnic politics. Since the early 1990s, the Berom had voiced their claim to the land of Plateau State and the city of Jos in strong religious terms. The Plateau land was understood as 'inheritance' from God to the Berom people. As 'good Christians', the Berom were responsible for defending the land of their ancestors for future generations. Ethnic and religious organizations included youth wings and women's groups. The youth wings of BECO and JDA, as well as of churches and mosques, created further overlapping social networks of young men

---

[115] Modibbo 2012, p. 15.    [116] Modibbo 2012.    [117] Adetula 2005, p. 217.
[118] Adetula 2005.    [119] This Day 2012.

that included ordinary youth groups and vigilantes, with links to criminals and gangs. One vigilante member emphasized the links between vigilante community protection and political mobilization, highlighting the internalized religious dividing line on both sides: 'we only base our vote on religious affiliation; God forbid a Muslim brother should represent us, and God forbid a Christian brother to represent them.'[120]

In sum, alignment of politicized ethnic and religious networks with violence specialists from gangs and vigilantes formed violence networks with the organizational capacity for mass killings. Two of the largest and poorest neighbourhoods in the city of Jos – Angwan Rogo (Muslim) and Angwan Rukuba (Christian) – emerged as strongholds with mobile armed fighters after the minority population was driven from these neighbourhoods during the first two days of clashes in 2001. Thereafter, the strongest gangs and vigilantes further transformed into mobile groups that collaborated with residents from other mixed neighbourhood, thereby 'spreading' atrocities and mass killings.

## Social Polarization and the 'Religious War' Narrative

The long-standing polarization of ethnic and religious identities along political cleavages and the uncompromising political discourse prior to the 2001 clashes contributed to a normalization of the '*othering*' of the opponent ethnic and religious group. Traditionally, the Hausa had largely viewed Christians as 'infidels'.[121] Such attitudes caused resentment among the indigene communities. Intermarriages occurred mostly between Muslim men and indigene women who had converted to Islam; meanwhile, Muslim women were often forbidden from marrying Christians, a practice that continued to the present and caused much resentment among Christian men.[122] Social tensions over interreligious marriages increased with the onset of communal violence.

After the 2001 clashes and the state of emergency in 2004, numerous meetings between politicians, traditional and religious leaders, women, and youth representatives took place to ease tensions. However, as interview respondents who took part in some of these meetings stated, traditional and religious leaders seldom conveyed decisions made or messages of peace and reconciliation back to their local

---

[120] Mark, vigilante member from Angwan Rukuba, 2012.    [121] Plotnicov 1972.
[122] Christian residents in Jos, November/December 2010.

communities.[123] Top-down approaches to violence prevention included heavy deployment of security forces, the routine establishment of commissions of inquiry after major clashes, and meetings for conflict resolution with traditional and religious leaders. However, 'in present-day Nigeria, those in charge of community conflicts are youth leaders rather than the traditional rulers with whom a top-down peacemaker might want to strike an agreement.'[124]

After the September 2001 clashes, a conflict prevention initiative by the United States Agency for International Development (USAID) brought the Jasawa and the Berom elites together, but the meetings achieved little because internally neither group could compromise on its maximum demands.[125] In 2001, Berom elders stated that 'not only is Jos on Berom land, but Jos is our JERUSALEM and is indigenously inhabited by the Berom, Anaguta, and Afizere' (emphasis in original).[126] A few years later, the traditional Berom leader added that even if the Hausa had been in Plateau State for more than 1,000 years, they would remain non-indigene.[127] This uncompromising attitude fuelled polarization. Many Christians I interviewed subscribed to a strongly polarized religious conflict narrative, claiming that Muslims sought to capture Plateau State and convert people to Islam. Aida, a Christian journalist concluded, 'we are saying to them: you cannot change our religion for us.'[128]

The extremely deadly 2001 clashes had shocked many residents. People recounted how they grew up with Muslim and Christian friends in Jos, how they had moved freely through the city, and that clashes on such a scale had been unthinkable. One woman remarked:

Before 2001, we lived together, we [ate] together, we [did] a lot of things together. We went to the same schools; we shared celebrations. But we never thought that there was going to be a day when Christians attacked Muslims, and Muslims attacked Christians. I still feel like I am living in a horrible dream.[129]

Many respondents referred to the trauma of victimization after the 2001 clashes, and even more so after the 2008 clashes, which led to

[123] NGO staff members and spokespersons ethnic associations, Jos, 2010–2015.
[124] Albert 1999, p. 39.
[125] Program leader who led the initiative for USAID, Jos, 2010.
[126] Best 2007, p. 35.    [127] Albin-Lackey 2006, p. 42.
[128] Aida, December 2010.
[129] Muslim resident whose mother was a Christian indigene, December 2010.

further polarization. When I conducted interviews in Jos in November and December 2010, respondents feared another 'fight to the finish' because national and local elections were scheduled for the spring of 2011.[130] Soraya, a Muslim community activist from the large and central neighbourhood of Nassarawa, stated:

People have become more heartless, more ruthless, taking up measures to make sure they take revenge. . . . In 2008 and in 2010, you could see a lot of hatred and a lot of sophistication in the way people were attacked this time.[131]

Aida, a Christian journalist, expressed similar feelings of shock and trauma in the aftermath of the killings:

You would be sleeping in the night thinking the next day, God will show you the next day. But the next day will be something different! People will be in their houses, they will set your house ablaze, and as you come out, they use machetes on you! It was very brutal. It's dehumanizing.[132]

The recurrent violent confrontation over local government elections further fostered the transformation from an ethnic urban competition into a 'religious' crisis reflecting national and international dimensions. Even among senior religious leaders who supported peacebuilding and reconciliation, perceptions of the conflict changed and the situation became understood as a 'religious conflict'.[133] After the 2008 clashes, religious leaders pointed to the destruction of religious, rather than political, buildings. For example, the former chairman of the Plateau State CAN, Archbishop Ignatius Kaigama, known for his very active role in inter-faith peacebuilding initiatives, stated after the 2008 killings:

We were taken aback by the turn of events in Jos. We thought it was political, but from all indications it is not so. We were surprised at the way some of our churches and property were attacked and some of our faithful and clergy killed. The attacks were carefully planned and executed. The questions that bog our minds are why were churches and clergy attacked and killed? Why were politicians and political party offices not attacked if it were a political conflict? Why were the business premises and property of innocent civilians

---

[130] Residents in Jos, November and December 2010.
[131] Soraya, December 2010.       [132] Aida, November 2010.
[133] Muslim and Christian residents, 2010–2011.

destroyed? We strongly feel that it was not political, but pre-meditated act[s] under the guise of elections.[134]

The Muslim leadership in Jos vehemently protested the religious framing of the 2008 crisis. In the name of the Jos North Muslim Ummah, they stated:

The November 2008 violence in Jos was ethno-political in all ramifications; its antecedents, the circumstances, the principal actors and the reason so far adduced by all parties only point to one inevitable conclusion: the struggle by ethnic groups to capture political power and manipulate for selfish reasons or to keep as vehicle for attaining socio-political goals. ... We cannot deny the fact that Mosques and Churches were destroyed in the mayhem, so also schools, residential houses, markets and other places that serve the common needs of all, regardless of faith, were destroyed.[135]

After the 2008 riots, the Jasawa leadership refused engagement and communication with the Jang government. Their leaders complained about the governor's 'extremist mindset' as both a Berom and Christian, accusing him of leading a government exclusively for the indigene population of Jos.[136] Many Jasawa suspected him of having actively promoted violence against them. In contrast, many Christians praised the governor for standing up against their 'enemies', whom they feared would otherwise 'finish them'.[137] The strong polarization not only between Berom and Jasawa, but between Christians and Muslims in general, as well as the lack of dialogue between political elites, brought peacebuilding efforts to a standstill. Even residents who had close friends and family members within both religious communities were not immune to '*othering*', traumatization, and polarization. For example, Aida explained that her family was religiously mixed, but she still found herself unable to trust Muslim relations again:

You don't trust people anymore; you don't believe in any person anymore. People who used to be very close to you, you still lose trust because when the crisis broke out, it was like a religious thing. Because your neighbour who does not share your religious faith will turn against you. It creates enmity between neighbours, friends, and even family relations. It breaks families

---

[134] Okocha, Ruben, and Adinoyi 2008.
[135] Jos North Muslim Ummah, 2009a.
[136] Representative from the Jasawa Development Association, December 2010.
[137] Christian respondents, 2010–2011.

apart. I have lived with my Muslim friend for many years. We went to high school together, we slept in the same bed, but this crisis took us apart.[138]

The January 2010 clashes in Jos were followed by two major massacres in villages on the outskirts of the city. The killings of small children further shocked and traumatized many people and became seen as proof that the other side was 'monstrous' and fighting to finish them. Funmi, a Christian resident from the city, stated:

In the past they preach what is in the Holy Book, but now that society has changed. As you worship God, you pray for safety for yourself, you have to be wise, and you have to be security conscious. So they have improved upon what they have been preaching. People should be security conscious.[139]

Ethnic groups consolidated their political agenda in religious institutions. The following is an excerpt from a preaching from February 2010 at the COCIN church to which the past two governors, Jang and Dariye, belonged:

When the Hausa person arrived, the Plateau people in their characteristic spirit of love welcomed and accommodated them. Hence in most cases the Hausa became the Sarkin Kasuwa (chief of the market), Sarkin Tabirma (chief of the mats), Sarkin Mudu (chief of the measure), Sarkin Tasha (chief of the motor park), and Sarkin Yanka (chief of the butchers), among others. In the same way, when the Igbos and the others arrived, they were similarly welcomed.

This explains why today, the visitors have the privilege of controlling aspects of the economy, to the extent of determining the prices and price value of even the agricultural goods never produced by them. But while the other settlers appreciated the hospitality of the host community, the Hausa settlers misconstrued this love and kind gestures, considering it rather as weakness on the part of Plateau people, and exploited it to their advantage.

They want to take the land and the inheritance of the people. While we admit that we are all Nigerians, we must also admit that God is not foolish to have assigned each ethnic nationality a geo-political entity they can call their own. This explains why we cannot fold our arms and simply watch others rob us of our God-given inheritance.[140]

Some community leaders from conflict-affected neighbourhoods in Jos repeatedly criticized government-sponsored peace efforts as little more

---

[138] Aida, December 2010.     [139] Christian journalist in Jos, November 2010.
[140] Bewarang 2010.

than 'talk shops' that left many people wondering what measures were taken to protect them and prevent renewed fighting. Muslim respondents accused the government of deliberately inviting community representatives who would 'dance to their tune' while the actual stakeholders with strong connections to the communities concerned were excluded. Aisha, a Muslim female participant, explained after the clashes in 2010:

I don't think anyone can give you the accurate number of dialogues, conferences and workshops we had on peace. I have been a member of many of such gatherings. They have not made any positive impact. In fact, *it helps worsen the situation*, because in almost all of these meetings, the people invited are not actually the people that have any direct link or connection with the crisis. But you can't solve a problem when you don't call the stakeholders.[141]

In Ambon, Indonesia, senior militia stated that inter-religious peace meetings and peace pledges by top religious leaders only worsened the conflict because initial fights between thugs and gangs were increasingly seen as a religious conflict among ordinary people. Similarly, in Jos, Aisha stated that the numerous peace meetings of top-level ethnic and religious leaders only 'worsened the situation', reinforcing the people's perception of an ethno-religious conflict, in which ethnic and religious leaders would not honour their peace pledges because the fighting continued.

The brutality of the killings and the loss of entire families and livelihoods left many of those victimized outraged, advocating revenge. Mark, one former gang member from the violence-prone neighbourhood of Angwan Rukuba, discussed the challenges of supporting victims of the conflict who had moved into his neighbourhood and stated:

When you are at grief, you believe you are taken advantage of. These people did this to us. They started burning houses. People [who] lost their loved ones are traumatized. This trauma causes a lot of problems, like drug addiction and drunkenness. When somebody becomes traumatized, they may have vengeance in their hearts.[142]

Women were particularly affected by the killings and destruction because the majority of those killed in fighting were men. Female respondents frequently discussed how they would receive and pass on

[141] Aisha, December 2010.  [142] Mark, July 2015.

details about atrocities through their networks of women friends and market women, and how discussions among the women and outrage over atrocities could spark preparations for further attacks.[143] Mohammed, a vigilante member who had repeatedly taken part in fighting, stated:

> Sometimes, the women receive information about attacks and atrocities even faster than the men. One wife will tell another wife, and finally the information reaches men, and then men will take action.[144]

Tanko, another vigilante leader from Nassarawa, explained how feelings of trauma and vengeance were passed from women to men and could ignite further fighting:

> A woman may receive the news of atrocities and will think: 'When my husband comes home, he must know this, what they did to us. How can this be, how can they kill Muslims like that? I can't take this. Let my husband come back.' Or: 'They went and burned down the church. I won't take it. Let my husband come back and I will tell him to go and fight.' Women do this, even though the fighting will bounce back and they are the victims, losing husband and son.[145]

The horrific atrocities in Jos and Plateau State were not simply bygone events, but 'remained very present in the lives of the victims and survivors'.[146] Among Christians, perceptions of the Jos conflict have become interlinked with regional and national politics. Some Christians explained that the Jasawa agitation over political rights in Jos was only coverage for seeking total religious, economic, and political domination. Citing the historical dan Fodio jihad movement, Christian men from Congo-Russia, an area in the city centre where the 2001 clashes had broken out, viewed themselves as the last bastion of Christianity before the 'Muslim north' of the country and stated in simplistic terms, 'if the Muslims have Jos, they have Nigeria. And if they have Nigeria, they have Africa.'[147] Among many Christians, particularly from the Berom group, Old Testament verses were cited to legitimize claims to land and

---

[143] Female residents from the city centre and Anglo Jos, July 2015.
[144] Mohammed, July 2015.     [145] Tanko, July 2015.
[146] Human Rights Watch 2013.
[147] Male Christian residents from the city centre in Jos, November and December 2010.

inheritance. Agnes, a Berom woman who worked as a local radio journalist, explained this view:

They [the Jasawa] have a plan to evict us from the Plateau and take over Plateau. Not just evict us, they want to destroy us, and take over our father's land. And I believe in the Bible, and sometimes I blame our forefathers. They were very, very lenient, they welcomed everybody. And for that, they [the Jasawa] took them for granted.[148]

The mass killings and displacements destabilized local communities. The high numbers of displaced families and individuals living with relatives in other neighbourhoods were a burden for many families that already struggled to get by. The vast destruction of property increased levels of poverty within the poorest areas. Tony, a gang member from the poor Christian neighbourhood of Angwan Rukuba, explained that 'the crisis initiated a lot of things and affected people in many lasting ways; we now have severe problems with alcohol and drug abuse.'[149] Community activists from other central neighbourhoods similarly stated that drug and alcohol abuse became a much more severe community problem after the clashes.

When the city became segregated into 'no-go areas', residents who wanted to remain mobile and avoid being targeted adapted in various ways. Changing one's dress according to Muslim or Christian standards 'acceptable to each of the warring territories' became known as 'chameleon tactics' that people increasingly employed in the city.[150] After the 2008 riot, some residents were still willing to rebuild their destroyed houses for a second time, trusting that they could live peacefully once again among their neighbours of different faiths. But after the 2010 clashes, even families whose houses had not been destroyed voluntarily moved into areas dominated by their own religious group.

## Gangs, Militias, and Militarization of Local Communities

In addition to the political tensions and severe economic deprivation, the social impact of the 2001 clashes transformed violence networks and the neighbourhoods they were embedded in. The pre-existence of violent vigilante groups and the repression of community leaders

---

[148] Agnes, December 2010.     [149] Tony, December 2012.
[150] Residents in Jos, December 2012.

opposed to fighting allowed armed groups to remain deeply embedded within neighbourhood communities and organize further attacks. As a result of the conflict, vigilantes all over Plateau State adapted their functions and composition.[151] In Jos, this transformation resulted in increased social control within ethnic, religious, and neighbourhood communities, but did not reach levels of community militarization as in Ambon, Indonesia.

In many rural areas, the purpose of vigilante groups was primarily to protect villages against petty theft and stealing of livestock.[152] After the September 2001 clashes, seeking revenge, some Christian village communities turned their anger against the Muslim Fulani cattle herders. Overlapping ethnic and religious cleavages meant that land conflicts between farmers and pastoralists became interlinked with the political confrontation in the city of Jos and a narrative of 'religious violence'.

Once the news [of the Jos riot] filtered through to rural areas, there was significant pressure for the indigenous farming populations to attack the resident Fulbe pastoralists. This occurred at several sites around Jos.[153]

Researching rural militia violence in Plateau State, Higazi concluded that 'mobilization occurred very quickly' and 'no prompting or elite manipulation was needed.'[154] Between 2002 and 2004, more than 100 villages were attacked, damaged, or destroyed by well-armed militia groups, and 'the main protagonists were generally small, highly mobile, well-armed groups with excellent local knowledge and familiarity with the bush.'[155] Weapons were acquired through ethnic and religious networks throughout Plateau State. In some areas, 'church leaders seem to have turned funds collected for evangelisation to the purchase of modern weapons.'[156]

Ethnic and religious activities led to the collection of donations for relief services, which was partly used for the acquisition of weapons and the organization of self-defence groups. Respondents in Jos accused ethnic and religious associations of acquiring weapons for community militias, and researchers documented the illegal arms trade among such associations.[157] Vigilantes transformed into self-

---

[151] Higazi 2008, p. 107.     [152] Higazi 2008, p. 128.
[153] Blench 2004, pp. 54–55.     [154] Higazi 2008, p. 109.
[155] Higazi 2008, p. 109.     [156] Blench 2004, p. 55.
[157] Blench, Longtau, Hassan, and Walsh 2006.

defence groups, and their leaders rose to positions of authority within the neighbourhoods. One elder from the neighbourhood of Nassarawa in the city centre stated that everyone knew the most notorious Muslim gang leaders who moved around freely within the neighbourhood. Since they had reputations for extreme violence, none of the elders dared to intervene and prevent further mobilization for killings.[158] Lynda, a female resident from Gyel, a neighbourhood in the south of Jos from where many youth had taken part in the fighting in Bukuru and an attempted attack on Dadin Kowa in 2010 (see Chapter 7), spoke about the daily fear these armed groups incited in their neighbourhoods:

These people don't respect authority no matter what you do, no matter what you tell them. Most of them are into drugs and we always have problems with them. It's very hard to bring them under control. When they drink or take drugs, you dare not cross their path. You just let them be.[159]

The resettlement of people displaced during the first crisis, the loss of economic livelihoods, and the trauma of victimization strongly contributed to a major drug problem in many central neighbourhoods. Within religious communities, intimidation by gang members and youth who wanted to fight and retaliate was equally a problem. One female church leader recalled meetings during which she was challenged when advocating for a stop to the killings.

Some Christians, particularly the young people, say, 'look, you've been telling all this while that Jesus says that we should turn the other cheek. And we've been turning the other cheek and now we have no more cheeks to turn. It is time to retaliate. How long will it continue to be that we will sit down and these people will come and just start killing. We've had enough.' So some people felt that the churches needed to be more militant, that we were too stupid, that we were too naïve, just relying on prayer, and God is not going to come down and fight for us. Others tried to argue that as Christians, we cannot become like the attacker. So those were the tensions among Christians.[160]

Attacks by mobile gangs were always cloaked in narratives of self-defence: 'We never stood up and retaliated: only when we hear "An fara" [meaning fighting has started in Hausa] we do self-defence,'

---

[158] Elder from Nassarawa, 2010.    [159] Lynda, July 2015.
[160] Funmi, a Christian female religious leader, Jos November 2010.

Mark, a former gang member from Angwan Rukuba stated.[161] Aisha, a community activist from Nassarawa, further explained how fighting in Jos was organized:

We are talking about a particular set of people organizing an attack on a particular group of people, and it is impossible for it to just happen. In most of the fighting, it is not the people [who] live in that particular area that do the attack but people come in numbers to make the attack.[162]

Tony, another gang member from Angwan Rukuba, discussed the territorial fighting strategies with me as follows:

*Q: I understand that your primary enemies are the Muslim men in Angwan Rogo. But Angwan Rogo is quite far away from Angwan Rukuba. You would have to march all the way over through the city centre, through Dogon Dutse …*
Yes, we go through Dogon Dutse, and parts of Nassarawa, Dilimi, or Dutse Uko. Yes, people from Dutse Uko do attack. People from Rikkos attack too, and the men from Angwan Rogo will come down and fight.

*Q: But when security forces are deployed, moving around like this is difficult?*
Yes, it's quite far, because we have to go through Congo-Russia. From here we go through Congo-Russia, and the Angwan Rogo men come down to Angwan Rukuba.

*Q: And then you meet in Congo-Russia to fight?*
Yes, because that is the border community. Whenever they come, we push them backwards. Then if they attack areas on their return, and Christians come to fight from the other side, then they clash in the border areas. In 2001, we even fought in Angwan Rukuba; it was very bloody. Since then, we have pushed them back.

*Q: Do you just use the main road or do you go through the back roads?*
No, they don't take the main road; they take a short cut through Dogon Dutse.

*Q: Do you also fight alongside other Christian communities, for example Kabong, Ali Kazaure, or Tudun Wada?*
No. That is just too far away.[163]

---

[161] Mark, December 2012.    [162] Aisha, December 2010.
[163] Tony, December 2012.

Tony's account demonstrated the collaboration strategies of gangs and vigilante groups from different neighbourhoods and named some of the areas from the Jos city centre that hosted armed groups involved in the fighting. As he explained, other neighbourhoods further to the south of Jos, such as Tudun Wada, had their own armed youth groups that would coordinate fighting without the men from Angwan Rukuba or Angwan Rogo. Other Christian strongholds in the southern part of Jos included Hwolshe and Gyel, while Muslims from Bukuru and Anglo Jos had also been involved in the fighting.

Abraham, a resident from Bukuru, further explained how local residents would collaborate with outside armed groups to organize attacks on their Christian and Muslims neighbours, thus indirectly killing their neighbours:

When there is fighting, when there is a problem, if the Christians want to come from the one side to help the ones here from the other side, the boys from that area will gather together and say, 'ok, you Christians are coming to help us here. Let's show you the house that you are going to torch. Those houses don't belong to us.' The same for the Muslims. If the Muslims are going to help the Muslims, they will point out, 'this one is Christian owned, so we will burn it, this one is Muslim owned, so we will not burn it.' They will pick out the houses in the midst of it and burn. Because, if I am living in this one place, I know that all the people here are Christian. I know that all the people around here are Muslim. So I can point out, 'this one is a Muslim house; this one is a Christian house.' And when they have pointed out, the Muslims will pick all the Christian houses and burn. The same for the Christians. They will pick the Muslim houses in that environment and burn. That's how they do it. Even with the killings. They would say, 'oh, this is one of our people, don't kill him.' Sometimes, they will use colour marking on houses during the night and mark the houses. Then [they] will go back and tell the leader, this colour, on all the houses with this colour, is the Christian colour.[164]

Christian and Muslim armed groups learnt how security forces deployed and moved through the city. They adapted their mobilization and coordination strategies accordingly. Christian gangs moved through Christian-dominated neighbourhoods, particularly in the south of Jos, to reach places for fighting in the centre. When moving through the backstreets of densely populated neighbourhoods, they

[164] Abraham, July 2015.

could avoid the main streets patrolled by security forces. Armed men would call on youth on the streets to join them. Both sides only needed to shout that 'it has started' and people knew that another round of fighting was under way. Once the military effectively deployed, both Christian and Muslim fighters would be forced to stay near the area they fought in because the military would enforce curfews. Thus, mobile armed groups had to rely on unarmed civilian support to carry out attacks outside their own neighbourhoods.

The gang members and youth leaders I interviewed explained that peer group pressure was an important aspect in recruiting youth into violence. Even men who were not or no longer willing to participate would find it hard to ignore other men going out to fight when called upon to provide support. Mohammed, a former perpetrator who became active within a violence prevention network, explained:

With our peace efforts, we try to talk to the youth, not to go out and fight. Not to be manipulated by politicians. Just because somebody offers you money, and then you start the action. But it is difficult because sometimes even I get a phone call, and people are saying, 'we need backup here, we have problems; there is a security issue and people are dying.' And then what do you do? The person who receives such a phone call will be willing to join.[165]

In the years between major clashes, violence networks remained embedded within neighbourhoods either as vigilantes primarily for community protection or as gangs involved in crime and armed robbery. Neighbourhood problems and market disputes were channelled to the vigilantes before being taken to the police station. Mark, a vigilante leader, stated:

The neighbourhood, yes there are quarrels, but no fighting. We only come along and settle the issues. The crisis is between the Christian community and the Muslim community. That's what we call the real fight.[166]

After the January 2010 clashes, the federal government deployed an STF to Jos and other conflict-affected areas of Plateau State, comprised of the military, police, and navy forces. Throughout 2010 and 2011, until the Boko Haram crisis broke out, the STF remained very visible on the streets of Jos. While major clashes continued in rural areas close to Jos until late 2016, no heavy fighting broke out again in Jos, despite

---

[165] Mohammed, July 2015.    [166] Mark, July 2015.

tensions around national and local elections and several bombings perpetrated by Boko Haram. The STF, initially deployed as a temporary security measure, remained stationed in Jos throughout 2017.

## Conclusion

This chapter analysed how communal war in Jos and Plateau State erupted based on long-standing tensions over indigene rights and local politics that led to increasing ethnic and religious polarization. The daily violent practice of vigilantes and gangs, the mobilization and politicization of these networks, and their alignment with the politics of ethnic associations and religious institutions, provided the organizational potential for mass killings, as the more than 1,000 victims during five days of clashes in 2001 amply demonstrated. Polarization and traumatization increased unarmed civilian support to gangs (and militias in rural areas) and enabled mobile armed groups to perpetrate attacks even when security forces began deploying on the main streets. Support from local communities meant that armed men could march through backstreets, avoid military and police forces, and hide in family homes after clashes until the state of emergency ceased and they could return to their own areas.

Patterns of violence in the Jos conflict consisted of pogroms only during the very first days of clashes in 2001, when religious minority populations were expelled from large and central neighbourhoods, such as Angwan Rogo, Apata, and Angwan Rukuba. Thereafter, violence patterns consisted primarily of attacks by mobile fighters on the minorities of other neighbourhoods, often jointly organized with residents from the targeted area, and frontal battles between armed groups from different neighbourhoods. In rural areas, fighting was carried out by well-armed militias, and often resulted in massacres of families and village communities.

Compared to conflict escalation in Ambon and Maluku Province of Indonesia (Chapter 4), Nigerian security forces were better able to halt the escalation process in Jos. While Maluku is a small province in Indonesia's eastern periphery, Jos is centrally located in Nigeria. The military deployed in such heavy numbers that it contained the transformation of gangs into militias and prevented militia control over the city. Even though groups of fighters could reach other neighbourhoods for attacks when using backstreets, the long-term presence of military peacekeepers, particularly after the 2010 crisis, meant that armed groups did not become strong enough to attack anywhere within and around Jos. In rural areas, however, security forces were hardly able to bring militia fighting under control. Senior military officers in Jos understood their task as a temporary suppression of fighting. Despite widespread fears of renewed violence after the 2010 clashes, the lack of a political settlement of the conflict, and the legacy of previous mass violence, Jos did not suffer further clashes from late 2011. Residents credited local peacebuilding programs for bringing youth from violence-prone neighbourhoods and community leaders together for building resistance against further instigation of fighting. These peace efforts were partly modelled after the community efforts that effectively prevented killings in the largest non-violent neighbourhood in Jos, called Dadin Kowa. It is to the analysis of non-violence in Dadin Kowa, and failed prevention efforts in the neighbouring community of Anglo Jos, that we now turn.

# 7 | *(Non-)Violence and Civilian Agency in Jos, Nigeria*

This chapter focuses on the micro-level comparison of the violent and non-violent communities Anglo Jos and Dadin Kowa, which administratively belong to Jos South Local Government Area (LGA). Although the root causes of the Jos conflict lie in the creation of Jos North LGA and political competition over indigene status and land rights, in the southern neighbourhoods of Jos City, ethnic and religious relations have been similarly polarized. Bukuru, an urban area to the south of Jos, which has practically merged with Jos into one city and is home of the headquarters of Jos South LGA, suffered heavy clashes and much destruction in September 2001 and in January 2010. Years later, many streets remained littered with the remnants of houses burned down during the fighting. After the 2010 clashes, the major market of Bukuru became religiously segregated and markets sprang up in Christian- and in Muslim-dominated areas. Similar to the Jos city centre, Bukuru had a sizeable Hausa population who demanded recognition for their chief (traditional leader) by the state government, while the Berom insisted that Bukuru was built on Berom land.[1] In the neighbourhoods of Anglo Jos and Dadin Kowa, non-indigenes were the majority population, but the land was regarded as Berom land and a Berom chief was recognized as the traditional leader.[2]

Anglo Jos and Dadin Kowa both included poor settlements as well as middle-class houses. While Anglo Jos was a relatively small neighbourhood bordering Hwolshe to the north, Kufang and Dadin Kowa to the south, the express highway to the east and Rantya to the west, Dadin Kowa is a much larger area with open land towards the south, where Bukuru and Gyel are located. Anglo Jos and Dadin Kowa were very tense during all major clashes in Jos. While Dadin Kowa managed to

---

[1] Bukuru is part of Gyel and Du districts, which are Berom and have a Berom senior chief.

[2] Residents from Anglo Jos and Dadin Kowa, 2010, 2015.

Table 7.1 *Demographic estimates for Anglo Jos and Dadin Kowa*[3]

|  | Population Size | Ethnic Composition | Religious Composition |
|---|---|---|---|
| **Anglo Jos** | Approximately 27,000 | Berom: 10% Yoruba: 8% Hausa: 15% Igbo: 6% Others: 61% | **Christians: 70%** (COCIN 40%; Evangelical 40%; Catholic 10%; Pentecostal 10%) **Muslims: 30%** (Izala 35%; Darika 55%; Shi'a 10%) |
| **Dadin Kowa** | Approximately 45,000 | Berom: 10% Yoruba: 12% Hausa: 15% Igbo: 13% Others: 50% | **Christians: 60%** (COCIN 30%; Evangelical 35%; Catholic 15%; Pentecostal 20%) **Muslims: 40%** (Izala 30%; Darika 50%; Shi'a 20%) |

avert killings, Anglo Jos was devastated during the January 2010 violence.

## Local Geography of Violence

While both the city centre of Jos and Bukuru to the south were repeatedly hit by communal violence, several middle-class neighbourhoods in between these two worst-hit areas – such as Rantya and State and Federal Lowcost – were spared from killings. These neighbourhoods had arranged community meetings and mixed youth vigilante groups to preserve good inter-group relations. Residents in Jos did not regard these neighbourhoods as vulnerable to communal violence. Large and quiet streets, gated houses, and compounds protected by private security guards made effective policing in these areas much easier than in the

---

[3] These numbers are estimates based on information collected from community leaders, ward heads, religious leaders, and residents. No official statistics exist. Estimates were collected with support from a research assistant who had family ties in both neighbourhoods.

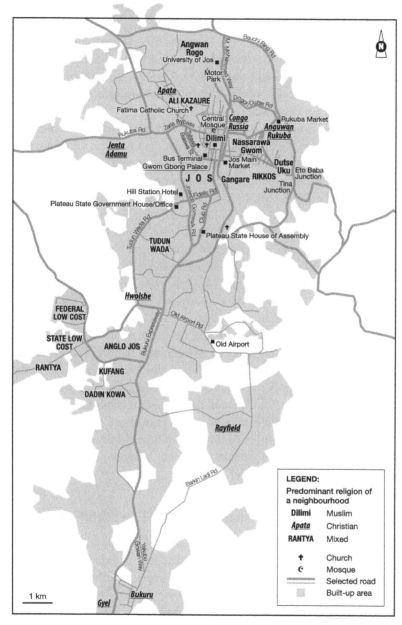

**Map 7.1** Religious segregation in Jos

overcrowded and violence-prone neighbourhoods. Security forces were present, private security was available to many middle-class houses, and community leaders agreed to prevent the instigation of violence. Killings of Muslim families took place in Mai Adiko, a poor area on the outskirts of the rich neighbourhood of Rayfield. The only religiously and socio-economically mixed and vulnerable neighbourhood in Jos that remained peaceful was Dadin Kowa.

Anglo Jos and Dadin Kowa lie in close proximity to the violence-prone neighbourhoods of Tudun Wada, Hwolshe, and Bukuru. Christian and Muslim youth from these neighbourhoods had fought during the clashes in 2001, and tensions remained high in these areas. Tudun Wada was also badly affected in 2008. The 2010 Jos clashes were sparked on 17 January by a dispute over the rebuilding of a house in the city centre, which had been destroyed during the November 2008 riot. On 19 January 2010, two days later, Berom men from Gyel and the villages Du and Zawan near Gyel fought the Hausa and other Muslim residents in Bukuru.[4] During the same morning, Christians fought Muslims in Anglo Jos in alliance with Berom Christians from the neighbourhoods of Hwolshe and Kufang. The next morning, when the military had deployed along the main roads, Christians from Gyel marched up to Dadin Kowa through the backstreets and tried to attack its Muslim population. The attack on Anglo Jos and the attempted attack on Dadin Kowa took place in the context of large-scale Berom militia mobilization. On 19 January, and during the following days, Christian Berom groups attacked a large number of Hausa and Fulani villages on the southern outskirts of Jos. According to representatives of the Plateau State Muslim Ummah, 726 Muslims were killed in attacks on rural villages south of Jos in January 2010.[5]

## Communal Violence in Anglo Jos: Failed Prevention Efforts

The population of Anglo Jos was ethnically and religiously very mixed. The predominantly poor settlement included middle-class areas and was surrounded by affluent neighbourhoods, such as Rantya and State and Federal Lowcost. Anglo Jos was centrally located near several large and important factories, and included a major neighbourhood market before the 2010 clashes. To the

---

[4] Higazi 2013, p. 55.   [5] Plateau State Muslim Ummah 2010.

north, it bordered Hwolshe, a predominantly Christian area with a sizeable Berom population, and to the south Kufang was located, a mostly Christian and Berom neighbourhood. Kufang included a small Muslim minority that remained unthreatened because some of them were ethnic Berom.[6]

Before the violence, Anglo Jos was 'a very busy area with many shops and a central marketplace'.[7] The main road entrance into Anglo Jos from the Bukuru Expressway led straight to the blackened remnants of the neighbourhood's market, burnt down during the January 2010 clashes. Thereafter, it served as the dividing line in a religiously segregated neighbourhood. Prior to those clashes, internal segregation had slowly grown in the aftermath of the 2001 and 2008 clashes because tensions were high even though violence was averted. Christians moved out of central Anglo Jos, which had been majority Muslim and Hausa, while Muslims left other settlements – Kambel, Owbolo and Folvorok – within Anglo Jos.

The Berom–Hausa conflict that dominated the situation in Jos North LGA reverberated in Anglo Jos. Christian respondents emphasized that the neighbourhood's land belonged to the Berom as the host community.[8] Some residents from Anglo Jos explained that they were deeply affected by the clashes in Jos in 2001 and 2008, having lost relatives and having seen the destruction in other neighbourhoods. Some stated that even though no fighting took place in their immediate area, they could hear the clashes in other neighbourhoods, see the smoke, and hear people scream. Market women stated that thereafter, a quiet segregation took place among many of them, and few talked about the killings with members from the other group. Given the high levels of tension, middle-class families who could afford to leave the neighbourhood moved into other areas, and internal segregation between Muslim and Christian settlements became more pronounced after the 2001 clashes.

## Violence Prevention Efforts

The political cleavage and claims to political representation that characterized the conflict over Jos North LGA impacted communal

---

[6] Muslim residents, Kufang, July 2015.
[7] Victor, Christian youth leader, Anglo Jos, June 2011.
[8] Christian resident, Anglo Jos, June 2011.

relations in Anglo Jos. Elections for neighbourhood-level political positions were contested between the Berom and the Hausa. According to a Muslim elder, the Muslim population of Anglo Jos respected the Berom chief as the traditional leader of the community. However, Christian Berom residents accused their Muslim neighbours of disrespecting Berom claims to the land. From their perspective, Muslims in Anglo Jos identified with the Jasawa[9] claims to political representation in Jos North LGA and recognition of their traditional leaders in Jos South LGA, including Bukuru.[10] According to a Muslim youth leader, in 2009, one of the Muslim Hausa residents from Anglo Jos had contested for the position of ward councillorship for the area that includes Anglo Jos, Kufang, and a part of Dadin Kowa. The man and his parents had lived in Anglo Jos all their lives, but he was an indigene from the neighbouring Taraba State in central Nigeria. Due to the minority of Muslims in Anglo Jos and a strong Berom population in Kufang, the Muslim Hausa candidate never had a realistic chance of winning this position.[11] Nevertheless, some Berom complained: 'How can somebody from another state contest for the councillorship? You give somebody a place to stay and he takes it away from you.'[12]

During the 2001 and the 2008 Jos clashes, residents feared fighting within Anglo Jos. Community and youth leaders met to set up a watch group to protect the neighbourhood. Anglo Jos was fortunate to be located outside Jos North LGA, some distance from the worst-affected neighbourhoods in the city centre. However, the September 2001 clashes lasted for five days, and the fighting spread when armed men who had driven out the minority group within their own neighbourhood sought to continue fighting in other parts of the city. In Hwolshe, a large and predominantly Christian neighbourhood next to Anglo Jos, Muslim residents were killed or expelled in 2001. Therefore, geographic location would not have kept Anglo Jos safe. Muslim and Christian respondents recounted that during the last two days of the clashes in 2001, an armed Christian youth group from Hwolshe marched into Anglo Jos to attack the Muslim population to revenge the killings of Christians in the city centre. These armed men had

---

[9] The term 'Jasawa' means 'Hausa of Jos' and is related to claims of political representation in Jos; see Chapter 7 for an explanation.
[10] Christian and Muslim residents in Anglo Jos, 2010–2015.
[11] Christian residents, Anglo Jos, July 2015.
[12] Usman, Muslim youth leader, Anglo Jos, July 2015.

already killed and expelled their own Muslim neighbours. However, a Christian pastor from Anglo Jos stopped them and forbade fighting in his neighbourhood, and no killings took place.[13]

According to the Christian youth leader, in 2008, tensions were again very high, but their Muslim neighbours 'brought down tensions' because 'their boys came out to the main road to block any advancing armed group and guard the neighbourhood.'[14] A Muslim elder stated that community leaders had meetings about violence prevention with members of the security forces and the district head in the context of the 2001 and 2008 clashes. However, youth leaders from Anglo Jos did not provide any details of these meetings in interviews.

## The January 2010 Clashes in Anglo Jos

Tensions remained high in Jos after the 2008 post-election violence. Despite the community's experience of vulnerability to external armed groups and having effectively prevented killings, violence prevention meetings died down prior to the 2010 clashes. Anglo Jos had some elders who supported prevention efforts, among them the traditional Berom leader of the neighbourhood and several Muslim elders. Almost a year after the clashes took place in Anglo Jos, the Berom leader explained:

I tried my best to get along with the community leaders here to prevent the crisis from happening. You may have heard about my efforts. We had meetings; we thought that we would preserve peace. We had a joint vigilante group. With everything that I did, I was trying to preserve the peace. In the end, the clashes came to us by surprise. Suddenly, there was smoke everywhere, and everyone was moving. My house was burnt and I took my family to the police station. Then I had to stay with relatives.[15]

Victor, the Christian youth leader who was part of the post-violence prevention network in Anglo Jos, only vaguely recalled the 2010 clashes in his neighbourhood:

One cannot understand what prompted the people of this community to go into violence; we heard gunshots, stones, and burning of houses within this

---

[13] Residents, Anglo Jos, 2010–2015. This Christian pastor had moved into a different state in Nigeria and I was not able to meet him.
[14] Victor, June 2011.
[15] Berom traditional leader of Anglo Jos, December 2010.

community ... and so the Christian community rose up to defend its territory.[16]

By contrast, Hassan, a Muslim elder, gave a very detailed account of how, on 19 January 2010, Anglo Jos was attacked by an armed Christian group from Hwolshe and Kufang:

> These are our neighbours, we grew up with them together, we went to school with them together, we played football with them together. All of a sudden, the peace was shattered. What happened in Jos metropolis came back to us. People came down from Kufang [and from Hwolshe]. We began to wonder what was happening. Previously, when something like this happened, we had an agreement that there should not be any violence. But this time the situation became uncontrollable. We cannot say what exactly was the reason, but I think it must have been a planned attack. If it had not been planned, it could not happen so coordinated and simultaneously like this, and we could have prevented fighting among neighbours in Anglo Jos. It was an attack and we were defenceless because we did not expect this to happen. You have seen the level of destruction. And why the violence? They are our friends. We socialized together. We have seen them. There is no way we don't identify them, no way![17]

According to Benjamin, a Christian resident from Hwolshe, among his Christian neighbours there 'was enmity towards Muslims even though there were no more Muslims in Hwolshe'.[18] He explained that people were angry over the 2010 clashes in the centre of Jos, and were saying, 'they are killing our people in town and we should support our people.'[19] The Muslims in Anglo Jos were the closest 'enemy population' to fight. Benjamin explained that the military first prevented the Hwolshe men from entering Anglo Jos and later prevented a larger number of casualties. He further remembered that community leaders in Hwolshe 'did not expect anything to happen and felt ashamed afterwards; they have strongly forbidden the youth from going out to fight again'. Mohammed, a Muslim respondent, said that the soldiers had done their best to prevent violence, but that they were outnumbered.[20]

According to some Christian respondents, Berom men from Kufang and Hwolshe forced them into collaborating against the Muslims by identifying their neighbours' houses and contributing to their

---

[16]  Victor, June 2011.    [17]  Hassan, June 2011.    [18]  Benjamin, July 2015.
[19]  Benjamin, July 2015.    [20]  Mohammed, Anglo Jos, June 2011.

destruction.[21] Emmanuel, a Christian respondent, stated that even though the Berom were a minority in Anglo Jos, in collaboration with Berom groups from other neighbourhoods they forced Christians in Anglo Jos to support the Berom political agenda and display loyalty. Furthermore, feelings of revenge were entertained within some churches.[22] Muslim respondents said that the Christian youth from Anglo Jos had invited the Berom Christians to fight their Muslim neighbours.[23]

My respondents from Anglo Jos, Hwolshe, and Kufang remained reserved about the motives behind the attack. Some referred to it as a 'criminal act', fighting in the name of enmity and revenge, with motivations to loot. One youth leader explained that he saw the killings as linked to the 2008 clashes in Jos because some Christians had relatives who were killed during post-election violence around Bauchi Road, a major Muslim area with a reputation for killings of Christians at road blocks. Christians from Hwolshe had also been affected by the 2008 killings and wanted revenge. He further confirmed that most of the people who participated in the killings came from outside Anglo Jos.[24]

I identified peer group pressure among the youth as one distinct factor. Young men from the neighbourhoods of Anglo Jos, Hwolshe, Kufang, and Dadin Kowa regularly met at a football pitch behind Anglo Jos. The youth from Anglo Jos and Dadin Kowa were often mocked as cowards for not having taken part in the fighting.[25] Apart from the youth in more affluent areas, such as Rantya, State and Federal Lowcost, and Rayfield, men from Anglo Jos, Dadin Kowa, and Kufang remained the only ones who did not fight in either 2001 or 2008. Knowing that the Christians in Dadin Kowa would not allow fighting in their neighbourhood, some of the youth from Kufang and Anglo Jos were eager to fight the Muslims in Anglo Jos, while the Hwolshe youth had already 'proven themselves' in fighting.[26]

According to Daniel, a Christian respondent who had family in Anglo Jos, Dadin Kowa, and Kufang, the Christian men from Kufang and Hwolshe first debated attacking the Muslim population of Dadin Kowa. Since they lacked support for an attack from Christians in

---

[21]  Christian youth in Anglo Jos, 2010–2015; see also Duffield 2010.
[22]  Emmanuel, November 2010.    [23]  Muslim residents, Anglo Jos, 2010–2015.
[24]  Usman, June 2011.    [25]  Christian and Muslim youths, Jos, 2010–2015.
[26]  Benjamin, July 2015.

Dadin Kowa, they decided to fight the Muslims in Anglo Jos instead.[27] Kufang is located between Anglo Jos and Dadin Kowa, therefore men from Hwolshe and Kufang could have planned an attack on Muslims in Dadin Kowa and entered the neighbourhood from Kufang. Instead, they assembled and attacked Anglo Jos.

According to Muslim respondents, the authority of the traditional Berom leader who had tried to preserve peace was undermined because Christians accused him of being too supportive of his Muslim neighbours.[28] The Christian pastor from Anglo Jos who had prevented fighting in 2001 had retired and left Anglo Jos, and no religious leader emerged in his place to forbid the youth from Hwolshe and Kufang from entering the area. Both Muslim and Christian youth were confident that if the Christian religious leader who previously prevented fighting had remained in Anglo Jos, he would have averted killings again.

Furthermore, a communication and collaboration gap between youth leaders and elders became instrumental for the clashes. One youth leader explained that when there were tensions in the community, people would not even think about going to the ward head to solve them. Instead, problems were handed down to the youth leaders directly.[29] As a result, the social dynamics among the youth from these neighbourhoods and plans for further attacks were not communicated to elders and religious leaders. Elders on both sides were unaware of the amount of pressure on the Christian youth to collaborate on attacks against their Muslim neighbours. They also underestimated the level of mobilization and preparations for a coordinated attack. No detailed discussions of threat and attack scenarios had taken place, and no agreements existed with youth leaders from Hwolshe and Kufang that could have prevented an attack on Anglo Jos. Mohammed, a Muslim youth leader active in violence prevention efforts, explained that such attacks on neighbourhoods were in principle preventable:

These things happened because there was no right person to talk to at that time. Because I remember that there was a time when there was a Reverend here in charge of the Hausa service. And during the conflict, people from Hwolshe came and wanted to engineer the fight [in 2001].

[27] Daniel, December 2010.    [28] Muslim residents, Anglo Jos, July 2015.
[29] Adib, June 2011.

*Q: Had they already come into Anglo Jos?*
Yes. And when they came, the Reverend stood and said: 'You will not go anywhere.' The only way you can go into this community to fight is when they kill him. And they went back.

*Q: Why did they not just attack anyway?*
You see, they cannot just do that. As things are, there were people behind the Reverend. There were youth who said, 'we don't want to fight.' So it was not just the Reverend standing there on his own. And also, the religious leaders are important. People respect them. That is why they need to be part of conflict prevention.

*Q: And the Reverend's house was on the way between Hwolshe and Anglo Jos, or how did he even know that an armed group was coming to attack?*
You see, the way it is with attacks, the leaders are aware. You will hear people talking about it. When we train people in violence prevention, we train them about the warning signs. If a Reverend, a Father or a pastor, or an imam, is within the community and he sees that people are grouping, people are discussing, then he knows that there is an issue. Maybe he begins to hear this group saying, 'we're going to fight Muslims,' and he hears another group saying this, and some people will try to hide such things from him. As a wise person – because before you become a clergy person, you're somebody who thinks deeply – you will see that they're saying some people are coming to cause problems. And you can decide, no we can't have this. You ask which way they are coming from. You tell them to go and block the roads. If religious leaders would do their best, we would not have these problems. You have to call bad people out by name.[30]

After the fighting in January 2010, community and youth leaders met again in efforts to prevent further killings. Many families in Anglo Jos were too poor to relocate, necessitating prevention and reconciliation efforts that would enable Christian and Muslim neighbours to continue living in the same area. Anglo Jos completely religiously segregated. A year after the fighting, vigilante leaders that I interviewed on both sides remained paranoid that 'outsiders' could infiltrate the neighbourhood and gather information on settlement patterns in preparation for another attack.[31] One Christian vigilante leader accused Muslim outsiders of entering his neighbourhood at night and spying out housing patterns. He explained that he was afraid that once Muslim groups had

---

[30] Mohammed, July 2015.
[31] Muslim and Christian vigilante leaders, June 2011.

enough information on the housing patterns and location of youth leaders and vigilantes, they would launch an attack against Christians in Anglo Jos.[32] A Christian youth leader stated that both sides made frantic efforts to prevent further killings:

You know what the situation is like within any deteriorated community. . . . We do our best as Christian community to bring people under control. But when the clashes happened, we could not control it. Our religious leaders have been brought together by an organization, but we still have difficulties. So this is how people are living now, with all the fears and tensions. In December 2010, after the Christmas bombings, another invited troop came into our neighbourhood and before we knew what was happening, we heard gunshots again. So people rose again to defend their territory, but fortunately the worst was prevented.[33]

Youth in and around Anglo Jos were among the first to retaliate against Muslims after the Christmas Eve bombings perpetrated by Boko Haram in 2010, and only the deployment of the special task force prevented further clashes. After the incident, youth leaders, together with security forces, improved communication networks to prevent further killings. In conclusion, collaboration of external armed youth with residents from Anglo Jos, and the lack of community leaders who intervened to prevent fighting, account for the January 2010 violence in this neighbourhood.

## Non-Violence in Dadin Kowa

Dadin Kowa was the only religiously, ethnically, and socio-economically mixed and vulnerable neighbourhood not devastated by clashes. The community became well known for its prevention efforts.[34] NGO peacebuilding programmes came to learn from Dadin Kowa's community leaders and facilitated replication of the model of community meetings and prevention strategies in other violence-affected neighbourhoods in Jos.

### Local Geography and Composition of the Neighbourhood

Many Jos residents regarded Dadin Kowa as the largest and most vulnerable mixed neighbourhood where no clashes took place. Parts

---

[32] Christian vigilante leader in Anglo Jos, December 2012.
[33] Victor, June 2011.     [34] Krause 2011c; Walker 2011.

**Figure 7.1** A street in Dadin Kowa[35]

of Dadin Kowa were predominantly poor, with high housing density and limited street infrastructure, while other newer settlements to the east and south of the area included middle-class compounds. To the east, Dadin Kowa bordered the middle-class neighbourhoods of Rantya and Federal and State Lowcost, where no killings had taken place. To the south, Dadin Kowa linked directly to Bukuru and Gyel.

Demographically, Dadin Kowa was as ethnically and religiously mixed as Anglo Jos. The area was divided into several subcommunities with different population mixes. The Jos conflict and the years of tensions impacted the resident population in Dadin Kowa despite the prevention of violence, and areas within the community became increasingly segregated after the 2008 Jos clashes. Around the first and second gates, the streets that lead from the Bukuru Expressway into the neighbourhood, central Dadin Kowa had been predominantly Muslim and Hausa. After the 2008 riot, Christians started moving out of this area. The settlement around the third and last gate remained religiously mixed, with Muslim and Christian houses standing side by side. The area called Angwan Baki had been predominantly Christian,

---

[35] Photo credit: Jana Krause.

and most of the few Muslim families left the area. New Abuja, a large area in the southern part of Dadin Kowa that included many new houses and middle-class compounds, had been majority Christian, and equally became almost exclusively so after 2008. Finally, the area called Akawu used to be majority Muslim but became almost exclusively Muslim after the 2008 riots.

The political conflict between Berom and Hausa elites also reverberated in Dadin Kowa. Non-indigene Christian leaders predominantly agreed with Berom claims to the land of the region and to political domination, criticizing the Hausa and Fulani elite for seeking political representation. Muslim respondents referred to the need to recognize the electoral results in Jos North LGA, which reflected the Hausa and Fulani elite's position that fair elections would give them an electoral victory in the LGA. During the 2001, 2008, and 2010 clashes, youth groups in Dadin Kowa mobilized to fight and rumours of clashes were circulating. In January 2010, one external Christian armed group from Gyel marched towards Dadin Kowa to fight its Muslim population, but the intervention of a community leader averted clashes. How did community leaders in Dadin Kowa prevent killings?

## Collective Agency and Violence Prevention

### Depolarization of Social Identities

Communal relations in Dadin Kowa reflected the political conflict cleavages as well as everyday conflicts between Muslim and Christian residents, such as competition at the local market or grievances over the use of loudspeakers at churches and mosques during prayer times. Moral outrage and traumatization over the killings of relatives and friends in other areas fuelled religious polarization and threatened to destabilize the community. In addition, community leaders held strong political views that largely reflected the Christian Berom and the Muslim Jasawa conflict narratives.

When I asked Festus, a Berom Christian religious leader, what he would do when he heard rumours, he said he had no idea whom to call among the community or youth leaders, demonstrating that not all religious leaders were part of Dadin Kowa's prevention networks.

*Q: Do you hear rumours here about imminent attacks?*
It's very common. Rumours are causing a lot of problems. Because sometimes we just hear 'people from that place are coming.' There are the ones who are always afraid, and I remember for many times people have been calling me, 'Pastor, we have heard that people from Bukuru are coming. And what can we do?' People from those areas, certain areas are coming. But I think this is a problem – the rumours, sometimes even the church, they will say, we have heard about Islam, the Muslims are planning to attack us. Somewhat like that.

*Q: And what do you do when you hear these rumours?*
We have not ever taken the time to confirm if the rumour is true. When it comes, it passes, and we forget about it.[36]

However, leaders contributed to an explicit meaning-making of the conflict situation that rejected the overall Jos conflict narrative and the implicit loyalties to the Berom Christian and the Muslim Jasawa political agendas. On the one hand, both sides disagreed with the political claims of the Berom Christian and Muslim Jasawa groups. On the other hand, they emphasized that all needed to be able to live together in Dadin Kowa, and that all belonged in this neighbourhood and required protection. Moreover, women's groups were very active in fostering a 'we-identity' across the religious divide that focused on being 'people of Dadin Kowa' and residents of a tolerant and peaceful place. Meaning-making and identity formation across the conflict cleavage were objectives painstakingly achieved by a committed number of community leaders and residents. Together, their efforts depolarized communal relations to a level that facilitated maintaining inter-group communication for violence prevention.

Christian elders in the community held strong opinions against the Jasawa elite of Jos. One of them was Timothy, a very influential Christian community leader. Timothy was originally from the south of Nigeria and could himself not obtain indigene rights for his children. He was strongly opposed to the Jasawa political elite and understood the situation in Jos as an attempt to overthrow the local people and take over their domain:

Jos is in the central geographical position of Nigeria. It has remained an un-Islamized patch in Northern Nigeria. They use politics and commerce to

[36] Festus, December 2010.

penetrate the local governments. But somehow, God has not allowed a full-scale Islamization of this place. During military rule, the Muslims dominated the affairs of the governors of this country. They worked on this area and created a local government [for the Muslims] and brought in aliens. But the Christians were more numerous, so they have been subjected to what I term a 'mental slavery'. In the sense that 'you are down, you will always remain down.' You don't need to aspire for rulership, you don't need to aspire for greatness. The Muslim attitude is 'we will give you and you will have to depend on us.' So Muslims have come to believe that they will always at all times have their way in Jos. And God has been helping us [Christians] here. They are getting the stiff resistance from us.[37]

Festus held similarly strong views against the Jasawa elite, even though he actively persuaded the youth not to mobilize for killings. Festus saw the Jos conflict as part of a broader regional confrontation:

Another problem we have in Jos is the treatment that has been meted out on our people outside, in other Muslim states. We see we are different. Because we have accepted everyone, everyone that comes to Plateau is accepted, but if we [Christians] go to other places we are not accepted. So when they [Jasawa] say 'indigeneship', they don't recognize that in other states that one has to recognize them [the Christians] there. And that is the problem. If in that state I am being denied from that right, if I come home I will also do the same thing. And I think that is the problem that is happening. But if [federal] government will tackle that problem, I think it would help.[38]

Even though Timothy and other leaders held very strong views against the Jasawa elite in Jos, he did not question the right of his Muslim neighbours to live in Dadin Kowa and to be protected by him and other Christians:

If somebody is living in our midst, then the person wants to live with us. You don't need another sign. You can be assured that this person who has built this house, no matter the type of house, and is living therein would want to stay. So you extend that person a hand of communality. Not that the person should interfere in indigenous rights, no. But the person should be protected, should be accommodated. So that there will be coexistence of one another. What made Dadin Kowa peculiar is that the parties are willing to live together. So if there is no willingness to seek peace, there is no way for peace. That's why I say that everything depends on enlightenment, education. You must preach peace, you must practise peace, you must live peace,

[37] Timothy, December 2010.     [38] Festus, December 2010.

you must accommodate the weaknesses of others and their faults. You must forget. And there will be peace. But where you are intolerant, where you believe it is you that must be adhered to, conflict will follow.[39]

Other elders similarly stated that they believed in living together with their Muslim and Christian neighbours, and that they saw themselves as a mixed and tolerant community. They emphasized their beliefs in common bonds of humanity to explain their actions of conflict management and depolarization. One Christian elder and former military officer, whom I call Nizar, concluded in the presence of a Muslim elder:

God created us all, we are all children of God. It is only the way we worship, but everybody calls on God when they pray. So, Muslims pray five times in the day; Christians say, pray without ceasing. So, we all fear God.[40]

I discussed with several elders how they dealt with the psychological impact of the crisis, having family members killed in other neighbourhoods, and hosting a large number of displaced persons and neighbours who wanted revenge. Moral outrage over atrocities and traumatization strongly polarized many other mixed neighbourhoods in Jos. Nurdeen, a Muslim elder, explained in the presence of Nizar that he strongly forbade revenge:

*Q: I can imagine that there is a lot of grief among the families and people might want revenge. Maybe it is difficult to talk about these things with the neighbours.*
God forbids revenge. We don't want revenge. It is better just to bear it. Leave everything to God, and just don't take law into our own hands.

*Q: And the other families in your community? Do they also think so?*
The majority of our families don't want to retaliate because there is no gain in fighting. The problem is the youth. They bring problems into the community, but the majority of people tell them, 'no, we don't want you to fight!' We don't allow it. Those who want to fight are a minority, so we can deal with them whenever problems arise. Like it is said in the Bible, if God did not protect this house, the builder, the owner, anything they do is in vain. It is only God that protects. So I believe that God will protect Dadin Kowa. Nothing will happen, since the majority agreed that nobody should fight, the youth should not fight. So I believe that nothing will happen and we will succeed.[41]

---

[39] Timothy, December 2010.　　[40] Nizar, December 2010.
[41] Nurdeen, December 2010.

Nurdeen made these interview statements in December 2010, several months before the 2011 presidential and state government elections, when most people in Jos feared renewed major clashes. At that time, no one in Dadin Kowa could know for certain that the community would remain able to prevent killings.

After the 2008 riots, women also played a major role in keeping peace in the community. A large number of displaced families fled to Dadin Kowa to settle with relatives, which upset the communal balance. Many residents began to worry about seeing strangers they had not grown up with and who were traumatized by what had been done to them in their neighbourhood. Women worried that their community could soon also be affected by violence. Some of the women who had found safety in Dadin Kowa had lost their husbands and children, their houses, and their businesses. They brought with them their grief, as well as stories of atrocities and loss. Seeing the state of the refugees and knowing the destruction within the city centre made some market women from Dadin Kowa aware of how much was at stake for them.

Prejudices and fears among women had a serious impact on everyday life because women ran the mixed market of Dadin Kowa. Tensions were so high that some women believed that the other religious group would try to sell them poisoned food to exterminate religious enemies. After the 2008 riot, women boycotted local food sellers and travelled into other neighbourhoods to buy from members of their own religious group even though the practice made food more expensive and threatened some sellers' livelihoods. In response to this tense climate, several mixed women's groups formed in Dadin Kowa with the objective of addressing communal tensions, building trust, and keeping the mixed market together to lessen the economic strain on families. Helena, one of the facilitators of these meetings from a local NGO, summarized her experiences in Dadin Kowa as follows.

*Q: What did the women talk about when you had your first women's meeting in Dadin Kowa?*
Many of the women were grieving about the fact that they were left widowed, they lost their sons, lost their children, they had to move house, they lost their houses, their businesses, their things. And they said, 'we are the ones left struggling. And nobody is noticing us. Nobody has ever asked us about peace, and we are the ones who are most affected.' They also said, 'we need to talk about peace and we need somebody to listen to us.'

*Q: And what was the result of this meeting?*
We encouraged the women to organize themselves. We told them, 'you all know who is your neighbour, so meet your neighbours and just organize yourselves.' And they organized into eleven different groups. And then we ran a workshop involving the group leaders and another person of the group. And they continued to meet without us.

*Q: And did these women become active during the 2010 riots?*
When the violence happened in January 2010, those women went to the imams and they went to the church leaders, and they said, 'we want no violence. We want you to come together and talk.' It was the women who called them to talk, and they did. They came together and nothing happened in that community.[42]

After the initial gathering through an NGO, the women regularly met in several smaller groups to address problems and establish dialogue with each other. When I asked a group of five women in Dadin Kowa, both Muslim and Christian, what they would do about problems and tensions in the community, they explained that they would deal with most of the problems among themselves. They would meet in groups of ten to fifteen women on an informal basis about once a month to discuss issues in the neighbourhood. These were not well-educated, middle-class women; none of them spoke English. We met (with my translator) in one of their houses, which was just as poor, dark, and crammed as many of the family homes I had visited in the most violence-prone parts of the city. The women stated, 'we tell our youth to stay at home if crisis happens and not to start fighting anywhere.'[43] Some of the women who joined these meetings explained that they did so secretly because their husbands did not approve of them meeting Muslim or Christian women. The women's peace efforts contributed to a sense of 'community' and 'we-thinking' in Dadin Kowa because the meetings fostered determination that their neighbourhood would not be devastated by clashes. Even though these women's activism was well known among the male elders and youth leaders, they did not reach all market women and tensions remained high. I interviewed one Muslim woman from the neighbourhood who expressed her worries and who had never heard of the women groups' meeting in her area:

[42] Helena, December 2010.    [43] Women group members, December 2012.

*Q: Do you meet with the women here in the community?*
No. The community, most of the people staying here, everybody is just on his own, nobody cares about anybody's problem. ... Us staying at this side, we don't meet each other and communicate about our problems, everybody just goes on his own.

*Q: Can you meet the Christian women at the marketplace?*
I will just go to the market and buy what I want to buy, afford what I can afford, and just go. I don't know if the market women discuss anything about the community. I don't know of that, but me, when I went to the market, I would just buy what I want to buy and just go. That's it.

*Q: Are you worried about the community?*
Yes, I'm worried. I'm very worried because of the situation that we are in. You can see the way children are staying at home. There is no work. Even the youths, they don't have work to do. They will just be roaming about and drinking. You will see them fighting, wounding themselves. A youth will finish his graduation and he will not have work to do. This is very bad. It's making the youth become rough. That's why you will see, when they say there is crisis, they will start burning things, fighting everybody, because they don't have work to do. That's the problem.[44]

## Consolidating Civilian Social Control
Respondents from Dadin Kowa explained that they worried much about idle and unemployed youth who abused drugs and alcohol and were easily mobilized. Residents, youth leaders, and elders worked together to persuade the youth not to start killings and to repress those they could not persuade with threats of physical punishment. When communal violence first broke out in September 2001, Dadin Kowa did not have any violence prevention networks or regular community meetings to address problems. The scale of the clashes in Jos was unprecedented and not anticipated by community leaders. Bem, a Berom youth leader from Dadin Kowa, remembered that tensions were very high in his neighbourhood because two Christian boys were shot.

In 2001, I remember, when Jos burst out into crisis. There was tension between us and our friends because I can remember, vividly, what brought about the tension was one Alhaji. He brought some soldiers to his house and

---

[44] Muslim female resident in Dadin Kowa, December 2012.

they shot down two boys [Christians] from here. Now when they shot down two boys from here, all of a sudden the communities from around heard rumours that the Muslims are killing Christians around here, and they all came in en masse. And so the traditional leader had to plead with them, no, no, no. It's not like that. He put more effort in calming the situation. And so as a result, well definitely, they damaged some mosques around us for vengeance.

*Q: From where did the Christians come? From which communities?*
All the surrounding communities.

*Q: Like Kufang, Anglo Jos?*
Yes, exactly. Because they learned that they were killing Christians around here. The traditional leader chose best to calm down the situation. But those two boys they shot down; as a result, it brought about some tension between us.[45]

Even though the clashes were concentrated in the city centre, rumours about imminent attacks reached Dadin Kowa. A newspaper report about the 2001 Jos riots stated:

Rumours were just flying about. There was stampede everywhere; rumours that some fake soldiers at Dadin Kowa were imported by one of the interest groups to kill people sent shivers down the spine of some people who would have loved to ply the road to their states for safety. It took the combined efforts of the deputy governor and the assistant inspector general of police in charge of zone four, Mr. Chris Obadan, to calm the situation at Dadin Kowa.[46]

The renewed escalation of fighting after the 9/11 attacks in 2001 that reverberated within the Muslim community in Jos was particularly challenging for people in Dadin Kowa because most security forces were bound up in the city centre. Violence prevention measures were ad hoc and not fully coordinated among all religious leaders and elders. Timothy stated that Dadin Kowa's Muslim leaders came to meet Christian elders for negotiation and collaboration. He remembered:

We tried to douse the tensions by talking to each other. We broke out the truth, that we want peace. Then we checkmated the dissidents, the boys that go anywhere. I believe that in any place where there is a problem of this type, the people [who] should be checked are those [who] smoke [drugs], you know, and the utterances of leaders. Because the utterances of leaders spark

[45] Bem, December 2012.   [46] *The Guardian Nigeria* 2001.

these wars. You know, they don't have anything at stake. They smoke, and then they say, 'let's go and destroy, let's go and destroy.' And the truth is that one destruction begets another destruction.[47]

Nizar, another Christian elder and retired military officer, also stated in the presence of a Muslim elder that Hausa elders from Dadin Kowa approached him to agree on non-violence:

> They came [the Hausa elders of Dadin Kowa], they came down here to meet us, and he [the leader] said he wanted negotiation, he wanted peace. He don't want fight. So we too, we don't want fight. But if you want it, we are ready for you! That's what I told him. So I summoned about four elders. We met and discussed, so please, go, no problem. Don't make trouble. And that's how they went back.[48]

Dadin Kowa did not host well-established gangs, as did other violence-prone neighbourhoods, but youth unemployment was as much a problem as elsewhere in town. Young men who spent their days around the first gate, the entrance from the main street into the neighbourhood, were seen as potential fighters. These were mostly unemployed men, who had often dropped out of school and who kept small jobs by selling fuel bottles on the street. These youth had neither formed into gangs nor were they completely religiously segregated. Although spending their time on the street, most of them still stayed with families or relatives in the community.

After the 2008 Jos clashes, the situation in Dadin Kowa became even more volatile because many displaced families from the city centre moved into the area. Their influx resulted in an economic burden to families in Dadin Kowa and increased the numbers of unemployed youth. Timothy explained how community leaders had to take particular care with the refugees who wanted revenge:

> Many refugees entered this place. And the refugees cry out what had happened to them. So then, some of them, they would have started, to their detriment. With the leaders, we all doused the tension, saying, 'No, no, no'.[49]

Respondents repeatedly explained that community leaders went to great effort to 'checkmate' these men. One resident recounted how he and his neighbours had tried to train some of the youth for jobs within

---

[47] Timothy, December 2010.   [48] Nizar, December 2010.
[49] Timothy, December 2010.

their small businesses to address their situation. Several women interviewed stated that they tried to keep these men under control by reporting any wrongdoing or suspicions to their husbands and elders. The potential threat that the 'youth of the first gate' represented was well recognized within the community.

On both religious sides, youth had tried to mobilize for fighting, and attempted to join the clashes in other neighbourhoods. Christian respondents acknowledged that some of the Christian youth had mobilized against their Muslim neighbours repeatedly and that it took community leaders much effort to calm the situation and prevent killings, while some of the Muslim youth had sought to fight alongside Muslims in other violence-affected neighbourhoods. In the presence of his friend, a Muslim elder, Nizar, a Christian elder who in 2010 persuaded the youth not to mobilize against Muslim neighbours, recalled:

I met the leader of the youth in this area. I am security conscious, and I know what war means. The youth wanted to fight when it started. From 11 o'clock at night they came out to me and said: 'Father, we want to deal with these people.' I said no. 'What do you have? If you want to go to war you must prepare yourselves. What do you have that you want to go out and fight?' And they said, 'We don't have weapons.' 'You don't have weapons? So you want to go and fight? And you think you will succeed? I tell you from my experience, if you have experienced war, you don't like to go out. Peace is the best here. So, I encourage you not to go out and fight and make trouble.' They were angry with me.[50]

Musa, the Muslim ward head, explained how he worked with other elders to establish control over the youth, and that his efforts were based on persuasion as much as repression of those who wanted to fight.

*Q: Did any of your youth go to the city to fight?*
We are telling our youth that they must be at home. Any time that something happens in town, we don't want anybody from here to enter town. You should be at home.

*Q: What do you do if some of the youths go to the city to fight?*
No.

*Q: But what if they do it anyways?*
Well, you don't always know what is in people's hearts. I can't say all the youths, but most of the youths do what I'm telling them all the time. All the

---

[50] Nizar, December 2010.

problem is with youth. If I gather my youth saying that I don't accept anybody to go outside, it's working. Everyone in this area here. So that is why I tell the youth not to go outside or not to camp out with anybody and that's how we did it.[51]

I also discussed these violence prevention efforts with Christian and Muslim youth leaders from Dadin Kowa. Tijian, one of the Muslim youth leaders, showed me the telephone list of community leaders in Dadin Kowa that indicated a clear hierarchy and the responsibilities of who was to inform whom about rumours and tensions. He summarized violence prevention efforts as follows:

We thank God because Dadin Kowa is a place of peace. It wasn't easy, but the people of the community said they need the peace and they tried to live in peaceful coexistence, and they do their best. We face challenges and we have learned to deal with things, such as idleness of some of our youth because they have nothing to do. Some use drugs. We do our best to create a very good network. We have built understanding between the Muslims and the Christians and also between the youth and then also the elders, whereby the youths do their own efforts. ... There is an elders' forum where they check-mate it [the youth who could incite violence] and we work well with the chairman of that elders' forum. We also have all the telephone numbers. It's the numbers, anything comes up we communicate, so there is a very good understanding between the religious leaders and also the community leaders. There is a lot of understanding, but it wasn't easy.[52]

Timothy and I also discussed the issue of mobilization in self-defence and acquiring weapons for self-protection. He acknowledged that weapons were circulating in his neighbourhood.

*Q: What do you do about weapons in Dadin Kowa? Do you have rules to enforce in the community? Maybe people are afraid and try to be prepared.*
People try to protect their lives. People don't wait for your rules and orders. They don't.

*Q: At the same time, it is dangerous if there are weapons.*
Yes, because everybody is afraid.

*Q: Do you think that both the Muslims in Dadin Kowa and the Christians acquire weapons because they are afraid?*
I cannot say Muslims. I cannot say Christians. I will say individuals.

---

[51] Musa, December 2012.   [52] Tijian, December 2012.

*Q: Do you think these individuals are using, for example, religious or ethnic networks to acquire weapons, or are they doing it individually?*
That is what I say I cannot say. I cannot say it is an association or it is they are Christians or they are Muslims. Why I say 'individuals' is that these individuals have no face. You cannot say whether they are Christians. You cannot say whether they are Muslims.[53]

Community leaders agreed to establish several basic rules and procedures to prevent fighting in their neighbourhood. They set up mixed youth patrol groups to guard the gates into Dadin Kowa, and approached the military and the police in a coordinated manner to maximize protection from often weak and unprofessional security forces. A community communication network involving the youth leaders on both sides was a further important aspect of violence prevention efforts. Nizar explained how the elders handled rumours about attacks and fighting:

*Q: When you hear rumours in your community about violence, plans to attack, what do you do about it?*
What we do, we call the youth. We are mounting three gates: one here, one this side, one at the back. So, if we hear any rumours, we quickly alert. I have the telephone number of the leader of the youth and summon all of them: 'This is what we have, this is what is happening. So, please, be careful. Don't take the law into your hands!' Because it is the youth that we are afraid of. So we have to talk to them, so that is what we do if we hear the rumour that something is likely going to happen, that's what we normally do. And the same do the Muslims too. They call their youth and talk to them.[54]

Some respondents who persuaded the youth not to mobilize explained that they perceived violence prevention as effective protection for themselves, their families, and their livelihoods. For example, one Berom elder who had also been part of the network that persuaded the youth not to fight in Dadin Kowa, stated: 'We think that the crisis has no achievement ... it is only loss, and loss mostly concerns the children and women.'[55] Women similarly stated that they actively tried to preserve the peace because fighting would cause much loss on all

---

[53] Timothy, December 2012.    [54] Nizar, December 2010.
[55] Berom elder, Dadin Kowa, December 2012.

sides. Festus remembered how in January 2010, he persuaded the youth not to mobilize and start killings:

What happened in the town angered the Christians here and they wanted to do something [i.e., fight]. On their own side, the Muslims, because they are a minority here, they came to us and they pleaded, 'Please don't allow, you should not allow.' And I went to our youth and asked them not to do anything.[56]

One respondent recounted that the Christians thought that they were stronger than the Muslims and they were ready to fight because 'they had long been accused of being cowards' by Christians from other neighbourhoods.[57] Timothy explained in detail how he used persuasion to work with the violence-prone youth, who included many Berom youth from the Berom-dominated settlement called Angwan Baki, within Dadin Kowa:

What we do is limited because we use persuasion. We use persuasion to call them to order. But I wonder how much persuasion you can use on an alcoholic. Be it as it may, persuasion is what we are using. Take, for instance, somebody from that area [Angwan Baki] who is a drunk and needs money to drink. When he doesn't have the money, he goes to look for menial work. If he doesn't find menial work, he steals. When you catch him, you throw him into prison, isn't it? When we catch him, we say, 'why did you steal?' He said, 'I'm hungry.' Will you call police to take him to prison? This person is hungry.

*Q: What do you do with this person?*
Well, you give him food first because food will make him to have sense. Then you can talk and say look, this attitude is not good. You see him respecting you. It does not deliver him from alcoholism but at least if he sees you, he tells you, he respects you. Hoping that when there is a problem and there are more people, perpetrators of this problem, if you come around, they will say, 'oh, we'll respect this person.'

*Q: Do you only have this problem with the youth in Angwan Baki, or also with the Muslim community?*
The Muslim community have their own youth who smoke a lot – marijuana, other things – they smoke a lot. They have their own. So it's the same method we are using.[58]

---

[56] Festus, December 2010.    [57] Daniel, December 2010.
[58] Timothy, December 2012.

## Engaging Armed Groups

Internally, elders, religious and youth leaders, and ordinary residents regularly met and persuaded the youth not to start killings and not to collaborate with outside armed groups for an attack on Dadin Kowa. While these prevention efforts were laborious, external negotiations and refusal to collaborate with armed groups was equally challenging but crucial for preserving local peace. Timothy and other community leaders established an extensive communication network in the region that included community and religious leaders from the neighbourhoods of Bukuru and Gyel, as well as Kufang and Anglo Jos. Elders and religious leaders met and agreed on a 'peace declaration' that was read out to the community of Dadin Kowa, but also announced in the neighbouring communities.[59]

Furthermore, Timothy and other elders negotiated regularly with security forces stationed within the area to solve problems, facilitate their patrolling, and secure favours with them. Internal consolidation of social control over the youth helped him and others to maintain relations with security forces, as he explained.

I persuade the youth to meet and discuss, for prevention. When they agree to meet, I carry their programme to the local police to inform them about who is meeting, and that the purpose is peace. Then the police will do their work.

*Q: Why are the police doing their work here? They don't function well in other communities.*
I am privileged to have an influence on them.

*Q: How do you have influence on them?*
First and foremost, I am a priest. We persuade the police, knowing that every human being has spiritual needs. They come to me with their needs. As you guide them, they respect you. At times, when they have official problems with their seniors and so on, they are afraid that their seniors will victimize them. And knowing that their senior comes for spiritual help and counsel to the Reverend, they come to me. They say, 'please, this and this, I have offended this person, this, this, this.' I said, 'okay, why will you do that? This is the way to go and then apologize.' Then on my own part, I will call their superior. . . . That's why if they hear that the Reverend calls, they will ask which Reverend. They will say, 'Reverend in New Abuja/Dadin Kowa', and they will rush.[60]

---

[59] Residents from Dadin Kowa, Bukuru, Anglo Jos, and Gyel, 2010–2015.
[60] Timothy, December 2012.

He further explained that he was not the only one who would regularly work with the police to secure local peace internally and externally. Muslim leaders and elders similarly worked with security forces to improve the safety of the neighbourhood.

Asked whether politicians would mobilize in Dadin Kowa and recruit followers among the youth, Timothy confirmed that politicians did try, but that Muslim and Christian leaders had frustrated their efforts and actively prevented the youth from being recruited into such networks.

The youth know that there are people of our likes in here. There are Muslims who think like me in this Dadin Kowa. They believe that there should be peace and they use their individual personal resources to go for it.

Q: *How do they use money?*
Ok, say for instance, you have a problem here. You call the police, the police will tell you they don't have fuel. You give them money for fuel because the government is not paying them. Then the police will come, 'Reverend, we've come to greet you. It's been a boring walk, we don't have food to eat and so on.' You give them food.

Q: *What about the soldiers?*
The soldiers are the same, but the soldiers move here and there. They should be taken care of. Their families are not here, so the communities plan and say, 'okay, we will cook them one meal a day.'[61]

Women from the women groups in Dadin Kowa confirmed that they regularly organized to cook for the soldiers to maintain good relations with them. These activities added another economic burden on poor families, and Timothy acknowledged that these were 'sacrifices for peace' that not everyone in the community was willing to make. The women's groups equally acknowledged that some of the women carried a disproportionate share of the burden of cooking for soldiers while other women did not join in.

In January 2010, two external Christian armed groups threatened Dadin Kowa. One was made up of the youth from Kufang, who in the end did not march into Dadin Kowa, but instead attacked Muslims in Anglo Jos, because they did not receive support from Christians in Dadin Kowa.[62] The second group came from Gyel. During the night and morning of 20 January, when the military had contained the

[61] Timothy, December 2012.    [62] Daniel, December 2012.

fighting in Bukuru, the fighters from Gyel marched through the back-streets into Dadin Kowa, calling on Christians to support them. Timothy confronted this armed group, refused to collaborate, and persuaded them to return without fighting. He recounted this incident at the end of year 2010 as follows:

*Q: What happened here during the 2010 riot?*
It has never been like that before early 2010. The tensions got to a point that many people attacked us.

*Q: How did they attack you?*
With guns, machetes, everything. They attacked me so that I should give way, so that they can kill. I said, 'you don't kill.'

*Q: And what happened then?*
I occupy a strategic position. If I am removed from here, the natives [Berom Christians] will come en masse and murder them [the Muslims]. So I am like the block, and the natives cannot come and cross this place and go against them because they would not want to hurt me or my people.

*Q: And what happened then? Did the police support you?*
The police really don't have enough people! We are talking of a population of 1,400,000 people [in Jos–Bukuru]. So how many policemen do we have? If you release the whole of Rukuba Barracks, the military, how many can there be? People started rumouring that Dadin Kowa is on fire already. People came out, but God took control.

*Q: And the people who threatened you?*
They went back to their places. Went back to their villages and organized to kill the Muslims. I said, 'you don't shed blood.'[63]

Although this account of single-handed violence prevention may surprise us, residents from Dadin Kowa and neighbouring areas confirmed the incident. One resident stated he had witnessed the Christian pastor delaying the approaching youth from Gyel. Christians in New Abuja supported Timothy by calling elders in Gyel to report on the armed group leaders and to enforce sanctions on them when they returned to Gyel.[64] They also called in the military. Timothy threatened the group leaders that they would not manage to finish their attack and move looted goods back to Gyel without serious risks to their lives. Daniel, a Christian resident who had observed the scene, commented that

[63] Timothy, December 2010.    [64] Daniel, December 2012.

tensions in Dadin Kowa were very high that morning and gunshots could be heard from the military moving into the surrounding areas. The discussion between the leaders of the armed group and Timothy slowed down the advancing group. Some started to leave as they lost the courage to proceed with an attack. Eventually, the Berom youth from Gyel and other Berom villages turned around and no attack took place, as he recounted:

There were people who wanted to come into Dadin Kowa, people from Gyel and other communities beyond Dadin Kowa. And there was a community leader from New Abuja who tried to convince them to go back. He is also a pastor. When they were coming they had to pass through his area. So he was able to stop them there and agree with them and convince them. I know he stopped them because I saw it with my own eyes. I know some people [armed groups] planned to go in [into Dadin Kowa]. Some of them were saying the Christians in Dadin Kowa are weak, and they are afraid, and things like that because they wanted support from the people in Dadin Kowa so that they would be able to come in. But people in Dadin Kowa did not support them, and that is why they were unable to come in.[65]

One respondent showed me the footpath that connected Gyel and New Abuja, explaining that the youth avoided being caught by soldiers already stationed on the Bukuru Expressway. The Gyel youth challenged Dadin Kowa's peace agreement, arguing that Muslims from Dadin Kowa had violated it first because some of them had fought alongside Muslims in Anglo Jos the previous day. However, Christians from Dadin Kowa refused to collaborate, instead following their leaders' orders.

## Triangulation

Why would external armed groups respect the position of Dadin Kowa's community leaders to reject fighting? In 2012 and in 2015, I questioned gang members from violence-prone neighbourhoods in the city centre, such as Nassarawa Gwom and Angwan Rukuba, about the prevention of killings in Dadin Kowa. I sought to verify that Dadin Kowa was indeed a community *vulnerable* to attacks from external armed groups, and that gang members believed that killings were prevented because of community leaders' decisive actions. Tony, one

[65] Daniel, June 2011.

former gang member from central Jos, described Dadin Kowa as 'part of the heartbeat of the town and an important area in Jos metropolis, because many economic activities take place there'.[66] Community developments in Dadin Kowa did not take place in isolation from the rest of the city of Jos. My respondents emphasized that during every Jos riot, Dadin Kowa was 'sitting on gunpowder'. Former perpetrators from the central neighbourhoods credited community leaders' effective prevention efforts, but noted that tensions remained high in Dadin Kowa because men were often mocked for not having fought. In 2015, after they had participated in several NGO-led peacebuilding programmes, they stated that they had links to some of the youth leaders from Dadin Kowa and encouraged them to preserve the local peace.[67]

Residents from Bukuru and Gyel explained that all the youth from neighbouring areas, including Gyel, Bukuru, Anglo Jos, and Hwolshe, knew that the community and youth leaders in Dadin Kowa had an agreement not to fight. The agreement was made public and presented at churches and mosques in other neighbourhoods, including Gyel. Timothy had met with the Berom traditional leader from Gyel and Christian pastors from neighbouring areas on a regular basis and ensured their support in preventing killings. Abraham, a Christian resident from Bukuru with family in Gyel and Dadin Kowa, explained why the armed group from Gyel and other villages was unable to enter Dadin Kowa for an attack:

*Q: If the men from Bukuru or Gyel want to fight in Dadin Kowa ...*
The boys from Dadin Kowa would show them where to fight.

*Q: And if the boys from Dadin Kowa say 'no' ...*
Then the boys will go back. If the boys from Dadin Kowa say, 'we don't want any problems because our fathers said we don't fight,' then no, they won't help, and all the boys will go back.

*Q: And if the boys from outside come in anyway and fight without the Dadin Kowa boys?*
No. ... There is an agreement with the church leaders and the Muslim leaders. If the boys from outside want to overcome them, then the Dadin Kowa boys will fight them. That's why Dadin Kowa in the whole of Jos was

---

[66] Tony, December 2012, July 2015.
[67] Former gang members from Angwan Rukuba and Nassarawa, July 2015.

saved. . . . Nobody goes there and comes back alive. They will also not help anybody go back safely to their places. . . . If you go there to fight, they will kill you. That's the agreement.[68]

When leaving their neighbourhood to fight in other parts of town, information regarding housing patterns and targets, the strength of opposing armed youth groups, and the strategies and location of security forces was essential for external fighters to lower their risk of being killed or detained in an attack. Mobile fighters without unarmed civilian support could be executed by security forces known for their brutality and extra-judicial killings.

In sum, Dadin Kowa averted killings because community leaders persuaded and controlled internal youths not to mobilize for killings; ordinary people – among them women groups – brought down tensions by addressing everyday conflicts and emphasizing a joint identity as 'people of Dadin Kowa' and neighbours with a right to live in the area and be protected; and community leaders engaged external community leaders, youth, gang and vigilante leaders in negotiations and refused collaboration for killings.

## Rescue Agency and Leadership

Dadin Kowa had no institutional framework in place that could have supported community leaders in the prevention of killings. Prevention efforts in 2001 and in 2010 took place on an ad hoc basis and were largely driven by the courageous initiative of Timothy, who was widely praised for his key role in preventing fighting, and other elders. Key leaders who persuaded the youth not to start killings had profound knowledge of conflict dynamics and previous experience of living in conflict environments. This experience taught them how to establish social control. Nizar, an influential Christian elder, had been a former military officer who had also been sent to peacekeeping missions abroad. Furthermore, Timothy, who was from the southeast of Nigeria, explained that he previously experienced the Nigerian civil war, and that those years had taught him how to deal with mobilized men:

One of the things that helped me was that I experienced the Nigerian civil war, because I come from the eastern part of the country. So, it informed me what to do and how to handle the people.[69]

---

[68] Abraham, July 2015.     [69] Timothy, December 2010.

Timothy and other elders stressed that in meetings with elders and youth leaders, potential threat scenarios were discussed in detail. Those who sought to prevent clashes anticipated which armed group could enter from where, and how to communicate to external community and youth leaders to prevent such attacks. Timothy summarized, 'we all repeatedly came together and strategized, and we made sure that this place is secure from insurgence and attack from outside armed groups.'[70]

Leaders and residents invested much time, resources and effort into the prevention of violence and the resolution of everyday conflicts. Dadin Kowa was no place of communal harmony. For example, I interviewed Bem, the Berom Christian youth leader from a Berom-dominated area within Dadin Kowa, who insisted that he was unable to negotiate with the Muslim youth leader because Muslims had no youth leaders. Bem made such statements even though other community leaders confirmed that several Muslim youth leaders were well recognized in Dadin Kowa. Bem acknowledged that some of the women who had organized in groups to address problems served as intermediaries between him and Muslim youth leaders, reliably transmitting information without requiring the youth leaders to meet in person. In 2012, Bem further explained that he found it increasingly difficult to calm the youth and prevent mobilization for an attack:

You might have a relative in town who lost his life due to crisis and so your grievances begin to build. So when it keeps building, our leaders, they try to calm the youth. And it has gotten to a stage that the youth don't listen anymore because they feel the elders are not leading them properly. Every time they tamper with you, you've been slapped, you complain, the traditional leader tries to calm you down, and then tomorrow you've been slapped again, they begin to withdraw from the traditional leaders. In fact, right now most of the youths in this area ... for me now, they trust me to some certain level. I've been trying to protect the trust because once you try to calm them down, and they don't see a positive result coming, the violence keeps escalating. They begin to stop trusting you.[71]

Despite having avoided violent clashes, Dadin Kowa remained highly volatile, and meetings to discuss conflicts did not always take place regularly with all relevant stakeholders. In an interview

---

[70] Timothy, December 2010.  [71] Bem, December 2012.

in December 2010, Festus , a Berom pastor, confirmed that he had not been in a meeting since the emergency situation in January 2010:

At the time of the crisis, we were able to meet, the Muslims and the Christians. I advise that if we want to maintain the peace a meeting should not be at the time when something is happening or something has happened. But it should be constant. It should be frequent. But the people responsible for the meeting are not calling the meeting.

*Q: And who is responsible for calling the meeting?*
Hmm ... We have the community leaders who are responsible to call the meeting. But nothing has been done since January [2010].

*Q: And who are your community leaders? Do you mean religious leaders, or traditional leaders?*
Traditional leaders! We have those who are in charge of the land, apart from us religious leaders. They are the ones responsible to call for this.

*Q: And do the Muslims also have a traditional leader whom everyone recognizes here?*
I don't think so. I am not sure.[72]

Dadin Kowa and Anglo Jos were under the rulership of the same traditional leader, who had been displaced during the January 2010 crisis when his own house was burned. Thus, he was unable to further call for official meetings, and passed away soon after. Muslims had no traditional leaders because these leaders were not officially recognized by the local government.

Youth leaders and elders stressed that they learned to deal with the tensions and challenges and that they adapted violence prevention efforts over time. After averting an attack in January 2010 and in anticipation of strong tensions over the 2011 national and state elections, Timothy and other community leaders proactively developed a stronger framework of rules and regulations to maintain social control and prevent clashes.

Similarly to Pastor John Sahalessy, who initiated violence prevention efforts in Wayame in Ambon, some residents from Dadin Kowa stressed that although Timothy had prevented clashes and was acknowledged as the most influential community leader, he was strongly disliked among many of his Christian neighbours. One

---

[72] Festus, December 2010.

Muslim woman from the neighbourhood explained that she greatly admired him for his courageous actions, particularly in confronting the armed group from Gyel and preventing killings.

> Some Christians dislike him and what he is doing because he confides in the Muslims, asks them for advice, for their opinions, and goes the extra mile to help them when there is need in the community. We always look up to him. Every time there is crisis in Jos he meets the religious leaders and they calm the youth. That is why crisis has never erupted in Dadin Kowa.[73]

## Conclusion

This chapter's comparative analysis of violence and non-violence in two neighbouring areas of Jos has demonstrated that non-violence in the mixed and vulnerable neighbourhood of Dadin Kowa was not an outcome predicted by structural factors, such as geography, demography, or the intervention of security forces. Instead, non-escalation was contingent on civilian agency and prevention efforts. Both the community of Anglo Jos and Dadin Kowa were threatened by internal youth mobilization and by external armed groups. Collaboration between external fighters and internal youth led to killings in Anglo Jos, while in Dadin Kowa leaders asserted social control over their youth and engaged external armed groups in negotiations to refuse collaboration in attacks. Community leaders announced their peace agreement in the neighbourhoods that hosted armed youth who could have attacked Dadin Kowa, and maintained a network for gathering information about potential attacks and for the strategic dissemination of messages to deter them.

Dadin Kowa was no place of harmony. Relations were tense, but leaders and residents actively worked on a sense of community and interpretation of the conflict situation that halted polarization. Civilian violence prevention efforts were proactive, foresighted, and laborious, and extended much beyond rumour control. Community leaders had the social knowledge to handle mobilizing youth and maintain violence prevention networks. Key leaders, particularly the Christian pastor Timothy, who displayed high-risk rescue agency, acted upon social knowledge and previous experience that he had gained during

---

[73] Muslim resident, Dadin Kowa, July 2015.

Nigeria's civil war, when he lived in the east of the country. This previous exposure to armed conflict informed him how to approach and engage mobilized youth, and how to anticipate and strategically counter potential attacks. Leaders were able to imagine threat scenarios, anticipate risks, and collectively strategize their efforts to maximize protection.

By contrast, violence prevention efforts in Anglo Jos eroded with the departure of the one Christian pastor who had most actively persuaded the youth not to start killings. The traditional leader of Anglo Jos and other community leaders did not maintain communication networks with community and youth leaders from the surrounding neighbourhoods, did not regularly gather information to be warned about imminent attacks, and did not strategically inform external fighters of their resolve to deter attacks. Consequently, when armed youth groups from the neighbouring areas of Hwolshe and Kufang coordinated an attack on Anglo Jos, community leaders were unprepared, overwhelmed, and unable to control the situation and prevent killings.

# Conclusion

This book set out to answer two puzzles. First, how could communal conflicts, which started with gang fights in the city of Ambon in eastern Indonesia and protests around a local political appointment in the city of Jos in central Nigeria, escalate to a level of lethality commonly associated with a small civil war, and in the case of Jos in only a matter of days? Second, how did ethnically, religiously, and socioeconomically mixed communities, vulnerable to mobilization for violence from their own youth and to attacks by external armed groups, prevent killings over years of armed conflict? This chapter summarizes the book's findings and discusses implications for prevention and social resilience, the protection of civilians, and local peacebuilding.

The book first developed the concept of communal war as a nonstate conflict between social groups, whereby casualty numbers reach beyond the civil war threshold. I have argued that such casualty numbers imply mobilization dynamics and sophistication in organization not captured in the ubiquitous term 'riot'. Chapter 1 advocated for an analysis of the patterns of violence in communal conflicts and distinguished four dimensions: geography (urban/rural); type of killings (one-sided pogroms versus dyadic communal clashes); categories of armed actors (neighbours, thugs, vigilantes, gangs, militias, state security forces); and the national context and the role of the state (e.g. context of regime change or civil war). In addition, a complementary analysis of the repertoires of violence can support a more nuanced understanding of the organization of armed groups and inform prevention.[1] This typology allows for a detailed analysis of the variation of violence in communal conflicts. Such analysis is important for countering myths of faceless 'outsiders' and 'provocateurs', which are common in narratives and reports about communal violence but disguise local agency and obstruct accountability for killings. A nuanced analysis

---

[1] See Gutiérrez-Sanín and Wood 2017.

of patterns of violence in a communal conflict should inform de-escalation and prevention measures, peacebuilding, transitional justice and reconciliation.

Using a mobilization framework, the book has traced the emergence of communal violence 'from below'. The theoretical framework focused on three escalation processes; the political mobilization of everyday violence networks (thugs, vigilantes, gangs) and their alignment with political and religious actors; the polarization of social identities and traumatization after victimization, which renders civilians more vulnerable to exclusive conflict narratives and more likely to support armed groups for self-protection and revenge; and the emergence of mobile gangs and militias and the militarization of local orders in the context of weak security forces and a retreat of the state. These three social processes of mobilization and conflict escalation are path-dependent and interlink. In their concatenation, they explain how fights between thugs and gangs can escalate into communal wars.

This focus on communal violence emerging from below is not meant to obliterate elite responsibility for inciting communal violence or failing to effectively prevent it. Instead, it aims to fully incorporate the causal role of civilian agency into explanations for the production of violence and the dynamics of escalation and non-escalation. The framework also underlines the mundane origins of large-scale communal violence as rooted in violent forms of community order upheld by vigilantes, thugs, and gangs long before the outbreak of communal clashes.[2] Consequently, prevention needs to start by addressing everyday forms of violent social orders, particularly in neighbourhoods and areas that suffer from poor policing and state service provision.

A careful analysis of the patterns of violence that distinguishes between pogroms; battles between armed groups; attacks by mobile armed groups on other settlements, sometimes in collaboration with unarmed civilians from a mixed area; and massacres provides more nuance to the often raised argument of 'neighbours killing neighbours'. In some instances in Ambon and in Jos, neighbours indeed killed neighbours when carrying out pogroms against the minority within their own neighbourhood. In many cases, however, as my interview material has shown, residents from mixed areas did not want to see their neighbours killed and did not fear being killed by their immediate

---

[2] See also Brass 1997, 2003; Berenschot 2011b.

neighbours. Instead, they feared external armed groups entering their settlement for an attack, potentially aided by a handful of local residents. Those who facilitated such joint attacks were a minority. The majority did not indirectly kill their neighbours through denunciation and the provision of target-relevant information to armed groups.

Second, this book developed a theoretical framework to study how *vulnerable communities* located in conflict zones *developed social resilience*. My empirical analysis demonstrates that the outcome of non-violence in the vulnerable communities of Wayame in Ambon and Dadin Kowa in Jos was not a mere by-product of local conflict dynamics or predicted by structural factors, such as geography, demography, or the intervention of security forces, as riot research would suggest. Instead, non-violence was an outcome contingent on civilian agency for prevention. Non-escalation resulted from three interlinking and path-dependent social processes.

The first such process is the depolarization of inter-group relations and rejection of narratives of a 'religious conflict'. Community leaders and residents engaged in 'meaning-making' and constructed a social identity as 'people of Wayame' or 'people of Dadin Kowa', emphasizing common ground and bridging the religious divide. These acts of meaning-making and identity formation drew on a set of cosmopolitan values, including tolerance, patience, citizenship, and community engagement. Meaning-making and identity formation helped people resist mobilization for pride or revenge. Research has argued that social resilience fundamentally concerns the production of hope.[3] Narratives and meaning-making enable agency in the face of adversity and are an integral part of positive adaptation to adversity, which builds social resilience. In non-violent communities, meaning-making and narrative formation were not accidental but served to mitigate polarization and prevent the dehumanization of the other religious group.

Second, leaders in non-violent communities consolidated civilian social control, as opposed to control by gangs or militia groups. They persuaded residents – particularly those who wanted to fight – to actively preserve peace instead of preparing attacks. Leaders also used repression and violent forms of punishment against men who wanted to instigate violence or were found to have fought in other areas. Establishing social control was based on a sense of a common

---

[3] Panter-Brick and Eggerman 2012, pp. 369–386.

identity. A key aspect was rule making and the creation of procedures and informal institutions for conflict management. Thus, in non-violent communities, institutional capacity for collective action was not pregiven. Instead, this capacity emerged when key leaders displayed high-risk rescue behaviour, confronted mobilizing men, and demonstrated their willingness and capability to protect residents and prevent attacks. Such extraordinary leadership motivated collective action, which sustained depolarization and social cohesion. Consequently, in non-violent communities, ad hoc violence prevention efforts became institutionalized and new social orders emerged, in marked contrast to violence-prone neighbourhoods.

Third, community leaders actively engaged external gangs and militias, negotiated neutrality, and deterred attacks. They continuously collected information regarding conflict dynamics, rumours, and preparations of attacks, and strategically disseminated their message of non-collaboration. They threatened to report to elders and to security forces – or to kill – anyone who dared to attack. Against militia leaders who demanded religious allegiance, community leaders argued that they had been neither threatened nor victimized by the other religious group and therefore provided no opportunity for attacks in the name of defence or revenge.

To further support my argument, I provide a counterfactual analysis. If demographic composition could explain the outcome of non-violence, no youth mobilization for killings should have taken place in the non-violent communities. If geography were the explanatory factor, no external armed group should have tried to attack. However, in both Wayame and Dadin Kowa, tensions were very high and a significant number of men wanted to fight their neighbours. In Jos, an external Christian armed group from a neighbourhood adjacent to Dadin Kowa approached the area to attack its Muslim population, but a community leader persuaded them to return without killing. In Ambon, external militia groups repeatedly threatened the community of Wayame. Lastly, if the willingness of security forces to prevent killings in certain neighbourhoods were the explanatory factor, security forces should have intervened and stopped armed groups that tried to attack. However, none of the militia fighters from Ambon or the gang and vigilante members from Jos whom I interviewed pointed to the threat of security forces as an explanation for not attacking Wayame or Dadin Kowa. Instead, all respondents from within the

two communities, as well as many respondents from other neighbourhoods, agreed that the communities' prevention efforts account for the
outcome of non-violence.

## The Resilience Lens

This book has developed a *resilience lens*, which sharpens an analytical
perspective that identifies the emergence of new forms of coping strategies, collective agency, and community adaptation to changing conflict dynamics. The key element of socio-ecological resilience is
*adaptation*. In the literature on climate change, community adaptation
has been linked to the social dynamics of knowledge and learning,
anticipation, and scenario-building. In Wayame and Dadin Kowa,
community leaders were guided by *social knowledge* concerning the
organization of violence and had previously gained *lived experience* in
other conflict zones.

I return to the question of why fear leads some people to see violence
prevention as in their best interest, while others choose to evade and flee
or actively join in killings. Following Kristen Monroe's theory of
altruism and rescue behaviour, individuals' sense of agency and their
confidence to act are crucial for how people perceive themselves in
relation to others, and what menu of behavioural choices they see
available for themselves.

The two key leaders who initiated prevention efforts, the Christian
pastor John Sahalessy in Wayame in Ambon and the Christian pastor
whom I call Timothy in Dadin Kowa in Jos, both had previously
experienced armed conflict. In Indonesia, John Sahalessy, who repeatedly negotiated with militias, stated that before the Ambon conflict, he
was often called on to mediate inter-communal clashes in other parts of
Maluku Province and had previously confronted armed groups.
Timothy, who stopped an armed group from attacking Dadin Kowa,
explained that he had lived through the Nigerian civil war in the east of
the country, which taught him how to negotiate with mobilizing men.
Both leaders displayed an altruistic attitude of rescue behaviour and
high confidence in their ability to act and prevent. In narrative interviews, both described how they saw themselves as called upon to lead
and to protect those under their domains.

Both religious leaders were recognized for their crucial prevention
efforts, particularly among the Muslim populations of the non-violent

communities. Both were also disliked and threatened by Christians from within and outside their communities who objected to efforts to protect the Muslim population.

By contrast, in the two case study communities where prevention efforts had failed, no such leaders were present. Prevention efforts remained ad hoc and leaders lacked either the knowledge or the willingness to effectively engage those who wanted to fight. Some fellow residents from these areas accused their religious leaders of having been half-hearted in their peace efforts. Community members were not convinced that leaders' peace assurance would eventually protect them. Some participated in the fighting in other areas, and people began mobilizing for attack and in self-defence.

Further factors that sustained adaptation and prevention in the non-violent communities over years of armed conflict were *social learning* with regard to the changing conflict environment, and the collective *anticipation* of potential threats based on imagination and scenario-building for contingency planning. In social resilience research, 'social learning' refers to 'the capacity and processes through which new values, ideas, and practices are disseminated, popularized, and become dominant in society or a sub-set, such as an organization or a local community'.[4] The anticipation of threats and scenario-building of potential attacks enabled proactive adaptation to a changing conflict zone. Such actions assured community members that leaders were willing and able to protect them.

## Implications

The book's findings challenge a number of assumptions about non-violent communities in war zones. First, non-violent communities were no 'islands of peace' or places of communal harmony. They were not isolated but deeply embedded in the conflict environment. Both communities were ripe with social conflicts, and some among their own youth repeatedly threatened to mobilize and attack their neighbours. Leaders' and residents' efforts to depolarize communal relations enabled collaboration and collective action for prevention. Supporting a common identity and we-thinking provided social glue

---

[4]  Pelling 2010, p. 59.

and hope that sustained prevention, but did not fully eradicate inter-communal tensions.

Furthermore, the outcome of non-violence is not necessarily linked to pacifist attitudes and exclusively non-violent forms of behaviour. Violence prevention and preserving local peace resulted primarily from the persuasion of potential fighters not to attack, but also on the use of violent means, such as repression, physical punishment, and expulsion of violence instigators. Violent punishments and threats were used to establish and maintain social control and credibly engage and negotiate with external armed groups. Consequently, social orders in non-violent communities were not necessarily open and tolerant, despite referring to cosmopolitan values. This is particularly evident in the case of Wayame in Ambon, where people had to prevent fighting during a very intense conflict period of more than three years. A highly restrictive form of social order, discipline, and control emerged, where the Christian pastor, the 'lone commander',[5] demanded obedience to the rules and guaranteed safety.

It is also important to note the gender dimensions of non-violent communities. Generally, male community leaders led prevention efforts, negotiated the terms of peaceful coexistence and the rules of everyday engagement, and punished those who broke rules. Women's groups supported violence prevention through distinct practices, such as advocating for peace among male leaders, shaming men for behaviour that would transgress community norms of violence prevention, and upholding a social identity that integrated both religious groups and supported the management of everyday conflicts. Women also helped community leaders in keeping potential fighters under control, and repeatedly demanded that male leaders fully support organized prevention. They collectively cooked food to support meetings and night watches, and maintained good relations with security forces. Some women served as communicators and messengers across polarized religious lines and stepped in when male leaders refused to communicate with one another, particularly in the case of Dadin Kowa in Jos. In sum, women's efforts contributed to the neighbourhood's protection. However, their activities were less visible and often received less

---

[5] This pastor described himself as the 'lone commander' and stated that the youth did not dare to break his rules; author interview, Palu, April 2015.

praise and acknowledgement by male and female residents in the community.

Civilian violence prevention and self-protection efforts are particularly relevant in the context of non-state armed conflicts, where security forces often deploy slowly and unprofessionally. Critics may object that civilians have little leverage over advancing armed groups when these are strong enough to 'overrun' a community and perpetrate massacres. Such dynamics primarily characterize the contexts of some civil wars, when armed groups do not need to rely on civilian support,[6] and militia attacks on villages in rural areas.[7] In communal conflicts, and particularly in urban or peri-urban neighbourhoods, where these conflicts often originate, security forces may deploy too late to save lives, but their eventual presence renders a safe return for mobile fighters difficult without support from residents of the targeted area. The rural dynamics of communal violence around Ambon and Jos were locally understood as having been triggered by fighting in the city, even though in the case of Plateau State in Nigeria farmer–herder conflicts later dramatically escalated regionally. Although the causes of rural violence may differ, the effects and legacies of urban violence undermined rural institutions of conflict management and rendered communities more vulnerable to clashes. Thus, in communal war – a type of conflict with often extremely high casualty numbers during short episodes of fighting – civilian agency for prevention can be highly effective. Even if violence can be held off only temporarily, a delay increases the likelihood that security forces may deploy to prevent or stop killings.

## Building Social Resilience in Conflict

I argue that social knowledge of violence prevention is crucial, and such knowledge can be partially trained and transplanted. Training can supplement a lack of lived experience in conflict environments and strengthen confidence and belief in the achievability of prevention

---

[6] For a more detailed discussion of the conditions under which civilians have bargaining power over armed groups in the context of civil wars, see Arjona 2016a and Kaplan 2017.

[7] The patterns of rural communal violence in Plateau State in Nigeria may in part be characterized as massacres rather than joint attacks. See Higazi 2016 for further details.

even when inter-group tensions and prejudices are high. Strengthening micro-level knowledge of violence prevention strategies may foster civilian resistance to armed groups based on instrumental motives to protect oneself, one's family, and one's livelihood. For example, research into gang violence prevention programmes has recognized how important it is that lived experience with dynamics of violence informs preventive agency. In the city of Chicago, which implemented a programme that relied in part on former gang members working as 'violence interrupters' with current gang members, the impressive success in reducing homicide rates was partly attributed to the intimate knowledge of gang dynamics and the credibility of the 'interrupters'.[8]

Intervention can empower ordinary people through knowledge and training and strengthen their confidence to act for prevention and self-preservation. In other words, if micro-level intervention can turn some 'bystanders' into 'rescuers',[9] then this is a significant contribution to civilian protection, local peace, and restraint.

However, also note that civilians in Ambon and Jos paid a price for protecting themselves. It is important to recognize that resilience approaches imply that the vulnerable, who often already struggle for daily survival, anticipate risks and prepare for their own protection.[10] Some scholars have argued that resilience thinking serves a neo-liberal policy agenda,[11] whereby the consequences of political interventions within the frame of resilience thinking become 'as inescapable as the weather'.[12] Without adequate external protection, the suffering of civilians, even when they employ sophisticated self-protection strategies in the face of war, is almost inevitable.[13]

This raises critical questions about policy approaches to resilience building but should not lead us to discard the resilience concept altogether. Ignoring how people mobilize to protect themselves may only increase community vulnerability because opportunities for adaptation and support are missed.[14] A realistic acknowledgement of international limits to civilian protection should inform a critical engagement with social resilience and resilience building. For example, peacekeeping operations should take civilian self-protection strategies into account to support and sustain social resilience.[15] Civilian self-protection

---

[8] Ritter 2009, pp. 20–25.    [9] Monroe 2012.    [10] Pelling 2003.
[11] Chandler 2014; Duffield 2012; Hall and Lamont 2013; Joseph 2013.
[12] Walker and Cooper 2011, p. 145.    [13] Corbett 2011, p. 60.
[14] Walker and Salt 2006, p. 9.    [15] Williams 2013.

strategies need to be the starting point for designing protection[16] because in many conflict environments, 'much of the de facto responsibility for providing protection will always remain with the vulnerable civilians themselves.'[17]

Theorizing adaptation and refocusing on communities' abilities to self-organize and prevent violence should not imply negating state responsibility to protect and support vulnerable communities. Climate change researchers have rightfully criticized such ideas as a 'misguided translation of self-organisation in ecological systems into self-reliance in social systems' that would 'advocate a kind of social Darwinism'.[18] Instead, civilian empowerment needs to remain the core objective of resilience building. After all, for civilians living with the threat of violence and oppression, social resilience implies sustained hope, against all odds, of a better outcome.[19]

The positive and prosocial legacies of civilian violence prevention efforts should motivate further research. The communities of Wayame in Ambon and Dadin Kowa in Jos became symbols of hope in both conflicts zones, demonstrating that living together, jointly preventing violence, and working for reconciliation were valuable and realistic objectives shared among members from both religious communities. Furthermore, even though violence prevention efforts in the communities of Poka–Rumahtiga in Ambon and Anglo Jos in Jos failed to prevent fighting, they reduced victim numbers and the overall lethality of clashes as neighbours warned neighbours and often facilitated escapes.

Consequently, the 'resilience lens' is an important analytical tool because it focuses on the strength of vulnerable communities in conflict zones and supports analysis of potential processes of adaptation for mitigating vulnerability, which is a crucial first step for protection and prevention.

---

[16] Baines and Paddon 2012, pp. 231–247.    [17] Corbett 2011, p. 9.
[18] Davoudi 2012.
[19] Almedom, Brensinger, and Adam 2010; Eggerman and Panter-Brick 2010.

# Bibliography

ABC News. 2000. *Spite Islands*. Journeyman Pictures. www.journeyman.tv/film/700.

Adam, Jeroen. 2008. 'Downward Social Mobility, Prestige and the Informal Economy in Post Conflict Ambon'. *South East Asia Research* 16(3): 461–479.

——— 2010. 'Post-Conflict Ambon: Forced Migration and the Ethno-Territorial Effects of Customary Tenure'. *Development and Change* 41(3): 401–419.

Adetula, Victor A. O. 2005. 'Ethnicity and the Dynamics of City Politics: The Case of Jos'. In *Urban Africa: Changing Contours of Survival in the City*, edited by Simone AbdouMaliq and Abouhani Abdelgani, 206–234. London: Zed Books.

Adger, W. Neil. 2000. 'Social and Ecological Resilience: Are They Related?' *Progress in Human Geography* 24(3): 347–364.

Adger, W. Neil, Terry Hughes, Carl Folke, Stephen R. Carpenter, and Johan Rockström. 2005. 'Social-Ecological Resilience to Coastal Disasters'. *Science* 309 (5737): 1036–1039.

Aditjondro, George J. 2001. 'Guns, Pamphlets and Handie-Talkies: How the Military Exploited Local Ethno-Religious Tensions in Maluku to Preserve Their Political and Economic Privileges'. In *Violence in Indonesia*, edited by Ingrid Wessel and Georgia Wimhöfer, 100–128. Hamburg: Abera.

Agbu, Osita. 2004. *Ethnic Militias and the Threat to Democracy in Post-Transition Nigeria*. Research Report No. 127. Nordic Africa Institute. www.files.ethz.ch/isn/95522/127.pdf.

Ake, Claude. 2000. *The Feasibility of Democracy in Africa*. Dakar: CODESRIA.

Albert, Isaac O. 1999. 'New Directions in the Management of Community Conflicts in Nigeria: Insights from the Activities of AAPW'. In *Community Conflicts in Nigeria: Management, Resolution and Transformation*, edited by Kenneth Onigu-Otite and Isaac Olawale Albert. Ibadan: Spectrum Books Limited.

Albin-Lackey, C. 2006. 'They Do Not Own This Place: Government Discrimination against "Non-Indigenes" in Nigeria'. Human Rights Watch, 25 April. www.hrw.org/report/2006/04/25/they-do-not-own -place/government-discrimination-against-non-indigenes-nigeria.

Allansson, Marie, Erik Melander, and Lotta Themnér. 2017. 'Organized Violence, 1989–2016'. *Journal of Peace Research*. 54(4): 574–587.

Almedom, Astier M. 2005. 'Resilience, Hardiness, Sense of Coherence, and Posttraumatic Growth: All Paths Leading to 'Light at the End of the Tunnel"?' *Journal of Loss and Trauma* 10(3): 253–265.

Almedom, Astier M., Evelyn A. Brensinger, and Gordon M. Adam. 2010. 'Identifying the "Resilience Factor": An Emerging Counter Narrative to the Traditional Discourse of "Vulnerability" in "Social Suffering"'. In *Global Perspectives on War, Gender and Health: The Sociology and Anthropology of Suffering*, edited by Hannah Bradby and Gillian Lewando Hundt, 127–146. London: Ashgate Publishing Company.

Anderson, David M. 2002. 'Vigilantes, Violence and the Politics of Public Order in Kenya'. *African Affairs* 101(405): 531–555.

Anderson, Mary B. and Marshall Wallace. 2013. *Opting Out of War: Strategies to Prevent Violent Conflict*. Boulder, CO: Lynne Rienner Publishers.

Aradau, Claudia. 2014. 'The Promise of Security: Resilience, Surprise and Epistemic Politics'. *Resilience* 2(2): 73–87.

Arjona, Ana. 2016a. *Rebelocracy*: Social Order in the Colombian Civil War. New York, NY: Cambridge University Press.

    2016b. 'Institutions, Civilian Resistance, and Wartime Social Order: A Process-Driven Natural Experiment in the Colombian Civil War'. *Latin American Politics and Society* 58(3): 99–122.

Azca, Muhammad N. 2006. 'In between Military and Militia: The Dynamics of the Security Forces in the Communal Conflict in Ambon'. *Asian Journal of Social Science*, 34(3): 431–455.

Bagudu, Nankin and C. J. Dakas. 2001. *The Right to Be Different: Perspectives on Minority Rights and the Cultural Middle-Belt and Constitutionalism in Nigeria. Report of the Proceedings of the Peoples of the Cultural Middle-Belt of Nigeria Conference and the 1999 Constitution*. Jos: League for Human Rights.

Baines, Erin and Emily Paddon. 2012. '"This Is How We Survived": Civilian Agency and Humanitarian Protection'. *Security Dialogue* 43(3): 231–247.

Barker, J. 2007. 'Vigilantes and the State'. In *Identifying with Freedom: Indonesia after Suharto*, edited by Tony Day, 87–94. New York, NY: Berghahn Books.

Barron, Patrick, Kai Kaiser, and Menno Pradhan. 2009. 'Understanding Variations in Local Conflict: Evidence and Implications from Indonesia'. *World Development* 37(3): 698–713.

Barron, Patrick, M. Najib Azca, and Tri Susdinarjanti. 2012. *After the Communal War: Understanding and Addressing Post-Conflict Violence in Eastern Indonesia*. Yogyakarta: CSPS Books.

Barron, Patrick, Sana Jaffrey, and Ashutosh Varshney. 2016. 'When Large Conflicts Subside: The Ebbs and Flows of Violence in Post-Suharto Indonesia'. *Journal of East Asian Studies* 16(2): 191–217.

Bartels, Dieter. 1977. *Guarding the Invisible Mountain: Intervillage Alliances, Religious Syncretism and Ethnic Identity among Ambonese Christians and Muslims in the Moluccas*. Ithaca, NY: Faculty of the Graduate School of Cornell University.

2001. 'Your God Is No Longer Mine: Muslim–Christian Fratricide in the Central Moluccas (Indonesia) after a Half-Millennium of Tolerant Co-Existence and Ethnic Unity'. In *A State of Emergency: Violence, Society and the State in Indonesia*, edited by Sandra Pannell, 128–153. Darwin: Northern Territory University Press.

Barter, Shane. 2014. *Civilian Strategy in Civil War: Insights from Indonesia, Thailand, and the Philippines*. New York, NY: Palgrave Macmillan.

Bates, Robert. 1983. 'Modernization, Ethnic Competition, and the Rationality of Politics in Contemporary Africa'. In *State versus Ethnic Claims: African Policy Dilemmas*, edited by Donald Rothchild and Victor A. Olunsorola. Boulder, CO: Westview Press.

Bateson, Regina. 2012. 'Crime Victimization and Political Participation'. *American Political Science Review* 106(3): 570–587.

BBC News. 2015. 'Nigeria's Boko Haram Crisis: Jos Blasts Kill Scores', 1 July. www.bbc.com/news/world-africa-33406537.

Bekoe, Dorina A. O. 2012. *Voting in Fear: Electoral Violence in Sub-Saharan Africa*. Washington, DC: US Institute of Peace.

Bellows, John and Edward Miguel. 2009. 'War and Local Collective Action in Sierra Leone'. *Journal of Public Economics* 93(11): 1144–1157.

von Benda-Beckmann, Franz and Keebet von Benda-Beckmann. 2007. *Social Security between Past and Future: Ambonese Networks of Care and Support*. Münster: LIT Verlag.

von Benda-Beckmann, Franz and Tanja Taale. 1996. 'Land, Trees and Houses: Changing (un) Certainties in Property Relationships on Ambon'. Food and Agriculture Organization of the United Nations. http://agris.fao.org/agris-search/search.do?recordID=NL2012064709.

von Benda-Beckmann, Keebet. 2004. 'Law, Violence and Peace Making on the Islands of Ambon'. In *Healing the Wounds: Essays on the*

*Reconstruction of Societies after War*, edited by Marie-Claire Foblets and Truth von Trotha, 221–239. Oxford: Hart.

Bennett, Andrew and Alexander L. George. 2005. *Case Studies and Theory Development in the Social Sciences*. Cambridge, MA: MIT Press.

Berenschot, Ward. 2011a. 'The Spatial Distribution of Riots: Patronage and the Instigation of Communal Violence in Gujarat, India'. *World Development*, 39(2): 221–230.

   2011b. *Riot Politics: India's Hindu–Muslim Violence and the Everyday Mediation of the State*. London: Hurst & Company.

Berkes, Fikret. 2001. 'Back to the Future: Ecosystem Dynamics and Local Knowledge'. In *Panarchy: Understanding Transformations in Human and Natural Systems*, edited by Lance H. Gunderson and C. S. Holling, 121–146. Washington, DC: Island Press.

Berkes, Fikret, Carl Folke, and Johan Colding. 2000. *Linking Social and Ecological Systems: Management Practices and Social Mechanisms for Building Resilience*. Cambridge: Cambridge University Press.

Berkes, Fikret, Johan Colding, and Carl Folke. 2003. *Navigating Social-Ecological Systems: Building Resilience for Complexity and Change*. Cambridge: Cambridge University Press.

Bertrand, Jacques. 2004. *Nationalism and Ethnic Conflict in Indonesia*. Cambridge: Cambridge University Press.

   2008. 'Ethnic Conflicts in Indonesia: National Models, Critical Junctures, and the Timing of Violence'. *Journal of East Asian Studies* 8(3): 425–449.

Best, Shedrack G. 2007. *Conflict and Peacebuilding in Plateau State, Nigeria*. Ibadan: Spectrum Books Limited.

   2008. *The Causes and Effects of Conflict in Southern Zone of Plateau State, Nigeria*. Edited by Shedrack G. Best. Jos: University of Jos.

Best, Shedrack and Dimieari Von Kemedi. 2005. 'Armed Groups and Conflict in Rivers and Plateau States, Nigeria'. In *Armed and Aimless, Armed Groups, Guns and Human Security in the ECOWAS Region*, edited by Nicolas Florquin and Eric Berman, 13–45. Geneva: Small Arms Survey.

Bewarang, Rev. Dr Soka. 2010. 'COCIN Vice President to the COCIN Church Leaders, Sermon on the Jos Crisis at the COCIN Conference Hall on Monday 8th February 2010'. www.google.ch/url?sa=t&rct=j&q=the %20address%20of%20rev.%20dr.%20soja%20bewarang%2 C%20c ocin%20vice%20president%20to%20the%20cocin%20church%20lea ders&source=web&cd=8&ved=0CF8QFjAH&url=http%3A%2 F%2F www.cfaithministries.org%2Fuploads%2Ffiles%2FCOCIN_Vice_Presi dent_Address.doc&ei=5wJrT_OjKomI4gTh6omRBg&usg=AFQjCNF7 sgV6O8qr7F1q7WExFWZ6sQtgQA.

Bitrus Jat, Rauta and Pam Sha Dung. 2005. *The Performance of Local Government Councils in the North Central Geo-Political Zone of Nigeria*. Stirling: Horden Publishers Ltd.

Blattman, Christopher. 2009. 'From Violence to Voting: War and Political Participation in Uganda'. *American Political Science Review* 103(2): 231–247.

Blench, Roger. 2003a. 'The Transformation of Conflict between Pastoralists and Cultivators in Nigeria'. Unpublished working paper. www .rogerblench.info/Conflict/Herder-farmer%20conflict%20in%20Nige ria.pdf.

    2003b. 'Access Rights and Conflict over Common Pool Resources on the Jos Plateau, Nigeria'. Report to World Bank/UNDP/DFID-JEWEL (Jigawa Enhancement of Wetlands Livelihoods Project). http://rb .rowbory.co.uk/Conflict/Jos%20section%20only.pdf.

    2004. 'Natural Resource Conflicts in North-Central Nigeria'. Unpublished working paper. http://rogerblench.info/Development/Nig eria/Pastoralism/Nigeria%20Conflict%20Book.pdf.

Blench, Roger, Selbut Longtau, Umar Hassan, and Martin Walsh. 2006. 'The Role of Traditional Rulers in Conflict Prevention and Mediation in Nigeria'. Prepared for the UK Department for International Development. www.rogerblench.info/Development/Nigeria/Conflict% 20resolution/Final%20Report%20TRs%20September%2006.pdf.

Boehm, Cornelius J. 2005. *Brief Chronicle of the Unrest in the Moluccas, 1999–2005*. Ambon: Crisis Centre, Diocese of Amboina.

    2006. *Supplement to Brief Chronicle of the Unrest in the Moluccas 1999–2005: Reporting of the Aftermath Events during the Period May 2005–May 2006*. Ambon: Crisis Centre, Diocese of Amboina.

Bonkat, Lohna. 2014. 'Survival Strategies of Market Women and Violent Conflicts in Jos, Nigeria'. *Journal of Asia Pacific Studies* 3(3): 281–299.

Boone, Catherine. 2011. 'Politically Allocated Land Rights and the Geography of Electoral Violence: The Case of Kenya in the 1990s'. *Comparative Political Studies* 44(10): 1311–1342.

Bourbeau, Philippe. 2015. 'Resilience and International Politics: Premises, Debates, Agenda'. *International Studies Review* 17(3): 374–395.

Braithwaite, John. 2010. *Anomie and Violence: Non-Truth and Reconciliation in Indonesian Peacebuilding*. Canberra: Australian National University Press.

Brass, Paul. 1997. *Theft of an Idol: Text and Context in the Representation of Collective Violence*. Princeton, NJ: Princeton University Press.

    2003. *The Production of Hindu–Muslim Violence in Contemporary India*. Seattle, WA: University of Washington Press.

2006. *Forms of Collective Violence: Riots, Pogroms, & Genocide in Modern India*. State College, PA: Pennsylvania State University. Three Essays Collective.

Bratton, Michael. 2008. 'Vote Buying and Violence in Nigerian Election Campaigns'. *Electoral Studies* 27(4): 621–632.

Bräuchler, Birgit. 2003. 'Cyberidentities at War: Religion, Identity, and the Internet in the Moluccan Conflict'. *Indonesia* 75: 123–151.

2005. *Cyberidentities at War: der Molukkenkonflikt im Internet*. Bielefeld: Transcript Verlag.

2009. *Reconciling Indonesia: Grassroots Agency for Peace*. London: Routledge.

2015. *The Cultural Dimension of Peace: Decentralization and Reconciliation in Indonesia*. London: Palgrave Macmillan.

Brewer, Marilynn B. 1999. 'The Psychology of Prejudice: Ingroup Love and Outgroup Hate?' *Journal of Social Issues* 55(3): 429–444.

Brosché, Johan. 2014. *Masters of War: The Role of Elites in Sudan's Communal Conflicts*. Uppsala University: Department of Peace & Conflict Research. No. 102.

Brosché, Johan and Emma Elfversson. 2012. 'Communal Conflict, Civil War, and the State: Complexities, Connections, and the Case of Sudan'. *African Journal on Conflict Resolution* 12(1): 9–32.

Brown, David and Ian Wilson. 2007. 'Ethnicized Violence in Indonesia: The Betawi Brotherhood Forum in Jakarta'. Working Paper No. 145. Perth: Murdoch University Asia Research Center.

Brown, Rupert and Miles Hewstone. 2005. 'An Integrative Theory of Intergroup Contact'. *Advances in Experimental Social Psychology* 37: 255–343.

Browning, Christopher R. 1993. *Ordinary Men: Reserve Police Battalion 101 and the Final Solution in Poland*. New York, NY: HarperCollins Publishers.

Brubaker, Roger. 2004. *Ethnicity without Groups*. Cambridge, MA: Harvard University Press.

Brubaker, Roger and David Laitin. 1998. 'Ethnic and Nationalist Violence'. *Annual Review of Sociology* 24: 423–452.

van Bruinessen, Martin. 1996. 'Islamic State or State Islam? Fifty Years of State–Islam Relations in Indonesia'. In *Indonesien am Ende des 20. Jahrhunderts*, edited by Ingrid Wessel, 19–34. Hamburg: Abera.

2002. 'Genealogies of Islamic Radicalism in Post-Suharto Indonesia'. *South East Asia Research* 10(2): 117–154.

Bubandt, Nils. 2000. 'Malukan Apocalypse: Themes in the Dynamics of Violence in Eastern Indonesia'. In *Violence in Indonesia*, edited by Ingrid Wessel and Georgia Wimhöfer, 228–253. Hamburg: Abera.

2004. 'Violence and Millenarian Modernity in Eastern Indonesia'. In *Cargo, Cult & Culture Critique*, edited by Holger Jebens, 92–116. Honolulu, HI: University of Hawaii Press.

2008. 'Rumours, Pamphlets, and the Politics of Paranoia in Indonesia'. *The Journal of Asian Studies* 67(3): 789–817.

Campbell, John. 2011. *Nigeria: Dancing on the Brink*. Lanham, MD: Rowman & Littlefield.

Carpenter, Steve, Brian Walker, J. Marty Anderies, and Nick Abel. 2001. 'From Metaphor to Measurement: Resilience of What to What?' *Ecosystems* 4: 765–781.

Caruth, Cathy. 1995. *Trauma: Explorations in Memory*. Baltimore, MD, and London: Johns Hopkins University Press.

Cavelty, Myriam Dunn, Mareile Kaufmann, and Kristian Søby Kristensen. 2015. 'Resilience and (In)Security: Practices, Subjects, Temporalities'. *Security Dialogue* 46(1): 3–14.

Centre for Humanitarian Dialogue. 2011. 'Conflict Management in Indonesia: An Analysis of the Conflicts in Maluku, Papua and Poso'. Report. www.hdcentre.org/uploads/tx_news/5ConflictManagementinI ndonesia.pdf.

Chandler, David. 2014. *Resilience: The Governance of Complexity*. London: Routledge.

Chandra, Sudhir. 1993. 'Of Communal Consciousness and Communal Violence: Impressions from Post-Riot Surat'. *Economic and Political Weekly* 28(36): 1883–1887.

Chenoweth, Erica and Kathleen Gallagher Cunningham. 2013. 'Understanding Nonviolent Resistance: An Introduction'. *Journal of Peace Research* 50(3): 271–276.

Chenoweth, Erica and Maria J. Stephan. 2011. *Why Civil Resistance Works: The Strategic Logic of Nonviolent Conflict*. New York, NY: Columbia University Press.

Chirot, Daniel and Clark McCauley. 2010. *Why Not Kill Them All? The Logic and Prevention of Mass Political Murder*. Princeton, NJ: Princeton University Press.

Christie, Daniel J. 2006. 'What Is Peace Psychology the Psychology Of?' *Journal of Social Issues* 62(1): 1–17.

Christie, Daniel J., Richard V. Wagner, and Deborah D. N. Winter. 2001. *Peace, Conflict, and Violence: Peace Psychology for the 21st Century*. Englewood Cliffs, NJ: Prentice-Hall.

Christie, Daniel J., Barbara S. Tint, Richard V. Wagner, and Deborah DuNann Winter. 2008. 'Peace Psychology for a Peaceful World'. *American Psychologist* 63(6): 540–552.

Citizens' Monitoring Group. 2010. 'Plateau under Attack! Jos Crisis 2010: Eyewitness and Survivor Accounts'. February. www.scribd.com/doc/2 8479137/Plateau-Under-Attack-Jos-Crisis-2010.

Claassen, Christopher. 2014. 'Who Participates in Communal Violence? Survey Evidence from South Africa'. *Research & Politics* April–June: 1–8.

Clauss-Ehlers, Caroline S. and Liliana Lopez Levi. 2002. 'Violence and Community, Terms in Conflict: An Ecological Approach to Resilience'. *Journal of Social Distress and the Homeless* 11(4): 265–278.

Colobijn, Freek. 2002. 'Explaining the Violent Solution in Indonesia'. *Brown Journal of World Affairs* 9(1): 49–56.

Colobijn, Freek and J. Thomas Lindblad. 2002. *Roots of Violence in Indonesia: Contemporary Violence in Historical Perspective.* Leiden: KIVTL Press.

Conflict Prevention and Management Centre of Jos. 1993. 'The Settler Question in Nigeria: The Case of the Jos Plateau'. *Communities Seminar Series (CSS 1).* Jos: Africa Leadership Forum.

Cooley, Frank L. 1962. *Ambonese Adat: A General Description.* New Haven, CT: Yale University, Southeast Asia Studies.

Coppel, Charles A. 2006. *Violent Conflicts in Indonesia: Analysis, Representation, Resolution.* London: Routledge Curzon.

Corbett, Justin. 2011. 'Learning from the Nuba: Civilian Resilience and Self-Protection during Conflict'. Local to Global Protection, October. www .cmi.no/file/1908-Learning-from-the-Nuba-Civilian-resilience-and-self -protection-during-con64258ict.pdf.

Coser, Lewis A. 1956. *The Functions of Social Conflict.* Oxon: Routledge.
   1966. 'Some Social Functions of Violence'. *Annals of the American Academy of Political and Social Science* 364(1): 8–18.

Crouch, Harold. A. 2010. *Political reform in Indonesia after Soeharto.* Singapore: Institute of Southeast Asian Studies.

*Daily Trust.* 2010. 'Secret Killings Persist in Jos'. 23 March. www.nigeria70 .com/nigerian_news_paper/secret_killings_persist_in_jos/197149.

Danfulani, Umar H. D. and Sati U. Fwatshak. 2002. 'Briefing: The September 2001 Events in Jos, Nigeria'. *African Affairs* 101(403): 243–255.

Davidson, Jamie and David Henley, eds. 2007. *The Revival of Tradition in Indonesian Politics: The Deployment of Adat from Colonialism to Indigenism.* New York, NY: Routledge.

Davis, Michael 2002. 'Laskar Jihad and the Political Position of Conservative Islam in Indonesia'. *Contemporary Southeast Asia* 24(1): 12–33.

Davoudi, Simin. 2012. 'Resilience: A Bridging Concept or a Dead End?' *Planning Theory & Practice* 13(2): 299–333.

Denham, Aaron R. 2008. 'Rethinking Historical Trauma: Narratives of Resilience'. *Transcultural Psychiatry* 45(3): 391–414.

Dixon, Lawrence G. and Samuel Mokuwa. 2004. Sierra Leone: Making Sense of One Community's Experience during the War. Steps toward Conflict Prevention Project, CDA Collaborative Learning Projects.

Doughty, Kristin and David Moussa Ntambara. 2003. 'Resistance and Protection: Muslim Community Actions during the Rwandan Genocide'. CDA Collaborative www.conference.unitar.org/ny/sites/unitar.org.ny/files/stepsCase02Rwanda.pdf.

Dudley, Billy J. 1968. *Parties and Politics in Northern Nigeria*. London: Frank Cass and Company Ltd.

Dudouet, Véronique. 2008. 'Nonviolent Resistance and Conflict Transformation in Power Asymmetries'. The Berghof Handbook. http://edoc.vifapol.de/opus/volltexte/2011/2586/.

, ed. 2015. *Civil Resistance and Conflict Transformation: Transitions from Armed to Nonviolent Struggle*. New York, NY: Routledge.

Duffield, Caroline. 2010. 'Why I Burnt My Nigerian Friend's House Down'. *BBC News*, 26 April. http://news.bbc.co.uk/2/hi/africa/8640796.stm.

Duffield, Mark. 2012. 'Challenging Environments: Danger, Resilience and the Aid Industry'. *Security Dialogue* 43(5): 474–492.

Duncan, Christopher R. 2005. 'The Other Maluku: Chronologies of Conflict in North Maluku'. *Indonesia* 80: 53–80.

2013. *Violence and Vengeance: Religious Conflict and Its Aftermaths in Eastern Indonesia*. Ithaca, NY: Cornell University Press.

Dung, Pam Sha. 2005. *The Politicisation of Settler-Native Identities and Ethno-Religious Conflicts in Jos, Central Nigeria*. Ibadan: Stirling-Horden Publishers Ltd.

Dung-Gwom, John Y. and Laraba S. Rikko. 2009. 'Urban Violence and Emerging Land and Housing Markets in Jos, Nigeria'. *ISA Housing Conference*. www.sma.ie/wp-content/uploads/images/stories/media_129777_en.pdf.

Dunn, Kevin C. 2009. '"Sons of the Soil" and Contemporary State Making: Autochthony, Uncertainty and Political Violence in Africa'. *Third World Quarterly* 30(1): 113–127.

Earl, Jennifer, Andrew Marten, John D. McCarthy, and Sarah A. Soule. 2004. 'The Use of Newspaper Data in the Study of Collective Action'. *Annual Review of Sociology* 30: 65–80.

Egeland, Byron, Elizabeth Carlson, and E. Alan Sroufe. 1993. 'Resilience as Process'. *Development and Psychopathology*, 5(04): 517–528.

Eggerman, Mark and Catherine Panter-Brick. 2010. 'Suffering, Hope, and Entrapment: Resilience and Cultural Values in Afghanistan'. *Social Science & Medicine* 71(1): 71–83.

Egwu, Samuel G. 2010. 'Ethnicity and Citizenship in Urban Nigeria: The Jos Case, 1960–2000'. Doctoral Thesis. Jos: University of Jos.

Elfversson, Emma. 2015. 'Providing Security or Protecting Interests? Government Interventions in Violent Communal Conflicts in Africa'. *Journal of Peace Research* 52(6): 791–805.

Erikson, Kai T. 1976. 'Loss of Communality at Buffalo Creek'. *American Journal of Psychiatry* 133(3): 302–305.

    1994. *A New Species of Trouble: Explorations in Disaster, Trauma, and Community*. New York, NY: Norton & Company.

    1995. 'Notes on Trauma and Community'. In *Trauma: Explorations in Memory*, edited by Cathy Caruth, 183–199. Baltimore, MD: Johns Hopkins University Press.

Ernston, Henrik, Sverker Sörlin, and Thomas Elmqvist. 2008. 'Social Movements and Ecosystem Services: The Role of Social Network Structure in Protecting and Managing Urban Green Areas in Stockholm'. *Ecology and Society* 13: 29–39.

Falola, Toyin. 1998. *Violence in Nigeria: The Crisis of Religious Politics and Secular Ideologies*. Rochester, NY: University of Rochester Press.

Farman, Tarah. 2005. 'Mungoi Community Chidenguele, Mozambique'. CDA Collaborative. http://cdacollaborative.org/publication/mungoi -community-chidenguele-mozambique/.

Fealy, Greg. 2001. 'Inside the Laskar Jihad'. *Inside Indonesia* 65: 29.

Fearon, James D. 1999. 'Why Ethnic Politics and "Pork" Tend to Go Together'. Conference paper. University of Chicago. https://s3.amazo naws.com/academia.edu.documents/39725/1ojs4cbof49zq9gw4n05.p df?AWSAccessKeyId=AKIAIWOWYYGZ2Y53UL3A&Expire s=1511132122&Signature=OKsuZ0F385ZzH4t1tR5ozo7Odr0%3D &response-content-disposition=inline%3B%20filename%3DWhy_Et hnic_Politics_and_Pork_Tend_to_Go.pdf.

Fearon, James D. and David D. Laitin. 1996. 'Explaining Interethnic Cooperation'. *American Political Science Review* 90(4): 715–735.

    2000. 'Violence and the Social Construction of Ethnic Identity'. *International Organization* 54(4): 845–877.

    2003. 'Ethnicity, Insurgency, and Civil War'. *American Political Science Review* 97(1): 75–90.

    2011. 'Sons of the Soil, Migrants, and Civil War'. *World Development* 39 (2): 199–211.

Fein, Helen. 1979. *Accounting for Genocide: National Responses and Jewish Victimization during the Holocaust*. New York, NY: Free Press.

Folke, Carl. 2006. 'Resilience: The Emergence of a Perspective for Social-Ecological Systems Analyses'. *Global Environmental Change* 16(3): 253–267.

Folke, Carl, Johan Colding, and Fikret Berkes. 2003. 'Synthesis: Building Resilience and Adaptive Capacity in Social-Ecological Systems'. In *Navigating Social-Ecological Systems: Building Resilience for Complexity and Change*, edited by Fikret Berkes, Johan Colding, and Carl Folke, 352–387. Cambridge: Cambridge University Press.

Folke, Carl, Thomas Hahn, Per Olsson, and Jon Norberg. 2005. 'Adaptive Governance of Social-Ecological Systems'. *Annual Review of Environmental Resources* 30: 441–473.

Fujii, Lee A. 2009. *Killing Neighbors: Webs of Violence in Rwanda*. Ithaca, NY: Cornell University Press.

2010. 'Shades of Truth and Lies: Interpreting Testimonies of War and Violence'. *Journal of Peace Research* 47(2): 231–241.

2012. 'Genocide and the Psychology of Perpetrators, Bystanders, and Victims'. *Perspectives on Politics* 10(2): 415–417.

2015. 'Five Stories of Accidental Ethnography: Turning Unplanned Moments in the Field into Data'. *Qualitative Research* 15(4): 525–539.

Fwatshak, Sari Umaru. 2006. 'A Comparative Analysis of the 19th and 21st Century Religious Conflicts on the Jos Plateau, Central Nigeria'. *Swedish Missiological Themes* 94(3): 259–280.

2011. *African Entrepreneurship in Jos, Central Nigeria, 1902–1985*. Durham, NC: Carolina Academic Press.

Galtung, Johan 1965. 'On the Meaning of Nonviolence'. *Journal of Peace Research* 2(3): 228–256.

Garcia, Ed. 1997. 'Filipino Zones of Peace'. Peace Review 9(2): 221–224.

Gerring, John. 2007. *Case Study Research: Principles and Practices*. Cambridge: Cambridge University Press.

Ghassem-Fachandi, Parvis. 2012. *Pogrom in Gujarat: Hindu Nationalism and Anti-Muslim Violence in India*. Princeton, NJ: Princeton University Press.

Golwa, Joseph H. P., and Ochinya O. Ojiji, eds. 2008. *Dialogue on Citizenship in Nigeria*. Abuja: Institute for Peace and Conflict Resolution.

Gore, Charles and David Pratten. 2003. 'The Politics of Plunder: The Rhetoric of Order and Disorder in Southern Nigeria'. *African Affairs* 102(407): 211–240.

Gorur, Aditi. 2013. 'Community Self-Protection Strategies: How Peacekeepers Can Help or Harm'. *Civilians in Conflict*, Issue Brief No. 1. www.stimson.org/images/uploads/research-pdfs/Stimson_Community_Self-Protection_Issue_Brief_Aug_2013_1.pdf.

Goss, Jan. 2000. 'Understanding the Maluku Wars: An Overview of the Sources of Communal Conflict and Prospects for Peace'. *Cakalele: Maluku Research Journal* 7, 11–12.

Gould, Roger. 1999. 'Collective Violence and Group Solidarity: Evidence from a Feuding Society'. *American Sociological Review* 64: 356–380.

Gray, Vanessa Joan. 2012. 'Nonviolence and Sustainable Resource Use with External Support: A Survival Strategy in Rural Colombia'. *Latin American Perspectives* 39(1): 43–114.

Gross, Jan T. 2001. *Neighbors: The Destruction of the Jewish Community in Jedwabne, Poland*. Princeton, NJ: Princeton University Press.

Grossmann, Dave. 1996. *On Killing: The Psychological Cost of Learning to Kill in War and Society*. Boston, MA: Little, Brown and Company.

*The Guardian Nigeria*. 2001. 'Jos: Its Underbelly and the Carnage'. 14 September. http://allafrica.com/stories/200109140109.html.

Guichaoua, Yvan. 2007. *Who Joins Ethnic Militias? A Survey of the Oodua People's Congress in Southwestern Nigeria*. Oxford: University of Oxford, Centre for Research on Inequality, Human Security and Ethnicity.

Gutiérrez-Sanín, Francisco and Elisabeth Jean Wood. 2017. 'What Should We Mean by "Pattern of Political Violence"? Repertoire, Targeting, Frequency, and Technique'. *Perspectives on Politics* 15(1): 20–41.

Hadiz, Vedi. 2003. 'Reorganizing Political Power in Indonesia: A Reconsideration of So-Called Democratic Transitions'. *The Pacific Review* 16(4): 591–611.

Hall, Peter A. and Michèle Lamont, eds. 2013. *Social Resilience in the Neoliberal Era*. Cambridge: Cambridge University Press.

Hallward, Maia, Juan Masullo, and Cécile Mouly. 2017. 'Civil Resistance in Armed Conflict: Leveraging Nonviolent Action to Navigate War, Oppose Violence and Confront Oppression'. *Journal of Peacebuilding and Development* 12(3): 1–9.

Hancock, Landon E. 2017. 'Agency & Peacebuilding: The Promise of Local Zones of Peace'. *Peacebuilding* 5(3): 255–269.

Hancock, Landon E. and Christopher R. Mitchell, eds. 2007. *Zones of Peace*. Bloomfield, IL: Kumarian Press.

Hancock, Landon E. and P. Iyer. 2007. 'The Nature, Structure and Variety of Peace Zones'. In *Zones of Peace*, edited by Landon Hancock and Christopher Mitchel, 1–28. Bloomfield, IL: Kumarian Press.

Harragin, Simon. 2011. 'South Sudan: Waiting for Peace to Come'. *Local to Global Protection*, pp. 1–103. https://reliefweb.int/report/south-sudan-republic/south-sudan-waiting-peace-come-study-bor-twic-east-duk-counties-jonglei.

Hartman, Alexandra and Ben Morse. 2018. 'Wartime Violence, Empathy, and Inter-Group Altruism: Theory and Evidence from the Ivorian Refugee Crisis in Liberia'. *British Journal of Political Science*, 1–25. doi:10.1017/S0007123417000655.

Hasan, Noordhaidi. 2002. 'Faith and Politics: The Rise of the Laskar Jihad in the Era of Transition in Indonesia'. *Indonesia* 73: 145–169.

　　2006. *Laskar Jihad: Islam, Militancy, and the Quest for Identity in Post-New Order Indonesia*. Ithaca, NY: Cornell University Southeast Asia Program Publication.

Hefner, Robert W. 2000a. *Civil Islam: Muslims and Democratization in Indonesia*. Princeton, NJ: Princeton University Press.

　　2000b. 'Disintegration of Democratization? Muslim–Christian Violence and the Future of Indonesia'. In *Political Violence: Indonesia and India in Comparative Perspective*, edited by Olle Törnquist, 39–49. Oslo: Centre for Development and the Environment.

　　2002. 'Global Violence and Indonesian Muslim Politics'. *American Anthropologist* 104(3): 754–765.

Hewstone, Miles, Ed Cairns, Alberto Voci, Juergen Hamberger, and Ulrieke Niens. 2006. 'Intergroup Contact, Forgiveness, and Experience of "The Troubles" in Northern Ireland'. *Journal of Social Issues* 62(1): 99–120.

Hewstone, Miles, Mark Rubin, and Hazel Willis. 2002. 'Intergroup Bias'. *Annual Review of Psychology* 53(1): 575–604.

Hiariej, Eddy O. S., ed. 2007. *Format Ulang Birokrasi Kota Ambon*. Makassar: Penerbit Ininnawa.

Higazi, Adam. 2008. 'Social Mobilization and Collective Violence: Vigilantes and Militias in the Lowlands of Plateau State, Central Nigeria'. *Africa* 78(1): 107–135.

　　2011. 'The Jos Crisis: A Recurrent Nigerian Tragedy'. Working paper. Abuja: Friedrich Ebert Foundation.

　　2013. 'Rural Insecurity on the Jos Plateau, Nigeria: Livelihoods, Land, and Religious Reform among the Berom, Fulani, and Hausa'. Nigeria Research Network (NRN) Working paper. University of Oxford.

　　2016. 'Farmer–Pastoralist Conflicts on the Jos Plateau, Central Nigeria: Security Responses of Local Vigilantes and the Nigerian State'. *Conflict, Security & Development* 16(4): 365–385.

Höglund, Kristine. 2009. 'Electoral Violence in Conflict-Ridden Societies: Concepts, Causes, and Consequences'. *Terrorism and Political Violence* 21(3): 412–427.

Holland, John H. 1995. *Hidden Order: How Adaptation Builds Complexity*. Cambridge: Helix Books.

Holling, Crawford S. 1973. 'Resilience and Stability of Ecological Systems'. *Annual Review of Ecology and Systematics* 4(1): 1–23.
    1986. 'The Resilience of Terrestrial Ecosystems: Local Surprise and Global Change'. In *Sustainable Development of the Biosphere*, edited by W. C. Clark and R. E. Munn, 292–231. Cambridge: Cambridge University Press.
Horowitz, Donald. L. 1985. *Ethnic Groups in Conflict*. Berkeley, CA: University of California Press.
    2001. *The Deadly Ethnic Riot*. Berkeley, CA: University of California Press.
    2013. *Constitutional Change and Democracy in Indonesia*. Cambridge: Cambridge University Press.
Hudson, Heidi. 2014. 'Gendercidal Violence and the Technologies of Othering in Libya and Rwanda'. *Africa Insight* 44(1): 103–120.
Hull, Stephen. 2009. 'The "Everyday Politics" of IDP Protection in Karen State'. *Journal of Current Southeast Asian Affairs* 28(2): 7–21.
Human Rights Watch. 1999. 'Indonesia: The Violence in Ambon'. 16 March. www.hrw.org/news/1999/03/16/indonesia-violence -ambon.
    2004. 'Nigeria: Prevent Further Bloodshed in Plateau State. Government Should Investigate Yelwa Massacre, Provide Security'. 11 May. www .hrw.org/news/2004/05/11/nigeria-prevent-further-bloodshed-plateau -state.
    2009. Arbitrary Killings by Security Forces. Submission to the Investigative Bodies on the November 28–29, 2008 Violence in Jos, Plateau State, Nigeria. www.hrw.org/sites/default/files/reports/niger ia0709web.pdf.
    2011. 'Nigeria: New Wave of Violence Leaves 200 Dead'. 27 January. www.hrw.org/en/news/2011/01/27/nigeria-new-wave-violence-leaves -200-dead.
    2013. '"Leave Everything to God": Accountability for Inter-Communal Violence in Plateau and Kaduna States, Nigeria'. Human Rights Watch Report, 12 December. www.hrw.org/report/2013/12/12/leave -everything-god/accountability-inter-communal-violence-plateau-and -kaduna.
Ibrahim, Jibrin. 2000. 'The Transformation of Ethno-Regional Identities in Nigeria'. In *Identity Transformation and Identity Politics under Structural Adjustment in Nigeria*, edited by Attahiru Jega, 41–61. Uppsala: Nordiska Afrikainstitutet.
Idowu, William O. O. 1999. 'Citizenship Status, Statehood Problems and Political Conflict: The Case of Nigeria'. *Nordic Journal of African Studies* 8(2): 73–88.

Institute for Peace and Conflict Resolution (ICPR). 2003. *Strategic Conflict Assessment of Nigeria: Consolidated and Zonal Reports*. Abuja: Institute for Peace and Conflict Resolution and the Presidency.

2008. *Strategic Conflict Assessment of Nigeria: Consolidated and Zonal Reports*. Abuja: Institute for Peace and Conflict Resolution.

Ikelegbe, Austine. 2005. 'State, Ethnic Militias, and Conflict in Nigeria'. *Canadian Journal of African Studies* 39(3): 490–516.

International Crisis Group. 2000. 'Indonesia: Overcoming Murder and Chaos in Maluku'. Asia Report No. 10, 19 December. www.crisisgroup.org/asia/south-east-asia/indonesia/indonesia-overcoming-murder-and-chaos-maluku.

2002. 'The Search for Peace in Maluku'. Asia Report No 31, 8 February. www.crisisgroup.org/asia/south-east-asia/indonesia/indonesia-search-peace-maluku.

2011. 'Indonesia: Trouble Again in Ambon'. Asia Briefing No 128, 4 October. www.crisisgroup.org/asia/south-east-asia/indonesia/indonesia-trouble-again-ambon.

IRIN News. 2010. 'Politics of Identity – the Jos Conflict'. 26 May. www.irinnews.org/report/89243/analysis-politics-identity-jos-conflict.

Janzen, John M. 2000. 'Historical Consciousness and a "Prise de Conscience" in Genocidal Rwanda'. *Journal of African Cultural Studies* 13(1): 153–168.

Jentzsch, Corinna, Stathis N. Kalyvas, and Livia Isabella Schubiger. 2015. 'Militias in Civil Wars'. *Journal of Conflict Resolution* 59(5): 755–769.

Jos North Muslim Ummah. 2009. 'Report on the 2008 Jos Crisis'. Unpublished document. Manuscript obtained in Jos, Nigeria.

Joseph, Jonathan. 2013. 'Resilience as Embedded Neoliberalism: A Governmentality Approach'. *Resilience* 1(1): 38–52.

Kalyvas, Stathis N. 2006. *The Logic of Violence in Civil War*. Cambridge: Cambridge University Press.

2009. 'Conflict and the Explanation of Action'. In *Oxford Handbook of Analytical Sociology*, edited by Peter Hedstrom, 592–618.Oxford: Oxford University Press.

Kaplan, Oliver. 2013. 'Protecting Civilians in Civil War: The Institution of the ATCC in Colombia'. *Journal of Peace Research* 50(3): 351–367.

2017. *Resisting War: How Civilians Protect Themselves*. Cambridge: Cambridge University Press.

Kastor, R. 2000. *Fakta, Data, dan Analisa Konspirasi Politik RMS dan Kristen menghancurkan ummat Islam di Ambon-Maluku: Mengungkap konflik berdarah antar ummat beragama dan suara hati warga Muslim yang teraniaya*. Yogyakarta: Wihdah Press.

Khamidov, Alisher, Nick Megoran, and John Heathershaw. 2017. 'Bottom-Up Peacekeeping in Southern Kyrgyzstan: How Local Actors Managed to Prevent the Spread of Violence from Osh/Jalal-Abad to Aravan, June 2010'. *Journal of Nationalism and Ethnicity* 45(6): 1118–1134.

Kenny, Joseph. 1996. 'Sharia and Christianity in Nigeria: Islam and a "Secular" State'. *Journal of Religion in Africa* 26(4): 338–364.

Killian, Beverly. 2004. 'Risk and Resilience'. In *A Generation at Risk? HIV/ Aids, Vulnerable Children and Security in Southern Africa*, edited by Robyn Pharoah, 33–63. Pretoria: Institute for Security Studies.

King, Charles. 2004. 'The Micropolitics of Social Violence: Review Article'. *World Politics* 56: 431–455.

Klaus, Kathleen and Matthew I. Mitchell. 2015. 'Land Grievances and the Mobilization of Electoral Violence: Evidence from Côte d'Ivoire and Kenya'. *Journal of Peace Research* 52(5): 622–635.

van Klinken, Gerry. 2001. 'The Maluku Wars: Bringing Society Back In'. *Indonesia* 71: 1–26.

2007. *Communal Violence and Democratization in Indonesia: Small Town Wars*. London: Routledge.

Krause, Jana. 2011a. 'Explaining Nigeria's Christmas Killings'. OpenDemocracy, 3 January. www.opendemocracy.net/jana-krause/ex plaining-nigerias-christmas-killings.

2011b. 'A Deadly Cycle: Ethno-Religious Conflict in Jos, Plateau State, Nigeria'. Report, Geneva Declaration. www.files.ethz.ch/isn/142958/ GD-WP-Jos-deadly-cycle.pdf.

2011c. 'Jos: Guarding Peace in the Midst of Ethno-Religious Violence'. *Comunidad Segura* Magazine, October. www.genevadeclaration.org/fi leadmin/docs/regional_seminars/Good_Pratices_magazine_8_-_web .pdf.

2017. 'Non-Violence and Civilian Agency in Communal War: Evidence from Jos, Nigeria'. *African Affairs* 116(463): 261–283.

2018. 'Gender Dimensions of (Non-)Violence in Communal Conflict: The Case of Jos, Nigeria'. Working paper. University of Amsterdam.

Kreidie, Lina Haddad and Kristen Renwick Monroe. 2002. 'Psychological Boundaries and Ethnic Conflict: How Identity Constrained Choice and Worked to Turn Ordinary People into Perpetrators of Ethnic Violence during the Lebanese Civil War'. *International Journal of Politics, Culture, and Society* 16(1): 5–36.

Krug, Etienne G., Linda L. Dahlberg, James A. Mercy, Anthony B. Zwi, and Rafael Lozano. 2002. 'World Report on Violence and Health. Geneva: World Health Organisation'. http://apps.who.int/iris/bitstream/10665/ 42495/1/9241545615_eng.pdf.

Last, Murray. 1967. *The Sokoto Caliphate*. London: Longmans.

2007. 'Muslims and Christians in Nigeria: An Economy of Political Panic'. *Round Table* 96(92): 605–616.

Lederach, John Paul, ed. 1997. *Building Peace: Sustainable Reconciliation in Divided Societies*. Washington, DC: US Institute of Peace.

2005. *The Moral Imagination: The Art and Soul of Building Peace.* Oxford: Oxford University Press.

Leonard, Madeleine. 2004. 'Bonding and Bridging Social Capital: Reflections from Belfast'. *Sociology* 38(5): 927–944.

Lewis, Peter. 1996. 'From Prebendalism to Predation: The Political Economy of decline in Nigeria'. *The Journal of Modern African Studies* 34(01): 79–103.

1999. 'Nigeria: An End to the Permanent Transition?' *Journal of Democracy* 10(1): 141–156.

Liddle, William. 2002. 'Indonesia's Democratic Transition: Playing by the Rules'. In *The Architecture of Democracy: Constitutional Design, Conflict Management and Democracy*, edited by Andrew Reynolds, 373–399. Oxford: Oxford University Press.

Lindsey, Tim. 2001. 'The Criminal State: Premanisme and the new Indonesia'. *Indonesia Today. Challenges of History*, edited by Grayson Lloud and Shannon Smith, 283–297. Lanham, MD: Rowman & Littlefield.

Longman, Timothy. 2010. *Christianity and Genocide in Rwanda.* Cambridge: Cambridge University Press.

Lubkemann, Stephen C. 2008. *Culture in Chaos: An Anthropology of the Social Condition in War*. Chicago, IL: University of Chicago Press.

Luthar, Suniya S. 2000. 'The Construct of Resilience: A Critical Evaluation and Guidelines for future Work'. *Child Development* 71 (3): 543–562.

Luthar, Suniya S. and Dante Cicchetti. 2000. 'The Construct of Resilience: Implications for Interventions and Social Policies'. *Development and Psychopathology* 12(4): 857–885.

Lynch, Megan F. 2014. 'Civilian Agency in Times of Crisis: Lessons from Burundi'. In *The Human Rights Paradox: Universality and Its Discontents*, edited by Steven J. Stern and Scott Straus, 81–106. Madison, WI: University of Wisconsin Press.

MacGinty, Roger. 2014. 'Everyday Peace: Bottom-Up and Local Agency in Conflict-Affected Societies'. *Security Dialogue* 45(6): 548–564.

Maier, Karl. 2000. *This House Has Fallen: Midnight in Nigeria*. New York, NY: Public Affairs.

Malik, Ichsan. 2003. *Bakubae: The Community-Based Movement for Reconciliation Process in Maluku*. Jakarta: BakuBae Maluku, Tifa Foundation and Yayasan Kemala.

Marc, Alexandre. 2009. 'Making Societies more Resilient to Violence: A Conceptual Framework for the Conflict, Crime, and Violence Agenda'. World Bank Brief, 1 January. http://documents.worldbank.o rg/curated/en/287621468155136976/Making-societies-more-resilient -to-violence-a-conceptual-framework-for-the-conflict-crime-and-vio lence-agenda.

Masten, Ann S., Karin M. Best, and Norman Garmezy. 1990. 'Resilience and Development: Contributions from the Study of Children Who Overcome Adversity'. *Development and Psychopathology* 2(4): 425–444.

Masullo, Juan J. 2017. 'Civilian Noncooperation in Armed Conflicts. Refusing to Cooperate with Armed Groups as a Self-Protection Strategy'. Unpublished Working paper.

McLoughlin, Stephen. 2014. *The Structural Prevention of Mass Atrocities: Understanding Risk and Resilience.* London: Routledge.

McNair, Rachel. 1996. *The Psychology of Peace: An Introduction.* Santa Barbara, CA: Praeger.

McRae, Dave. 2013. *A Few Poorly Organized Men: Interreligious Violence in Poso, Indonesia.* Leiden: Brill.

Mearns, David. 1996. 'Class, Status and Habitus in Ambon'. In *Remaking Maluku: Social Transformation in Eastern Indonesia,* edited by David Mearns and Chris Healy, Northern Territory University, Special Monograph No. 1, 95–105. Darwin: Centre for Southeast Asian Studies.

Mearns, David J. and Christopher J. Healey. 1996. *Remaking Maluku: Social Transformation in Eastern Indonesia.* Northern Territory University, Special Monograph No. 1. Darwin: Centre for Southeast Asian Studies.

Mehta, Mona G. 2013. 'Networks of Death and Militant Vegetarianism: The Mechanics of Communal Violence in Gujarat'. *India Review* 12(2): 108–117.

Merriam Webster Online Dictionary. 2017. 'Resilience'. www.merriam-webster.com/dictionary/resilience.

Mietzner, Marcus. 2009. Military politics, Islam, and the state in Indonesia: From turbulent transition to democratic consolidation. Singapore: Institute of Southeast Asian Studies.

Milligan, Maren. 2013. 'Fighting for the Right to Exist: Institutions, Identity, and Conflict in Jos, Nigeria'. *Comparative Politics* 45(3): 313–334.

Misol, Lisa. 2006. 'Too High a Price: The Human Rights Cost of the Indonesian Military's Economic Activities'. Human Rights Watch Report, 21 June. www.hrw.org/reports/2006/indonesia0606/.

Mitchell, Christopher. 2007. 'The Theory and Practice of Sanctuary'. In *Zones of Peace,* edited by Landon Hancock and Christopher Mitchell, 1–28. Bloomfield, IL: Kumarin Press.

Mitchell, Christopher R. and Landon E. Hancock, eds. 2012. *Local Peacebuilding and National Peace: Interaction between Grassroots and Elite Processes*. London: Continuum International Publishing Group.

Modibbo, Muhammad Sani Adam 2012. 'Survey of Muslim Groups in Plateau State, Nigeria'. Nigeria Research Network Working Paper No. 4. Oxford. https://www.qeh.ox.ac.uk/sites/www.odid.ox.ac.uk/files/BP4Modibbo.pdf.

Mohammad, Zulfan Tadjoeddin and Syed Mansoob Murshed. 2007. 'Socio-Economic Determinants of Everyday Violence in Indonesia: An Empirical Investigation of Javanese Districts, 1994–2003'. *Journal of Peace Research* 44(6): 689–709.

Mohammed, Abubakar Sokoto. 2004. 'The Impact of Conflict on the Economy: The Case of Plateau State of Nigeria'. Overseas Development Institute. http://citeseerx.ist.psu.edu/viewdoc/download?doi=10.1.1.517.8276&rep=rep1&type=pdf.

Monroe, Kristen R. 2001a. 'Morality and a Sense of Self: The Importance of Identity and Categorization for Moral Action'. *American Journal of Political Science* 45(3): 491–507.

2001b. 'Paradigm Shift: From Rational Choice to Perspective'. *International Political Science Review* 22(2): 151–172.

2003. 'How Identity and Perspective Constrain Moral Choice'. *International Political Science Review* 24(4): 405–425.

2004. *The Hand of Compassion: Portraits of Moral Choice during the Holocaust*. Princeton, NJ: Princeton University Press.

2008. 'Cracking the Code of Genocide: The Moral Psychology of Rescuers, Bystanders, and Nazis during the Holocaust'. *Political Psychology* 29(5): 699–736.

2009. 'The Ethical Perspective: An Identity Theory of the Psychological Influences on Moral Choice'. *Political Psychology* 30(3): 419–444.

2012. 'Ethics in an Age of Terror and Genocide: Identity and Moral Choice'. *PS Political Science and Politics* 44(3): 503–507.

Monroe, Kristen R., Michael C. Barton, and Ute Klingemann. 1990. 'Altruism and the Theory of Rational Action: Rescuers of Jews in Nazi Europe'. *Ethics* 101(1): 103–122.

Muluk, Hamdi and Ichsan Malik. 2009. 'Peace Psychology of Grassroots Reconciliation: Lessons Learned from the Baku Bae Peace Movement'. In *Peace Psychology in Asia*, edited by Noraini M. Noor and Cristina Jayme Montiel, 85–103. New York, NY: Springer Social Science and Business Media.

Mustapha, Abdul R. 2000. 'Transformation of Minority Identities in Post-Colonial Nigeria'. In *Identity Transformation and Identity Politics under Structural Adjustment in Nigeria*, edited by Attahiru Jega, 86–108. Uppsala: Nordic Africa Institute.

Mustapha, Abdul R., Adam Higazi, Jimam Lar, and Karel Chromy. 2018. 'Jos: Top-down and Bottom-Up Approaches to Conflict Resolution'. In Abdul R. Mustapha and David Ehrhardt, eds., *Creed & Grievance: Muslim–Christian Relations and Conflict in Northern Nigeria*. Suffolk: Boydell & Brewer.

Narula, Smita. 2002. 'India: "We have no orders to save you": State Participation and Complicity in Communal Violence in Gujarat'. Human Rights Watch Report, 30 April. www.hrw.org/reports/2002/india/India0402.htm.

Nelson, Donald R., W. Neil Adger, and Katrina Brown. 2007. 'Adaptation to Environmental Change: Contributions of a Resilience Framework'. *Annual Review of Environmental Resources* 32: 395–419.

Newman, Lenore and Ann Dale. 2005. 'Network Structure, Diversity and Proactive Resilience Building: A Response to Tompkins and Adger'. *Ecology and Society* 10(1): 1–32.

Nina, Daniel 2000. 'Dirty Harry Is Back: Vigilantism in South Africa – The (Re)Emergence of the "Good" and "Bad" Community'. *African Security Review* 9(1): 18–28.

Nnoli, Okwudiba 1978. *Ethnic Politics in Nigeria*. Enugu: Fourth Dimension Publishers.

1995. *Ethnicity and Development in Nigeria*. Aldershot; Brookfield, VT: Avebury.

2003. 'Ethnic Violence in Nigeria: A Historical Perspective'. In *Communal Conflict and Population Displacement in Nigeria*, edited by Okwudiba Nnoli, 13–45. Enugu: Pan African Centre for Research on Peace and Conflict Resolution.

Nordlinger, Eric. 1972. *Conflict Regulation in Divided Societies*. Cambridge, MA: Harvard University Center for International Affairs.

Nordstrom, Carolyn. 1997. *A Different Kind of War Story*. Philadelphia, PA: University of Pennsylvania Press.

1998. 'Deadly Myths of Aggression'. *Aggressive Behavior* 24(2): 147–159.

2007. 'War on the Front Lines'. In *Ethnographic Fieldwork: An Anthropological Reader*, edited by Antonius C. G. M. Robben and Jeffrey A. Sluka, 129–153. Chichester: Wiley-Blackwell Publishers.

Nordstrom, Carolyn and Antonius C. G. M. Robben. 1995. *Fieldwork under Fire: Contemporary Studies of Violence and Survival*. Berkeley, CA: University of California Press.

Norris, Fran H., Susan P. Stevens, Betty Pfefferbaum, Karen F. Wyche, and Rose L. Pfefferbaum. 2008. 'Community Resilience as a Metaphor, Theory, Set of Capacities, and Strategy for Disaster Readiness'. *American Journal of Community Psychology* 41: 127–150.

Obateru, Taye. 2001. 'Nigeria: Youth Association Condemns Crisis in Middle Belt'. *The Vanguard*, 16 July. http://allafrica.com/stories/2001 07180423.html.

Oberschall, Anthony. 1973. *Social Conflict and Social Movements.* Englewood, NJ: Prentice-Hall.

Obi, Cyril. 2004. 'Nigeria: Democracy on Trial'. Occasional Electronic Paper No 1. Uppsala: Nordiska Afrikainstitutet.

Ojukwu, Chris C., and C. A. Onifade. 2010. 'Social Capital, Indigeneity and Identity Politics: The Jos Crisis in Perspective'. *African Journal of Political Science and International Relations* 4(5):173–180.

Okocha, Chuks, Buhari Ruben, and Seriki Adinoyi. 2008. 'Death Toll in Jos Rises to 350'. *This Day Nigeria*, 30 November. http://allafrica.com/stor ies/200811300001.html.

Olaniyi, Muideen. 2010. 'Nigeria: Fulanis Massacred in Front of Jang's House'. *Daily Trust*, 24 January. http://allafrica.com/stories/20100125 0169.html.

Oliner, Samuel P. and Pearl. M. Oliner. 1988. *The Altruistic Personality: Rescuers of Jews in Nazi Europe.* New York, NY: Free Press.

Olsen, Mancur. 1971. *The Logic of Collective Action: Public Goods and the Theory of Groups.* Cambridge, MA: Harvard University Press.

Onoja, Adoyi. 2015. 'Remapping Secured Neighbourhoods in Conflict Prone Nigeria: The Jos Example'. *Developing Country Studies* 5(7): 118–128.

Onuoha, Freedom C. 2010. 'The Islamist Challenge: Nigeria's Boko Haram Crisis Explained'. *African Security Review* 19(2): 54–67.

Oommen, Tharrileth K. 2005. *Crisis and Contention in Indian Society.* New Delhi: Sage Publications.

Ostien, Philipp. 2009. 'Jonah Jang and the Jasawa: Ethno-Religious Conflict in Jos, Nigeria'. *Muslim–Christian Relations in Africa*, August. https:// papers.ssrn.com/sol3/papers.cfm?abstract_id=1456372.

Paden, John N. 2005. *Muslim Civic Cultures and Conflict Resolution: The Challenge of Democratic Federalism in Nigeria.* Washington, DC: Brookings Institution Press.

Pamudji, M. Dr Nanang, Akiko Horiba, Mohamad Miqdad, Nerlian Gogali and Loury Sipasulta. 2008. 'The Success Story of Community Mechanism in Handling and Preventing Conflict: Case Studies at Wayame Village (Ambon-Moluccas) and Tangkura Village

(Poso-Central    Sulawesi)'.    Report.    Jakarta:    Friedrich    Ebert
    Foundation.
Panter-Brick, Catherine. 2010. 'Conflict, Violence, and Health: Setting
    a New Interdisciplinary Agenda'. *Social Science and Medicine* 70(1):
    1–6.
    2015. 'Culture and Resilience: Next Steps for Theory and Practice'.
    In *Youth Resilience and Culture*, edited by Linda C. Theron,
    Linda Liebenberg, and Michael Ungar, 233–244. New York, NY:
    Springer.
Panter-Brick, Catherine and Mark Eggerman. 2012. 'Understanding
    Culture, Resilience, and Mental Health: The Production of Hope'.
    In *The Social Ecology of Resilience*, edited by Michael Ungar,
    369–386. New York, NY: Springer.
Pariela, Tonny. 2008. *Damai di Tengah Konflik Maluku. Preserved Social
    Capital Sebagai Basis Survival Strategy*. Ambon: Universitas Kristen
    Satya Wacana.
Para-Mallam, Oluwafunmilayo J., and Kate Hoomlong. 2012. 'A Critical
    Investigation into the Role of Security Sector Agencies in the Jos
    Conflict: Issues and Strategies for Institutional/Security Sector
    Reform'. African Peacebuilding Network. Social Science Research
    Council. Research Report, 10–55.
Pasquini, Margaret W. and Michael J. Alexander. 2005. 'Soil Fertility
    Management Strategies on the Jos Plateau: The Need for Integrating
    "Empirical" and "Scientific" Knowledge in Agricultural Development'.
    *Geographical Journal* 171(2): 112–124.
Pelling, Mark 2003. *The Vulnerability of Cities: Natural Disasters and Social
    Resilience*. London: Earthscan.
    2010. *Adaptation to Climate Change: From Resilience to Transformation*.
    London: Routledge.
Petersen, Roger Dale. 2002. *Understanding Ethnic Violence: Fear, Hatred
    and Resentment in Twentieth Century Eastern Europe*. Cambridge:
    Cambridge University Press.
Pfefferbaum, Betty, Dori B. Reissman, Rose L. Pfefferbaum, Richard
    W. Klomp, and Robin H. Gurwitch. 2005. 'Building Resilience to
    Mass Trauma Events'. In *Handbook on Injury and Violence
    Prevention Interventions*, edited by Lynda S. Doll, Sandra E. Bonzo,
    James A. Mercy, David A. Sleet, and E. N. Haas, 347–358. New York,
    NY: Springer.
Plateau State Muslim Ummah. 2010. 'Muslims Massacred Toll Recorded
    January 17, 2010'. Report by the Central Mosque in Jos, Nigeria.
    Unpublished document obtained in Jos.

Plotnicov, Leonard. 1967. *Strangers to the City: Urban Man in Jos, Nigeria*. Pittsburgh, PA: University of Pittsburgh Press.

1972. 'Who Owns Jos? Ethnic Ideology in Nigerian Urban Politics'. *Urban Anthropology* 1(1): 1–13.

Posner, Daniel N. 2005. *Institutions and Ethnic Politics in Africa*. Cambridge: Cambridge University Press.

Pratten, David. 2008. 'The Politics of Protection: Perspectives on Vigilantism in Nigeria'. *Africa* 78(1): 1–15.

Prunier, Gerard. 1995. *The Rwanda Crisis: History of a Genocide*. New York, NY: Columbia University Press.

Purdey, Jemma. 2004. 'Describing Kekerasan: Some Observations on Writing about Violence in Indonesia after the New Order'. *Bijdragen tot de Taal-, Land- en Volkenkunde* 160: 189–225.

Putnam, Robert D. 1995. 'Bowling Alone: America's Declining Social Capital'. *Journal of Democracy* 6: 65–78.

2001. *Bowling Alone: The Collapse and Revival of American Community*. New York, NY: Simon and Schuster.

Reno, William. 1999a. 'Crisis and (No) Reform in Nigeria's Politics'. *African Studies Review* 42(1): 105–124.

1999b. *Warlord Politics and African States*. Boulder, CO: Lynne Rienner Publishers.

Ritter, Nancy. 2009. 'Cease Fire: A Public Health Approach to Reduce Shootings and Killings'. *National Institute of Justice Journal*, 264: 2–25.

Rittner, Carol and Sondra Myers, eds. 1986. *The Courage to Care: Rescuers of Jews during the Holocaust*. New York, NY: New York University Press.

Robben, Antonius C. G. M. and Jeffrey A. Sluka, eds. 2007. *Ethnographic Fieldwork: An Anthropological Reader*. Chichester: Wiley-Blackwell Publishers.

Roberts, Adam and Timothy Garton Ash, eds. 2009. *Civil Resistance and Power Politics: The Experience of Non-Violent Action from Gandhi to the Present*. Oxford: Oxford University Press.

Rosenberg, Sherry P. 2012. 'Genocide Is a Process, Not an Event'. *Genocide Studies and Prevention* 7(1): 16–23.

Rubin, Mark and Miles Hewstone. 1998. 'Social Identity Theory's Self-Esteem Hypothesis: A Review and Some Suggestions for Clarification'. *Personality and Social Psychology Review* 2(1): 40–62.

Rutter, Michael 1987. 'Psychosocial Resilience and Protective Mechanisms'. *American Journal of Orthopsychiatry* 57(3): 316–331.

1999. 'Resilience Concepts and Findings: Implications for Family Therapy'. *Journal of Family Therapy* 21(2): 119–144.

2012. 'Resilience as a Dynamic Concept'. *Development and Psychopathology* 24(2): 335–344.

Ryter, Loren. 1998. 'Pemuda Pancasila: The Last Loyalist Free Men of Suharto's Order?' *Indonesia* 66: 45–73.

Sarkees, Meredith Reid. 2014. 'Patterns of Civil Wars in the Twenty-First Century. The Decline of Civil War?' In *Routledge Handbook of Civil Wars*, edited by Edward Newman and Karl DeRouen, 236–256. London: Routledge.

Scacco, Alexandra. 2010. 'Who Riots? Explaining Individual Participation in Ethnic Violence'. PhD dissertation excerpt. New York: Columbia University.

Schulze, Kirsten S. 2002. 'Laskar Jihad and the Conflict in Ambon'. *Brown Journal of World Affairs* 9(1): 57–69.

Shehu, Sani. 2007. *The Killing Fields: Religious Violence in Northern Nigeria*. Ibadan: Spectrum Books.

Sidel, John T. 2006. *Riots, Pogroms, Jihad: Religious Violence in Indonesia*. Ithaca, NY: Cornell University Press.

Simmel, Georg. 1955. *Conflict and the Web of Group Affiliations*. New York, NY: Free Press.

Smit, Barry and Johanna Wandel. 2006. 'Adaptation, Adaptive Capacity and Vulnerability'. *Global Environmental Change* 16(3): 282–292.

Smith, Daniel J. 2004. 'The Bakassi Boys: Vigilantism, Violence, and Political Imagination in Nigeria'. *Cultural Anthropology* 19(3): 429–455.

South, Ashley. 2010. 'Conflict and Survival: Self-Protection in South-East Burma'. Asia Programme paper. April. London: Chatham House.

Spyer, Patricia. 2002. 'Fire without Smoke and Other Phantoms of Ambon's Violence: Media Effects, Agency, and the Work of Imagination'. *Indonesia* 74: 21–36.

Staniland, Paul. 2014. 'Violence and Democracy'. *Comparative Politics* 47 (1): 99–118.

Staub, Ervin. 1989. *The Roots of Evil: The Origins of Genocide and Other Group Violence*. Cambridge: Cambridge University Press.

2000. 'Genocide and Mass Killing: Origins, Prevention, Healing and Reconciliation'. *Political Psychology* 21(2): 367–382.

Stockholm Resilience Centre. 2017. "Resilience Dictionary." www .stockholmresilience.org/research/resilience-dictionary.html.

Straus, Scott. 2006. *The Order of Genocide: Race, Power, and War in Rwanda*. Ithaca, NY: Cornell University Press.

2012. 'Retreating from the Brink: Theorizing Mass Violence and the Dynamics of Restraint'. *Perspectives on Politics* 10(2): 343–362.

2015. *Making and Unmaking Nations: War, Leadership, and Genocide in Modern Africa*. Ithaca, NY: Cornell University Press.

Straus, Scott and Charlie Taylor. 2009. 'Democratization and Electoral Violence in Sub-Saharan Africa, 1990–2007'. American Political Science Association Annual Meeting, Toronto. https://ssrn.com/abstract=1451561.

Suberu, Rotimi T. 2001. *Federalism and Ethnic Conflict in Nigeria.* Washington, DC: US Institute of Peace.

    2009. 'Religion and Institutions: Federalism and the Management of Conflicts over Sharia in Nigeria'. *Journal of International Development* 21(4): 547–560.

Sukma, Rizal. 2005. 'Ethnic Conflicts in Indonesia: Causes and the Quest for Solution'. In *Ethnic Conflicts in Southeast Asia*, edited by Kusuma Snitwongse and W. Scott Thompson, 1–41. Singapore: Institute of Security and International Studies.

Sundberg, Ralph, Kristine Eck, and Joakim Kreutz. 2012. 'Introducing the UCDP Non-State Conflict Dataset'. *Journal of Peace Research* 49(2): 351–362.

Tadjoeddin, Mohammed Z. 2002. 'Anatomy of Social Violence in the Context of Transition: The Case of Indonesia'. UNSFIR Working paper. 1 February. www.conflictrecovery.org/Zulfan%20-%20Anatomy%20of%20social%20violence%20-%20April%202002.pdf.

    2004. 'Civil Society Engagement and Communal Violence: Reflections of Various Hypotheses in the Context of Indonesia'. https://papers.ssrn.com/sol3/papers.cfm?abstract_id=767364.

    2007. 'Socio-Economic Determinants of Everyday Violence in Indonesia: An Empirical Investigation of Javanese Districts, 1994–2003'. *Journal of Peace Research* 44(6): 689–709.

Tadjoeddin, Mohammed Z. and Anis Chowdhury. 2009. 'Socioeconomic Perspectives on Violent Conflict in Indonesia'. *Economics of Peace and Security* 39: 39–49.

Tajfel, Henri. 1972. 'Social Categorization'. English manuscript of 'La categorisation sociale'. In *Introduction a la Psychologie Sociale*, edited by Serge Moscovici, 272–302. Paris: Larousse.

    1982. 'Social Psychology of Intergroup Relations'. *Annual Review of Psychology*, 33(1): 1–39.

Tajfel, Henri and John C. Turner. 1979. 'An Integrative Theory of Intergroup Conflict'. In *The Social Psychology of Intergroup Relations*, edited by William G. Austin and Stephen Worchel, 33–47. Monterey, CA: Brooks/Cole.

Tajima, Yuhki. 2013. 'The Institutional Basis of Intercommunal Order: Evidence from Indonesia's Democratic Transition'. *American Journal of Political Science* 57(1): 104–119.

Tambiah, Stanley. J. 1990. 'Presidential Address: Reflections on Communal Violence in South Asia'. *The Journal of Asian Studies* 49(4): 141–160.
  1996. *Levelling Crowds: Ethnonationalist Conflict and Collective Violence in South Asia.* Berkeley, CA: University of California Press.
Tanamal, Pieter and Lambang Trijono. 2004. 'Religious Conflict in Maluku: In Search of Religious Community Peace'. In *The Making of Ethnic and Religious Conflicts in Southeast Asia: Cases and Resolutions,* edited by Lambang Trijono, 231–255. Yogyakarta: CSPS Books.
Tarrow, Sidney. 2010. 'The Strategy of Paired Comparison: Toward a Theory of Practice'. *Comparative Political Studies* 43(2): 230–259.
Tec, Nechama. 1986. *When Light Pierced the Darkness: Christian Rescue of Jews in Nazi-Occupied Poland.* Oxford: Oxford University Press.
  1993. *Defiance.* Oxford: Oxford University Press.
Tempo. 2001. 'Belajar Damai dari Waiyame'. Tempo, 30 December, https://majalah.tempo.co/konten/2001/12/26/NAS/86656/Belajar-Damai-dari -Waiyame/43/30.
Tertsakian, Carina. 2005. 'Revenge in the Name of Religion: The Cycle of Violence in Plateau and Kano States'. Human Rights Watch Report, 25 May. 375 www.hrw.org/report/2005/05/25/revenge-name-religion/ cycle-violence-plateau-and-kano-states.
Tertsakian, Carina and Malcom Smart. 2001. 'Jos: A City Torn Apart'. Human Rights Watch Report, 18 December. www.hrw.org/report/200 1/12/18/jos/city-torn-apart.
Thalhammer, Kristina E. 2012. 'Genocide and the Psychology of Perpetrators, Bystanders, and Victims'. *Perspectives on Politics* 10(2): 418–421.
Thapa, G. B. and Othniel M. Yila. 2012. 'Farmers' Land Management Practices and Status of Agricultural Land in the Jos Plateau, Nigeria'. *Land Degradation & Development* 23(3): 263–277.
Theidon, Kimberly. 2012. *Intimate Enemies: Violence and Reconciliation in Peru.* Philadelphia, PA: University of Pennsylvania Press.
*This Day.* 2012. '8 Killed as Bombers Target Jang's Church'. 27 February. www.thisdaylive.com/articles/8-killed-as-bombers-target-jang-s-churc h/110170.
Tilly, Charles. 1986. 'European Violence and Collective Action since 1700'. *Social Research* 53(1): 159–184
  2003. *The Politics of Collective Violence.* Cambridge: Cambridge University Press.
Tilly, Charles and Sidney. G. Tarrow. 2007. *Contentious Politics.* New York, NY: Oxford University Press.
Tronto, Joan C. 2012. 'Genocide and the Psychology of Perpetrators, Bystanders, and Victims'. *Perspectives on Politics* 10(2): 421–424.

Turiel, Elliot. 1983. *The Development of Social Knowledge: Morality and Convention*. Cambridge; New York, NY: Cambridge University Press.

Turkmani, Rim, with Ali A. K. Ali, Mary Kaldor, and Vesna Bojicic-Dzelilovic. 2015. Countering the Logic of the War Economy in Syria: Evidence from Three Local Areas. LSE Department of International Development, Civil Society and Human Security Research Unit. www.securityintransition.org/wp-content/uploads/2015/08/Countering-war-economy-Syria2.pdf.

Tyoden, Sonni G. 1993. *The Middle Belt in Nigerian Politics*. Jos: AHA.

Ukiwo, Ukoha. 2003. 'Politics, Ethno-Religious Conflicts and Democratic Consolidation in Nigeria'. *Journal of Modern African Studies* 41(1): 115–138.

2005. 'The Study of Ethnicity in Nigeria'. Centre for Research on Inequality, Human Security and Ethnicity. Working paper. June. University of Oxford.

USAID West Africa. 2010. 'Early Warning and Response Design Support (EDWARDS): Jos Conflict Assessment'. Final Report. http://pdf.usaid.gov/pdf_docs/pdacu129.pdf.

Varshney, Ashutosh. 2001. 'Ethnic Conflict and Civil Society: India and Beyond'. *World Politics* 53(3): 362–398.

2002. *Ethnic Conflict and Civic Life: Hindus and Muslims in India*. New Haven, CT: Yale University Press.

2007. 'Ethnicity and Ethnic Conflict'. In *Oxford Handbook of Comparative Politics*, edited by Carles Boix and Susan C. Stokes, 274–295. Oxford: Oxford University Press.

Varshney, Ashutosh, Mohammed Z. Tadjoeddin, and Rizal Panggabean. 2008. 'Creating Datasets in Information-Poor Environments: Patterns of Collective Violence in Indonesia, 1990–2003'. *Journal of East Asian Studies* 8(3): 361–394.

Verkaaik, Oskar. 2003. 'Fun and Violence: Ethnocide and the Effervescence of Collective Aggression'. *Social Anthropology* 11(1): 3–22.

Vigil, James Diego. 2003. 'Urban Violence and Street Gangs'. *Annual Review of Anthropology* 32(1): 225–242.

De Waal, Frans B. M. 2008. 'Putting the Altruism Back into Altruism: The Evolution of Empathy'. *Annual Review of Psychology* 59: 279–300.

Walker, Brian and David Salt. 2006. *Resilience Thinking: Sustaining Ecosystems and People in a Changing World*. Washington, DC: Island Press.

Walker, Jeremy, and Melinda Cooper. 2011. 'Genealogies of Resilience from Systems Ecology to the Political Economy of Crisis Adaptation'. *Security Dialogue* 42(2): 143–160.

Walker, Rob. 2011. 'Jos Violence: "Everyone Lives in Fear of His Neighbour"'. BBC News, 7 April. www.bbc.co.uk/news/world-africa -12985289.

Wallace, Marshall 2002. 'Tuzla, Bosnia: Cross-Ethnic Solidarity in the Face of Ethnic Cleansing'. *CDA Learning Collaborative*. http://cdacollabora tive.org/wordpress/wp-content/uploads/2016/01/Tuzla-Bosnia-Cross -Ethnic-Solidarity-in-the-Face-of-Ethnic-Cleansing.pdf.

Waller, James. 2007. *Becoming Evil: How Ordinary People Commit Genocide and Mass Killing*. Oxford: Oxford University Press.

Watanabe, John M. 1992. *Maya Saints and Souls in a Changing World*. Austin, TX: University of Texas Press.

Wax, Emily. 2002. 'Islam Attracting Many Survivors of Rwanda Genocide'. *Washington Foreign Post Service*, 23 September. www.washingtonpost .com/wp-dyn/articles/A53018-2002Sep22.html.

Wedeen, Lisa. 2010. 'Reflections on Ethnographic Work in Political Science'. *Annual Review of Political Science* 13: 255–272.

Weiner, Myron. 1978. *Sons of the Soil: Migration and Ethnic Conflict in India*. Princeton, NJ: Princeton University Press.

Wilkinson, Steven I. 2004. *Votes and Violence: Electoral Competition and Ethnic Riots in India*. Cambridge, New York, NY: Cambridge University Press.

   2009. 'Riots'. *Annual Review of Political Science* 12: 329–343.

   2012. 'A Constructivist Model of Ethnic Riots'. In *Constructivist Theories of Ethnic Politics*, edited by Kanchan Chandra, 359–386. New York, NY: Oxford University Press.

   2013. Electoral Competition, the State, and Communal Violence: A Reply'. *India Review* 12(2): 92–107.

Williams, Paul D. 2013. 'Protection, Resilience and Empowerment: United Nations Peacekeeping and Violence against Civilians in Contemporary War Zones'. *Politics* 33(4): 287–298.

Wilson, Ian D. 2006. 'Continuity and Change: The Changing Contours of Organized Violence in Post–New Order Indonesia'. *Critical Asian Studies* 38(2): 265–297.

   2008. 'As Long as It's Halal: Islamic Preman in Jakarta'. In *Expressing Islam: Religious Life and Politics in Indonesia*, edited by Greg Fealy and Sally White, 192–211. Canberra: Australian National University.

Wimmer, Andreas. 2008. 'Elementary Strategies of Ethnic Boundary Making'. *Ethnic and Racial Studies* 31(6): 1025–1055.

Wood, Elisabeth J. 2003. *Insurgent Collective Action and Civil War in El Salvador*. Cambridge: Cambridge University Press.

   2006. 'The Ethical Challenges of Field Research in Conflict Zones'. *Qualitative Sociology* 29(3): 373–386.

2008. 'The Social Processes of Civil War: The Wartime Transformation of Social Networks'. *Political Science* 11(1): 539–561.

2015. 'Social Mobilization and Violence in Civil War and Their Social Legacies'. *The Oxford Handbook of Social Movements*, edited by Donatella Della Porta and Mario Diani, 452–466. Oxford: Oxford University Press.

Ya'u, Yunusa Zakari 2000. 'The Youth, Economic Crisis and Identity Transformation: The Case of the Yandaba in Kano'. In *Identity Transformation and Identity Politics under Structural Adjustment in Nigeria*, edited by Attahiru Jega, 161–180. Uppsala: Nordic Africa Institute.

Zimmermann, Marc and Alison B. Brenner 2010. 'Resilience in Adolescence: Overcoming Neighbourhood Disadvantage'. In *Handbook of Adult Resilience*, edited by John W. Reich, Alex J. Zautra, and John S. Hall, 283–308. New York, NY: Guilford Press.

# Index